THE CRISIS OF
ELEMENTARY EDUCATION IN INDIA

THE CRISIS OF
ELEMENTARY EDUCATION IN INDIA

Editor

Ravi Kumar

SAGE Publications
New Delhi ◆ Thousand Oaks ◆ London

First published in 2006 by

Sage Publications India Pvt Ltd
B-42, Panchsheel Enclave
New Delhi 110 017
www.indiasage.com

Sage Publications Inc 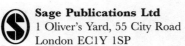 **Sage Publications Ltd**
2455 Teller Road   1 Oliver's Yard, 55 City Road
Thousand Oaks, California 91320   London EC1Y 1SP

Published by Tejeshwar Singh for Sage Publications India Pvt Ltd, phototypeset in 11/13 pt. Baskerville MT by Star Compugraphics, Delhi and printed at Chaman Enterprises, New Delhi.

Library of Congress Cataloging-in-Publication Data

The crisis of elementary education in India/editor Ravi Kumar.
   p.   cm.
   Includes bibliographical references and index.
   1. Education, Elementary—India. I. Kumar, Ravi, 1975–

LA1152.C75   372'.954—dc22   2006   2006020392

ISBN: 10: 0-7619-3499-5 (HB)   10: 81-7829-654-3 (India-HB)
       13: 978-0-7619-3499-8 (HB)   13: 978-81-7829-654-8 (India-HB)

Sage Production Team: Payal Dhar, Roopa Sharma, Mathew P.J. and Santosh Rawat

My Mamu, Professor Navin Chandra, and Mamani, Sushila Chandra, who taught me the basics of critical engagement

and

Professor Avijit Pathak from whom I have learnt the art of tireless endeavour to practice what we believe in

Contents

List of Tables

ACKNOWLEDGEMENTS

After the enactment of the Constitution (86th Amendment) Act in December 2002, debates in the education sector further sharpened. The government's performance since then came under more rigorous scanning and its policies became a matter of great debate. At such a critical conjuncture when the Indian State has been struggling to fulfil its responsibilities amidst serious debates on a vast range of educational tools and policies, the Council for Social Development organised a seminar in October 2004 to deliberate on the crucial issues confronting the elementary education sector and make relevant policy contributions. In this exercise, scholars and activists from different segments of society participated.

I must express my thanks to the Ford Foundation for supporting this endeavour, and the scholars and activists, especially Anil Sadgopal, Karuna Chanana, Vasudha Dhagamwar, Geetha B. Nambissan, Padma Velaskar, Sadhna Saxena, Amarjeet Sinha, Madan Mohan Jha, Shyam Menon, Rohit Dhankar, Jaya Srivastawa, Arun Bhandari, Anita Ghai, Sukhdeo Thorat, Avijit Pathak and Nalini Juneja, who provided valuable inputs to make the process furthermore live and productive. I will fail in my duty if I do not thank Professor Muchkund Dubey, President of the Council for Social Development, for making this whole exercise possible. He not only compelled me to be alert to the developments taking place in the education sector through his guidance, but also provided me sufficient space to evolve. Dr N.J. Kurian, Director, Council for Social Development, consistently encouraged me through the protracted task of developing a volume out of the papers. I enjoyed the encouraging support of faculty members and administrative staff of the Council during this process. Mr R.S. Somi deserves special mention for helping me wade through the administrative procedures while Jaya Lekshmi Nair lent her undaunting research support during this exercise. Mimi Choudhury, Anamika Mukharji and Roopa Sharma from Sage Publications have been of great help and they made the publication process look quite interesting to me.

Lastly, this volume would have been inconceivable without the support of Rama, who not only corrected my language through her copy-editing skills but also engaged on diverse themes while I had been developing this volume.

Ravi Kumar
New Delhi, 2006

1

INTRODUCTION

EQUALITY, QUALITY AND QUANTITY—MAPPING THE CHALLENGES BEFORE ELEMENTARY EDUCATION IN INDIA*

Ravi Kumar

During recent years no other issue has dominated the development discourse more fiercely than elementary education. The impulse of this single issue led the apex judicial institution, the Supreme Court, to pass a judgement that the Right to Education must be seen in conjunction with the Right to Life. Subsequently, the Indian Parliament amended the Constitution through the 86th Constitutional Amendment, making the Right to Education a fundamental right for children between 6 and 14 years of age. The Government of India and governments of different states that were already popularising non-formal education schemes, launched the Sarva Shiksha Abhiyan (SSA) aimed at educating all out-of-school children. In this rush to bring all children to 'teaching centres' many of the important aspects responsible for keeping children out of school were either diluted or overlooked. Structural issues responsible for keeping children out of school, for instance, have

* I would like to thank Rama Paul for her comments on the content as well as language, and for helping me sharpen my arguments.

failed to find a place in the conceptual as well as operational framework of education policy. Recent emphasis on education also institutionalised all non-formal education schemes as a substitute to
formal schooling, and 'literacy' has become synonymous with 'education'. Due to these conceptual ramifications and ignorance about
educational deprivation as emanating out of systemic deficiencies,
we are still confronted with a serious crisis in the Indian education
system.

This acute crisis is overtly manifested with a vast mass of illiterates
on one hand, while on the other there is a subterranean process
under way that delegitimises the role of the state as service provider.
The crisis further entrenches itself in tacit acknowledgement with
the State wherein formal schooling will not be available to every
child and, hence, one encounters the preponderance of non-formal
methods of education on a mass scale. Though such policies have
been critiqued by many activists and academicians as discriminatory, a vast literature is simultaneously generated by various State
apparatuses to strengthen the current policy focus on non-formal
methods as the panacea for all ills. Despite the concerns for universal
free and compulsory elementary education for all children since
the days of Independence, a huge number of children are out of
school. In particular, the debate also questions whether the State,
with its policies that do not provide all children with a common
formal schooling system, is institutionalising inequality in education.
What appears more troublesome is that the dominant discourse
on education functions essentially within a framework where every-
thing is perceived as 'given', as a priori. Hence, there is an urgent
need to raise questions such as why not formal schooling for every
child; or why 'innovative' methods are employed only in case of
Dalits, girl children or underprivileged children; or how this transition from a promise of universal free and compulsory education
(read equality in access and access to quality education) by leaders
of the freedom movement to the current division into formal and
non-formal schools, with trained and well-paid teachers on one
hand, and partially trained and ill-equipped, underpaid teachers
on the other, has come about. Therefore, this book is founded on a
premise wherein leading educationists reflect on different dimensions of the educational crisis in the country.

To fully comprehend this crisis in education it is necessary to sketch the trajectory of how India's education system evolved. The debate on education began long before independence from colonial rule, with the emergence of a critique of colonial education policy from some quarters as well as support from a big section of the emergent English-educated elite. A major thrust to the debate occurred during the first half of the 20th century when the Congress party and many national leaders engaged with education on a priority basis. The following sections try to understand this in brief as a background to the whole debate that this book carries forward so that the current themes may be located in a historical context. Furthermore, it enables us to comprehend the changing education agenda of the Indian State from a welfarist regime in the early phase of post-Independence India to the contemporary phase of liberalised capitalist development.

EMERGENCE OF A NATIONAL SYSTEM OF EDUCATION

Colonial education was devised as an 'ideological apparatus' that sought to legitimise the privileges of colonisers and their domination. It has been argued that when the British came to India, it had a vibrant education system with good number of village schools. Some British estimates had put the total number of village schools in Bihar and Bengal alone at 100,000 in the 1830s (Pathak 2002: 72–76). The East India Company was least interested in spreading modern/European education in India. Instead, it began supporting the indigenous education system. However, 'even this involvement with the indigenous system of education was designed to control the Indian subcontinent politically' (ibid.: 77).

Things, however, began to change when Charles Grant advocated the need for modern education to civilise Indians. At an ideological plane, James Mill's *History of India* gave this an impetus. Thomas Babington Macaulay took it a step further to the realm of implementation and an order was passed on 7 March 1835 by

Bentinck, the Governor-General of India, making English education a priority. This order was based in the politico-economic dynamics of contemporary Indian colonialism. Though there were opposi-tions to this vehement Occidental critique of Oriental knowledge (as by the Woods Despatch, 1854, and the Hunter Commission, 1882), 'the idea of cognitive superiority of modern/English educa-tion remained unchallenged' (Pathak 2002: 81).

Modern education led to the emergence of a new educated élite among Indians. Raja Rammohan Roy upheld Western science and 'the Bengal *bhadralok* saw the affirmation of their class interests in English education' (ibid.). Another significant support for modern education emerged from a Dalit leader, Jyotirao Phule. He believed that the common man could benefit from the legal system and scientific reforms introduced by the British. His prime enemy was the traditional brahminical system. He did not only see

> positive/progressive features in the British rule ... he sought to construct a new society; a society that would be qualitatively different from traditional/ brahminical/hierarchical order; a society that would celebrate modern/ scientific knowledge as opposed to religious beliefs and practices; a society in which all men and women would enjoy equal rights, and occupations such as farming, artisanship and labour would not be allowed to degrade a man's dignity. (Ibid.: 88)

It is against this backdrop that the construction of the idea of a national system of education in the pre-Independence days needs to be located.

A strong current for compulsory education at the primary stage was seen during the pre-Independence days. There was a national awakening that emphasised mass education as against the British policy of education for a few. 'The period between 1905 and 1921 witnessed a great ferment of educational thought within the fold of the Indian struggle for freedom and the birth of the concept of national education' (Biswas and Aggarwal 1994: 36). After Jyotirao Phule's fight for mass education of *equitable character* in 19th century and Dadabhai Naoroji's demand for universal education, a major step was taken in this direction when Gokhale moved a resolution in the Imperial Council in 1910 for free and compulsory education.

The Nagpur Congress (1920) advised the withdrawal of children from schools and called for the establishment of parallel national colleges and schools. This move was upheld by Mahatma Gandhi. Gradually, the concept of a national system of education started to take shape with numerous debates on the theme. Lala Lajpat Rai clearly defined the idea of national education: 'Assume nothing, analyse every idea, examine every scheme in the light of the day, in the searchlight of scientific truth' (quoted in Biswas and Aggarwal 1994: 47). He was opposed to blind rejection of Western literature or scientific disciplines. A similar understanding of synthesising the progressive Western body of knowledge with the Indian was also seen in the works of Raja Rammohan Roy and others in Bengal.

There was a general national awakening on the anvil in the specific context of education. In 1937, when Congress ministries assumed office in seven provinces, they faced a dilemma: though committed to universal free and compulsory education, they lacked the monetary resources to implement it. At such a juncture Mahatma Gandhi came forward with elaborate proposals on how to make education self-supporting through useful and productive work (ibid.: 55). He wrote a series of articles explaining his idea of a national system of education in *Harijan* in 1937.

Gandhi opposed colonial education not only because of its Western origin, but also because of 'its inherent élitism, its irrelevance as far as the needs of India's rural/subaltern masses were concerned' (Pathak 2002: 89). He also perceived how it hampered the integral education of the child and emphasised the use of craft as a medium through which a child could be provided an integral education. A close look at his *basic education* 'would suggest that it was not limited merely to the craft; through the craft, he wanted to impart knowledge on all important branches of learning' (ibid.: 90). Gandhi's education policy needs to be located in his contemporary socio-economic and political realities; therefore, it needs to be understood that 'for Gandhi, basic education was a component of his political programmes' (Acharya 1997: 604). And through his scheme of education he wanted to effect far-reaching social transformation. He wrote, 'My plan to impart primary education through the medium of village handicrafts like spinning and carding, etc., is thus conceived as the spearhead of a silent social revolution fraught with the most far reaching consequences' (quoted in Acharya 1997: 604).

Consequently, the first Congress of National Education was called at Wardha on 22–23 October 1937 to discuss the proposed educational system. In the conference, resolutions approving Gandhi's proposals on 'free/compulsory education for seven years, mother-tongue as the medium of instruction, education centred around some form of manual/productive work and a self-supporting education in the sense that it would be able to cover the remuneration of teachers' were passed (Pathak 2002: 91). A committee under Zakir Hussain was appointed to look into the details. It submitted its report soon after the conference, known as the Wardha Scheme of Basic Education. Mahatma Gandhi and the Congress as a whole endorsed it at the Haripura Congress (1938), which passed a resolution. An all-India board called Hindustani Talimi Sangh was set up to work out a programme of basic national education.

The Wardha Scheme of Education made path-breaking recommendations such as the need for 'an integral all-sided education', which by educating children 'through some suitable form of productive work' would balance 'the intellectual and practical elements of experience' (Biswas and Aggarwal 1994: 56). It elaborated on the nature of the curriculum and the duty of teachers apart from making minute suggestions on diverse aspects of subjects to be taught. However, one major drawback of the scheme was its patriarchal tone as it recommended domestic science specifically for the education of girls (ibid.: 56–63).

Built into this unfolding national system of education was a thrust to provide equal educational opportunities to all. Together with the urge to have *mass education,* there was an emphasis on the quality of education as well. It was manifested, irrespective of criticism, so as to focus on teachers' roles and responsibilities, designing of curriculum, teaching pedagogy, etc.

It was in this series of serious educational deliberations that the recommendations and understanding of the Central Advisory Board of Education (CABE) committee of 1944 needs mention. Called the *Post-War Educational Developments in India,* the CABE report of January 1944, also known as the Sargent Commission, elaborated on the questions of equality, quality as well as quantity as aspects of education in India. It defined the character of a national system of education in following words:

> The minimum provision which could be accepted as constituting a national system postulates that all children must receive enough education to prepare them to earn a living as well as to fulfil themselves as individuals and discharge their duties as citizens. (Government of India 1944: 3)

Arguing against any kind of selective dissemination of education, the commission said:

> If there is to be anything like equality of opportunity, it is impossible to justify providing facilities for some of the nation's children and not for others. In the first place, therefore, a national system can hardly be other than universal. Secondly, it must also be compulsory, if the grave wastage which exists today under a voluntary system is not to be perpetuated and even aggravated. And thirdly, if education is to be universal and compulsory, equity requires that it should be free and common sense demands that it should last long enough to secure its fundamental objective. (Ibid.)

Arguing against proposals and debates of making education free and compulsory in stages, it cited that such a division of stages between junior basic (primary) and upper primary in England caused a lot of problems. It urged that 'basic education from 6–14 is an organic whole and will lose much of its value, if not so treated; in any case an education, which lasts only five years and ends about the age of eleven, cannot be regarded as an adequate preparation either for life or livelihood' (ibid.). It talked of a 1:30 teacher–pupil ratio in primary schools and 1:25 ratio in middle schools (see ibid.: Chapter 1, para 5). It even dwelt upon the important role of teachers in educating children. It said, 'Even though all the nation's children are brought to school, success will not be achieved unless the teaching is effective and efficient teachers will have to be properly paid' (ibid.). Hence, a national system of education was taking shape, which focused on equal educational opportunities for all and also brought forth the significance of quality education, working conditions of teachers, etc., as the essential components of an education system that could prepare children for life and livelihood.

Most certainly there were shortcomings; for instance, the gender dimension was defined within a patriarchal framework (as in the Wardha Scheme of Education) or the issues relating to caste or class-based inequality were not focused upon in detail. However, the agenda of an equitable quality education was being amply projected.

Post-Independence Educational Development

One of the landmarks of the post-Independence educational agenda in India was reflected in Article 45 of the Indian Constitution, which asked the state to make education free and compulsory for all children up to 14 years of age. However, this was a part of the Directive Principles of State Policy and was, therefore, non-justiciable. It could become a fundamental right only in the 21st century, that too with objections from many quarters.

The post-Independence educational agenda was a nationalist project having broadly two components: (a) it attached 'great importance to modernity', trying to put forth the image of an industrially advanced modern state having a scientific and rational paradigm of development; and (b) it was deeply concerned with the issue of national integration, which meant 'overcoming all local identities and regional differences; realising our shared Indianness and strengthening the centrality of the new nation-state' (Pathak 2002: 95). In fact, a close look at the different reports and recommendations post Independence reveals this agenda of national unity and integration trying to merge the distinctness of a varied social structure, region, ethnicity, etc., into one whole—the nation. The agenda of modernity was written clear and large in policy debates and documents. And when the *Report of the Committee of Members of Parliament on Education* (Government of India 1967: 1) emphasised making 'the rising generation conscious of the fundamental unity of the country in the midst of her rich diversity, proud of her cultural heritage and confident of her great future', it was clear that the agenda was to strengthen the emergent nation–state within the framework of modernity.

Indeed, a close observation of the agenda of a post-Independence nation–state in India discloses an interesting politics of development. It has been argued predominantly that India's mixed economy provided a more equitable pattern of development through its focus on welfarist measures and 'control of the monopoly capital'. On the other hand people have argued, through the example of the Bombay Plan (1944),[1] that the 'mixed economy' was a façade. Instead, 'it was the business community who guided the government to build an infrastructure for their "profit" accumulation and appropriation' (Bhattacharyya 2000). Aditya Mukherjee (2002) also explains how Indian planning was motivated by the interests of the Indian bourgeoisie. He shows, for instance, 'why the capitalist representatives in the National Planning Committee (1945) agreed to the state ownership or control in key and heavy industries and public utilities like heavy electricals, power, fuel, and so on' (ibid.: 400). Whatever the underlying logic of welfarist economy of India was, the stress on universalising primary education always remained on the agenda. However, this agenda was different from the Wardha Scheme of Education or Gandhi's conception. The post-Independence agenda(s) of education, whether envisaged by Jawaharlal Nehru, the Radhakrishnan Commission (1949), the Kothari Commission (1966) or the National Policy on Education (NPE) (1986), they all had science and technology on their scheme as the paramount goal of education. The Nehruvian era represented the triumph of scientific temper (Nehru 1998: 509–14). The agenda of modern nation building was expressed in developing the industrial capability of the nation and making it self-reliant, and this project could only be realised riding on the back of science and rationality.

This emphasis is apparent in all the reports and recommendations of the state post Independence. For instance, the Kothari Commission stressed on science to be made an integral part of school and university education; to be included in study of humanities and social sciences at university levels (see Government of India 1966: 6, para 1.23). It was seen as an important tool to fight dogma and superstition, and establish reason and free enquiry. However, emphasis was also given to higher values over material affluence and power, leading to 'mingle science and spirituality' (ibid.: para 1.24).

Nehru simultaneously called for equality of opportunity. He wrote: 'The spirit of the age is in favour of equality, though practice denies it almost everywhere.' He was concerned about commodification of individuals and wrote that 'in the name of individual freedom, political and economic systems exploit human beings and treat them as commodities.' He argued that 'the backwardness or degradation of any group is not due to inherent failings in it, but principally to lack of opportunities and long suppression by other groups' (Nehru 1998: 521). The notion of equality has been bestowed great importance by different committees and policy documents of the State as well. Thus, education came to be perceived as a right and not a privilege. The Kothari Commission's proposal for a common school system and its reaffirmation in the NPE in 1986 and review of NPE-1986 in 1992 was a clear-cut indication that equal access to education opportunities was also on the state's agenda.

The Kothari Commission saw the utility of education as an instrument of change.

Quantitatively, education can be organized to promote social justice or to retard it.... On the other hand, a social and cultural revolution has been brought about in a system where equality of education opportunity is provided and education is deliberately used to develop more and more potential talent and to harness it to the solution of national problems. (Government of India 1966: 4, para 1.16)

It argued that 'one of the important social objectives of education is to equalize opportunity, enabling the backward or underprivileged classes and individuals to use education as a lever for improvement of their condition' (ibid.: 97, para 6.01). Its concept of the common school system and neighbourhood schools were steps in this direction (see Government of India 1966: 231–36, paras 10.05 and 10.19). The *Report of the Committee of Members of Parliament on Education* (Government of India 1967) endorsed the proposals of the Kothari Commission saying that:

> To strengthen social unity and to provide equality of opportunity to the less advanced sections of the society, the unhealthy social segregation that now takes place between the schools for the rich and those for the poor should be ended; and the primary schools should be made the common schools of the nation by making it obligatory on all children, irrespective of caste, creed, community, religion, economic condition or social status, to attend the primary school in their neighbourhood. This sharing of life among the children of all social strata will strengthen the sense of being one nation which is an essential ingredient of good education. (Ibid.: 2)

The NPE (1986) reiterated the issues of equality of educational opportunity, and free and compulsory education for all children up to 14 years.

However, that very NPE included non-formal education (NFE) as part of a policy document in a major way for the first time. Though it argued that NFE 'can result in provision of education comparable in quality with formal schooling', hardly does one find any justification for introduction of newer streams of NFE. The NPE tried to justify non-formal education by presenting similar arguments as done by numerous contemporary programmes of alternative and parallel education: 'The essential characteristics of NFE are organizational flexibility, relevance of curriculum, diversity in learning activities to relate them to the learners' needs, and decentralization of management' (Government of India 1986: 25). The NPE (1986) in fact began a significant trend of proposing new methods of increasing enrolment without trying to delve into the reasons why children from particular sections of the population remained outside schools. Today, we see how NFE is proliferating and is being used by the State to shed its responsibility of providing equitable and quality education to all children up to the age of 14 years.

Post NPE (1986), the Indian State's policy on education has witnessed a major shift. The Directive Principles of State Policy were ignored for over half a century and the state evaded its responsibility to impart free and compulsory education of good quality. It began meeting demands for formal schooling by implementing non-formal schemes under the garb of increasing the literacy rate. These changes left their impressions on the reports of different education committees as well. The only departures from the customary stance were the National Policy on the Education Review Committee (1990) or the Ramamurti Committee Report and Yashpal Committee (1989). However, these recommendations were either rejected or shelved. The State's discomfort with the Ramamurti Committee was such that a CABE Committee on Policy was appointed in 1991 under Janardhan Reddy to review it. The ploy was to shelve some of the 'radical' recommendations made by the Ramamurti Committee. The CABE Committee was against the neighbourhood school concept, argued against a local context-based curricula, and supported a multiple-layered government education system of Navodaya Vidyalayas as well as NFEs, among many other things (Government of India 1992). We see a drastic turn in India's education policy in the post-1990 period when programmes of 'alternative' and 'innovative' education began mushrooming. This new trend can be appreciated in a more holistic and contextualised fashion after we take a cursory look at the international context of shifts in educational concerns.

International Provisions for the Right to Free and Compulsory Elementary Education

Education is cited as one of the prime indicators of development as well as a tool to develop human and social capital. Consequently, there is tremendous concern to educate the vast mass of the population. This concern is apparent in UN documents as well as the Indian government's effort to achieve 'literacy' through a variety of programmes. Article 26 of the UN Declaration on Human Rights underscored everyone's right to education: 'Education shall be free, at least in the elementary and fundamental stages. Elementary education shall be compulsory.' It defined the aim of education as 'directed to the full development of the human personality and to the strengthening of respect for human rights and fundamental freedoms'. At the same time it also made clear that 'parents have a prior right to choose the kind of education that shall be given to their children', linking the nature of education disseminated with the needs and context of the child.[2]

Principle 7 of the Declaration of the Rights of the Child states that apart from free and compulsory elementary education, the child 'shall be given an education which will promote his general culture and enable him, on a basis of equal opportunity, to develop his abilities, his individual judgment, and his sense of moral and social responsibility, and to become a useful member of society'.[3]

The International Covenant on Economic, Social and Cultural Rights also recognises, in its Article 13, the right of everyone to education, and maintains that 'primary education shall be compulsory and available free to all' and 'the development of a system of schools at all levels shall be actively pursued, an adequate fellowship system shall be established, and the material conditions of teaching staff shall be continuously improved'. The liberty of parents and legal guardians is also emphasised with regard to the choice of schools for their children. Article 14 makes it mandatory for its signatories 'to work out and adopt a detailed plan of action for the progressive implementation, within a reasonable number of years, to be fixed in the plan, of the principle of compulsory education free of charge for all' within a period of two years.[4] India acceded to the Covenant on 10 July 1979, but failed to take the follow-up steps towards achieving the promises made in it.

The United Nations Convention on the Rights of the Child, in its Article 1, defines 'child' as every human 'below the age of eighteen years unless under the law applicable to the child, majority is attained earlier'. Article 28 maintains that states shall

recognize the right of the child to education and with a view to achieving this right progressively and on the basis of equal opportunity, they shall, in particular:

(a) Make primary education compulsory and available free to all; (b) Encourage the development of different forms of secondary education, including general and vocational education, make them available and accessible to every child and take appropriate measures such as the introduction of free education and offering financial assistance in case of need.

It also stressed on the need to check drop-out rates. Simultaneously, Article 29 provides that education of the child shall be directed to 'the development of respect for the child's parents, his or her own cultural identity, language and values, for the national values of the country in which the child is living, the country from which he or she may originate, and for civilizations different from his or her own'.[5] India acceded to the Convention on the Rights of the Child (CRC) on 11 January 1993, and even after more than a decade it has not only failed to act upon it, but has enacted amendments in contravention of the CRC, most pernicious of which is the definition of the child under the Child Labour (Prohibition & Regulation) Act.

In March 1990, the First World Conference on Education was held at Jomtien, Thailand. It 'represented a collective attempt to address this quantitative crisis' of a vast mass of out of school children (Kumar et al. 2001a: 561). It propagated the slogans, 'education for all' and 'lifelong learning opportunities', without questioning the fundamental structural reasons for why children remain outside the school. The World Education Forum met in Dakar in April 2000 to reflect upon the status of educational achievements worldwide and chalk out strategies for the future. Before the Dakar meet, the Asia–Pacific Conference on Education for All (EFA) 2000 Assessment was organised, which prepared the Asia and Pacific Regional Framework for Action: Education for All—Guiding Principles, Specific Goals and Targets for 2015. It spelt out its priorities for quality-based care and education 'at all stages of life' for children. It highlighted the need for 'child-centered, family-focused, community-based, holistic care and education of pre-school children', and sought to forge a 'synergistic partnership among families, communities, civil society, NGOs and the government'. It said Early

Childhood Care and Education (ECCE) programmes should aim at promoting 'the child's optimum physical, psycho-social, emotional, cognitive and linguistic development in ways that are culturally and socially relevant'. The focus of educational agenda must be 'good quality that focuses on the "whole" person, including health, nutrition and cognitive and psycho-social development'. The education must also

> eliminate systemic gender disparities, where they persist, amongst girls and boys throughout the education system—in enrolment, achievement and completion; in teacher training and career development; in curriculum, and learning practices and learning processes. This requires better appreciation of the role of education as an instrument of women's equality and empowerment.

The excluded groups of society must be the focus of education programmes. Within this framework of education the 'public perceptions of teachers and teaching must be enhanced; incentives to identify, attract and retain good teachers must be provided'.[6]

Structural adjustment programmes were launched and educational crisis was seen to aggravate, especially in the developing countries. It became a matter of grave concern and, hence, the emphasis on education by international agencies emerged as a natural corollary to the events unfolding. 'Targets' of enrolment and making children literate became a priority. Target achievement came to be the measure of development, without any effort at analysing its pros and cons. The definition of development in terms of mere targets not only mechanised and centralised the whole process of development, but it also led to severe constraints regarding the way education should be perceived (see Goldstein 2004). In this new development paradigm, certain correlations became fixed categories without any space for alterations or critical re-examination, thereby entrenching itself in the educational discourse. In fact, this is how any dominant discourse in society establishes and maintains its unswerving hegemony. One such instance can be cited in the way literacy and women's empowerment have been correlated. The slogan of autonomy and empowerment is narrowed down to certain decontextualised categories like work participation rate (WPR) and literacy without considering the multiple variables that constitute the paradigm of 'empowerment'.

> How education supposedly enhances women's autonomy is rarely specified. Nevertheless a casual link between female schooling, female autonomy and low fertility is universally assumed. Both at national and international levels, policies to foster women's education and employment opportunities often have the ulterior goal of controlling population growth through reducing fertility. This instrumentality is common to many development policies. In the 1991 World Development Report, the World Bank lists the benefits of educating women as: reducing the need for community health programmes; lowering infant mortality thus compensating for the absence of medical facilities; increasing the use of contraception. (Swaminathan 2002: 70)

In brief, there has obviously been a shift in the discourse on education at international level as well and India experiences a similar fallout.

The goals for universal elementary education have been reemphasised on numerous occasions, as cited earlier. However, in the course of this there has been a change in the way education has come to be problematised. The changes can be seen in words as well as in aims, as the *World Education Report* (UNESCO 2000) argues that 'words matter, for they are used to express principles'. The Jomtien Conference, sponsored by the World Bank, according to some educationists, laid the 'groundwork for intervention by the international funding agencies in the national educational structures and processes of the developing nations' (Sadgopal 2001: 45). This emphasis on external funding was further enforced by the Dakar Framework for Action, which committed itself to 'increasing external finance for education, in particular basic education', among other aims.[7] The Dakar Framework continued on the same agenda set by the Jomtien Conference. Its addition of the 'ambiguous notion of Life Skills seems to be yet another mechanism for social manipulation and market control of the adolescent mindset, particularly girls' and 'India unfortunately gave up its progressive policy on women's education in favour of the international framework that was guided more by the considerations of market than by women's socio-cultural and political rights' (Sadgopal 2003: 99).

The changes in education discourse also had implications for the right to education agenda as formulated in the beginning by the United Nations itself. UNESCO's 2000 *World Education Report* notes:

> There has been a change in the world's perception of the right to education over the past few decades. Whereas the Universal Declaration of Human Rights proclaims that 'Everyone has the right to education', that elementary and fundamental education shall be 'free' and that 'elementary education shall be compulsory', the Declaration adopted by the World Conference on Education for All proclaims that 'Every person—child, youth and adult—shall be able to benefit from educational opportunities designed to meet their basic learning needs.'
>
> The Universal Declaration of Human Rights does not mention 'learners' or 'learning needs', and the World Declaration on Education for All does not mention 'elementary', 'fundamental', 'free', or 'compulsory education'. The twin notions of 'elementary and fundamental education' have been overtaken by the notion of 'basic education', while at the same time there has been a shift of emphasis from 'education' to 'learning': from what society should supply, so to speak, i.e., education that is 'free', 'compulsory', and 'directed towards', to what members of society are said to demand ('educational opportunities designed to meet their basic learning need'). (UNESCO 2000: 26)

EDUCATION IN DEVELOPMENT DISCOURSE

The understanding of education has been unravelled repeatedly by documents released by 'international/national development agencies'. Perspectives on education got encapsulated in the wider conception of development, with the aim of improving 'human development indicators'. The emphasis on education as a source of enhancing prospects of opportunities and capacity of human beings has come to dominate the development paradigm. Development economists like Dreze and Sen (1995) stressed on the need for 'participatory growth'. Amartya Sen set the discourse in terms of development as 'expansion of opportunities', or in terms of freedom enjoyed by individuals. Opportunities came to occupy centre-stage in guiding development programmes and policies, and, consequently, the elements that go into the making of such opportunities as health and education. This has been the guiding paradigm of developing nations today, with aid pouring in. To expand 'opportunities' and 'freedoms' of individuals, their capability needs to be enhanced, and it is this enhancement that is widely recognised as an indicator of development. Education came to be identified as one of the most 'enabling change agents', whether for an individual or society as whole.

In search of the ultimate development imagery, development agencies or bodies concerned with it held that economic planning is not sufficient unless supplemented by human resource development, which is viewed as 'the process of enlarging people's choices'. UNESCO argued that there is a need to alter our notion of development to a 'broader view', which encompasses other factors apart from schooling. UNESCO evolved the notion of *continuing education* aimed at integrating 'learning, working and living'. These three elements of personality development became very important to achieve an educated society.

> Logically, however, it is reasonable to infer that increases in knowledge and skills are needed for the introduction and expansion of modern technology and that education must grow and change if a technologically based socio-economic system is to grow and change. Education seen in this way is an enabling agent for development. (UNESCO 1997: 4)

It further argued that schooling has also alienated people from 'mainstream society' in many cases, and formal education has rendered many people unemployed due to its urban orientation.

> The crisis in education in many developing countries has come about largely because the formal system caters only to a handful of successful students and the rest become alienated and unproductive. *Continuing education*—the opportunity to engage in lifelong learning—therefore emerges as a way of compensating for the inadequacies of the formal system by giving people a second chance, and also of ensuring a continual growth and upgrading of human resources throughout the lives of all citizens. (Ibid.: 5)

It has been cited as a source for developing a community and individuals because education leads to equity. 'It provides knowledge, skills and values which enable people to add economic value to their labour beyond that necessary for mere subsistence'. It ultimately makes possible a 'rational, sustainable and humanistic' national development. The development of human resource has become the focus of attention, and numerous programmes have been launched or suggested by development agencies. Non-formal education, adult education and multi-grade teaching among many other methods/programmes have come to signify education. It blatantly puts conditions in which multi-grade teaching can be implemented—such as shortage of classrooms and teachers—to bring disadvantaged people into the education net, thereby proclaiming a different system for the disadvantaged and negating the plank of equality and of a welfare society (ibid.)

The spate of liberalisation unleashed in the aftermath of structural adjustment programmes (SAP) started the process of States gradually withdrawing from those sectors that were seen as non-profit-making. And one of the most noticeable aspects of the post-liberalisation phase has been the gradual withdrawal of the State from sectors believed to be a burden for its treasury. Naturally, if measurement or tangible outcome in terms of profit is the guiding principle, the social sector becomes the obvious target. The shift in the development discourse and location of education within that discourse could be observed starkly in India from the time structural adjustments began. For instance, 'the DPEP was initiated as a part of the larger Social Safety Net Credit Adjustment Loan under the Structural Adjustment Programme of the World Bank to India in 1991' (Ramachandran and Saihjee 2002: 1601). Indeed, the Jomtien Conference was important in the education history of India, but not because it opened the gates of mass education for the poor and underprivileged.

On a first reading it would appear that suddenly in the 1990s, the wealthy countries of the world converged on the agenda of educating the poor, and that this change of heart facilitated a substantial amount of resources in the form of both loan and aid for education in Africa, Latin America and South Asia. The Jomtien Conference of 1990 was seen as crystallising this support strategy.

However, to look at Jomtien as a biblical start of international devotion to children is to commit a willing methodological error—one of ignoring history and interconnections while looking at state policy inclinations or changes. These are seen as variables that can be explained by themselves, without a reference to their interconnections with society, politics, and culture. It is our contention that one of the chief characteristics of the smokescreen is its ahistorical character. (Kumar et al. 2001a: 560)

This caution also becomes necessary because of the way in which the District Primary Education Programme (DPEP) has been lauded and portrayed. It has been shown as based on the policy guidelines laid down in NPE (1986) and as a holistic programme of education (Ramachandran and Saihjee 2002: 1601). It has been argued that the Jomtien slogans in 'a language of benign benevolence' were response to the economic as well as educational crisis of the 1980s. 'The 1991 economic crisis provided leverage to the World Bank to insist that developing countries must borrow for primary education and health' (Kumar et al.: 561). Hence, began the DPEP programme. 'Behind the smokescreen then is a vivid story of the roll-back of the state, of contracting commitments for formal education, of the dismantling of the existing structures of formal education, proliferation of "teach anyhow" strategies, a thrust on publicity management, and a neo-conservative reliance on community' (ibid.).

The education policy underwent a drastic change. Education coincided with literacy. Though it was in 1988 that the National Literacy Mission was started, the overwhelming domination of the literacy paradigm—of short-term mechanisms to 'educate'—was seen during the post-1990 phase. Foreign aid began pouring in for elementary education. Beginning with the DPEP, it continued with many other programmes and the most recent addition to the list is Sarva Shiksha Abhiyan (SSA), India's answer to all educational problems. The proof of massive foreign investment in education is evident from the way the share of external aid in education expenditure increased from Rs. 374.7 million in 1993–94 to Rs. 12.1 billion in 2001–2 (budget estimates). The share of external aid in the total central budget plan account for elementary education as a percentage of the central government budget has risen from 9.60 per cent (in 1993–94) to 31.84 per cent (in 2001–2) (Tilak 2003: 46). The loans are not only conditional, but constitute a part of the larger neo-liberal framework of capitalist development wherein the State's role is pushed back and private capital is provided a free playing field. There is a continued effort to reinforce the centre–periphery relationship of development in which developing countries will be at the mercy of developed nations. It further entrenches education as a commodity in the market in the name of empowerment and skill development for sustainable living. Consequently, critical thinking is consistently ignored as a part of education. The relationship between 'apparently' diverse fields of social structure, opportunities incumbent upon it, and educational status are perpetuated as they are taken as autonomous variables in education debate and planning.

The understanding of education as an arena of critical thinking has been negated and replaced by the necessity of literacy. There is a common ground on which international agencies, development economists, as well as the Indian State works. The idea of capacity building and empowerment are being commonly used as buzzwords to justify all that is being implemented.

> Education, in the present day context is perhaps the single most important means for individuals to improve personal endowments, build capacity levels, overcome constraints and, in the process, enlarge their available set of opportunities and choices for a sustained improvement in well being. (Government of India 2002a: 48)

The 10th Plan clearly stated its intention of inviting private–public partnership (a subtle way of inducing privatisation) in education, ignoring the dynamics of capital and market, which seldom function on the basis of welfare motivations and commitments. The Approach Paper to the 10th Five-Year Plan suggested that 'laws, rules and procedures for private, cooperative and NPO supply of education must be modernised and simplified so that *honest and sincere individuals and organisations can set up universities, colleges and schools*' (Government of India 2001a: 38, para 3.64; emphasis added). The Plan document went a step further to define the role of private agencies. It argued:

> The task of providing basic education in a country with diverse conditions is so stupendous that it is difficult to expect the government sector alone to do this effectively. Even though private initiatives have always been a part of the school education endeavour, it has neither been large nor of a sizeable magnitude in the efforts to universalise elementary education. The private sector can contribute not only in monetary and material terms, but also in the form of expertise for improving quality through effective management of the system and the development of locally relevant teaching learning materials.... A synergetic public–private partnership would be built up during the Tenth Plan to achieve the objective of UEE. (Government of India 2001b: 39, para 2.2.70)

Perceptions that deemed education as an emancipatory tool are lost. Gandhi or Freire's ideas have been mutilated to unrecognisable extents. The Task Force on *India as Knowledge Superpower* of the Planning Commission (Government of India 2001c) expressed its concern at the 'commodification' of education as depriving rural and poor children of education. It also stressed the significance of developing the 'individuality and creativity' of the child (ibid.: 12). However, its suggestions of 'distance education as a means of bringing education to every school-aged child' (ibid.: 11) negates its prior observation and will effectively only feed information to passive recipients in villages, establishing the rule of mechanised ethos, while killing creativity, and what Tagore would have called 'freedom of mind'. Similarly, the *Report of the Committee on India Vision 2020* (Government of India 2002b) correctly observed:

> Literacy is an indispensable minimum condition for development, but it is far from sufficient. In this increasingly complex and technologically sophisticated world, 10 years of school education must also be considered as an essential prerequisite for citizens to adapt and succeed economically, avail of the social opportunities and develop their individual potentials'. (Ibid.: 5)

But eventually its understanding of education failed to talk of inculcating criticality as the prime aim of the education system. Like the other reports, it also failed to dwell upon the larger context within which any education system functions—such as the social structure, social relations, and curriculum and pedagogy as reflections of these structures and relations. It is these efforts that have contributed to the entrenchment of literacy in the mainstream discourse.

A survey of literature on 'education' overwhelmingly reflects this trend though there are attempts trying to focus on why literacy campaigns have proved ineffectual or the kind of problems that characterise them. The Total Literacy Campaigns (TLC), which represented the thrust of the Indian State to discharge its responsibilities 'somehow', was a precursor to the contemporary trends that are diluting the notion of formal schooling. Nevertheless, it must be kept in mind that formal schooling is not without its own drawbacks. A whole gamut of literature on how schooling serves the needs of market and how it furthers the aims of capitalist development can be found in writings of critical educationists (see Allman 2001; Giroux 1998; Rikowski 2002). The emphasis on strengthening formal schooling, as argued here, is aware of such complications, but it is seen as an important tool in enforcing the idea of equal educational opportunities in contemporary times. A formal schooling system of comparable quality, free for every Indian child, will also constitute a battle against inequality in the education system. The aim of the TLC was to achieve the following:

> Copying at the rate of seven words a minute, counting and writing from 1 to 100, adding and subtracting three digit numbers as well as being able to multiply and divide two digit numbers.... Basic general knowledge of the world and society as well as of institutions the learners were likely to encounter was to be imparted, and there was an emphasis on the development of what was called 'social and critical consciousnesses'. All this was to be taught in 200 learning hours in an environment which suited the learner. (Karlekar 2004: 20)

It is assumed from such 'schemes' of 'social engineering' that development in a smooth and mechanical way will take place, devoid of any complications, at the end of which will emerge the final product, a 'developed' and 'empowered' individual and society. Cautioning against the pitfalls of isolated literacy campaigns as a 'programme', Sadhna Saxena (2004: 179) argues that literacy needs to be considered in historical, socio-political and economic contexts because 'it is neither a neutral nor an isolated or an autonomous variable. It is an ideological construct, a double-edged sword that could help in reinforcing or reducing the inequality and inequity'.

The Indian State gradually decided to focus on 'schemes' such as the Education Guarantee Scheme (EGS) or Alternative and Innovative Education (AIE) to educate out-of-school children'. No concerted effort to strengthen formal schooling has been made despite evaluation studies citing the pitfalls of NFE (Government of India 1998). Interestingly, studies began to point out the ineffectiveness of government schools and the system, thereby justifying new 'methods' and 'schemes'.

FROM ARTICLE 45 TO THE 86TH AMENDMENT: QUALITY EDUCATION TO QUANTITY EDUCATION?

Despite such emphasis on education, the Indian State has failed to achieve the target set by Article 45. It is not only the status of the 'target' to be achieved in education, but the general educational scenario has been dismal as well. Gradually, the recommendations of various committees and even the constitutional provisions began to get diluted as the notion of 'knowledge' and 'education' was transformed into 'literacy'. From the aim of striving for all-round development of individuals in a congenial atmosphere, governments started implementing programmes that tried to educate a child in two years as opposed to five-year schooling through different schemes. Similarly, instead of providing every child sufficient facilities in form of a well-equipped school, the state implemented the District Primary Education Programme (DPEP), in collaboration with the World Bank. This focused on multi-grade teaching with low resources and under-trained para-teachers. A study conducted by the DPEP itself in 1999 belied the claim that para-teachers are more dependable than regular teachers. 'The report says that low salary, combined with the contractual character of the job, has been the major source of discontent and lack of motivation among para-teachers' (Kumar et al. 2001b).

A major step was taken when the fundamental right to education was passed by the Indian Parliament as the 86th Amendment. Following the recommendations of the Saikia Committee, the government introduced the 83rd Constitutional Amendment Bill in Parliament in 1997 to make the right to education from 6 to 14 years a fundamental right. The Supreme Court in its judgement in Unnikrishnan's case (in 1993) had already held that citizens of India have a fundamental right to education up to 14 years of age. Under pressure from international bodies and national civil society organisations, the Indian State, through the 86th Amendment, made elementary education a fundamental right by inserting Article 21A, which says that 'the State shall provide free and compulsory education to all children of the age of six to fourteen years in such manner as the State may, by law, determine'. It also substituted Article 45 by the text that 'the State shall endeavour to provide early childhood care and education for all children until they complete the age of six years'. Social activists claim that if the State's attitude towards the earlier version of Article 45 is any indication, the new version would imply dilution of the children's right to early childhood care and education (ECCE). The other opinion argues, citing the Unnikrishnan judgement, that the new amendment would provide a basis for legal intervention, though it also implies that it has gone against the Supreme Court ruling for educating all children till the age of 14. Scepticism towards the policy also increases because the amendment or the pending Bill does not clearly mention the nature of education to be provided or the State's financial commitment to the sector. According to the Ministry of Human Resource Development, the percentage of expenditure on education to GDP has been 4.02 in 2001–2 whereas the National

Policy on Education (1986) had put expenditure target on education at 6.0 per cent of GDP. Para 11.4 of the NPE (1986) states 'that:

> The investment on education be gradually increased to reach a level of 6% of the National Income as early as possible. Since the actual level of investment has remained far short of that target, it is important that greater determination is shown now to find the funds for the programmes laid down in this policy. While actual requirements will be computed from time to time on the basis of monitoring and review, the outlay on education will be stepped up to ensure that during the 8th Five Year Plan and onwards it will uniformly exceed 6% of the national income. (Quoted from the Ministry of Human Resource Development Web site: http://www.education.nic.in/htmlweb/natpol.htm#1)

Given such disposition of the state, implementation of the fundamental right becomes extremely problematic, and optimistic results should be expected with trepidation. It has not only been unable to implement the right to education sincerely, but has transformed the character of education, deviating from the ideals. The recent programme of SSA, EGS and AIE have implied a second-grade teaching for children of the poor, Dalits, disabled and girls. The 'alternative' programmes designate them as their 'targets' because they are the most needy ones due to their poor resource base. It is an irony that despite considering them so, the programmes deliver to them a substandard education.

It is also of great concern that these policies have seldom taken care of issues of curriculum (its relevance and attraction for the child), teacher training and teaching pedagogy, leave aside the infrastructural requirements of schooling. The pending Free and Compulsory Education for Children Bill, despite numerous revisions, is still to address structural issues and that of teaching pedagogy and quality of education. When the UPA government came to power, a member of the National Advisory Council in his *Draft Recommendations of the National Advisory Council for Provision of Universal Access to Quality Education through Sarva Shiksha Abhiyan* not only kept the spirit of a poor-quality education for the poor alive, but also suggested indirectly the provisions for professional management interventions, killing the space for any community participation (see http://www.nac.nic.in). Many review studies have pointed out that even the SSA is not being implemented in the manner the government had intended, especially with regard to participatory planning, community evaluation, etc. The SSA had 'promised that every child will be in school by 1 January 2003. With 35 million to 70 million children out of school, that promise stands broken' (Kaura 2004). A recent probe by *Outlook* magazine in different parts of the country shows what the new programmes aiming at educating everybody look like—without infrastructure, absent teachers, under-trained teachers and disinterested children (Wadhwa 2004).

INEQUITY IN EDUCATION: LOCATING THE SYSTEMIC CONCERNS

Built into the concerns of providing education to all has been the element of inequity. The systemic concerns in education need to be immediately addressed if the problem of high drop-out is to be checked and education of comparable quality is to be provided to every child. It is both the social system within which the school is located as well as the larger system of state initiatives and management that play the most significant roles in ensuring a good-quality education, which remains our most vital concern. Arguments have consistently demonstrated that certain sections of society are deprived of education. This deprivation has been attributed to systemic characteristics. Indian society has been caste-ridden and patriarchal with marginalisation perpetuated by inequitable distribution of wealth, and the logic of hegemonic interests controlling and dictating access to resources and facilities, thus, further complicating the issue. Consequently, we have a society where Dalits, women, the poor and tribal are marginalised, and the deprivation of education is just an accentuation of this marginalisation.

Inequity in education, as in other cases of social concern, reflects sharply the structural inequalities of our social system and its structures. These structures are driven by economic differentiation and corresponding cultural and social features, and which create hurdles for many down the structure in accessing education. It is manifested on one hand in the inaccessibility to formal schooling system due to lack of purchasing power, while on the other hand social and cultural norms are reinforcing this further. More importantly, structural inequalities, as argued by Geetha B. Nambissan in this book, have also determined access to 'valued resources'. This access has been overwhelmingly discriminatory due to accumulated consequences of social hierarchisation, with the poor, Dalits, tribals and women figuring at the margins.

It is in this context that one finds the caste system with its 'typical' hierarchy still creating hurdles for Dalits to access education of *comparable quality*. Even if Dalit children gain entry into schools, they confront a variety of problems as they attempt a total inclusion in the system at par with others. These problems may range from discriminatory behaviour of teachers, classmates and distribution of midday meals, to growing social pressure and poverty. The character of social system, its approach vis-à-vis diverse social sections such as poor, Dalits and women, must be explored if analyses into the reasons for their exclusion from the education system are to be undertaken. Karuna Chanana, for instance, argues in her chapter that the exclusion of girls from schools will continue so long as schools reflect the gendered relations embedded in society, characterised by the lower positioning of women vis-à-vis men.

Provisions aimed at tackling the issues of inequity inbuilt into the education system have been made from time to time, as the history of education indicates, but they have always proven insufficient on some account or the other and have, in fact, institutionalised systems such as that of NFE, as Vasudha Dhagamwar argues in her chapter. Due to the failure of education policies and the dubious commitment towards educating every Indian, we still find millions of children out of school. The challenge of education today is not only to bring in those children, belonging primarily to the poor sections, Dalits, disabled and girl children, into the formal schooling system, but also to reflect upon the issues of curriculum, teaching pedagogy, infrastructure, social relations/structure–education interface, etc. And these issues require a holistic approach that links these problems together, not fragmented truths meriting distinct responses. It is also about prioritisation and commitment, as Amarjeet Sinha contends that 'all arguments vanish into thin air as ultimately it is a matter of priority, a matter whether elementary education of poor children really matters'. The concern for addressing the educational backwardness of different communities must be located in terms of its relationship with the inequity characterising the society. Unless this is addressed the problems of educational development and equalisation of educational opportunities will remain mere wishful thinking.

The debate on education persists because of the acute crisis generated by skewed educational opportunities existing in the country in favour of those who can spend. Data has shown the stark discrimination in education. There is clear-cut correlation between economic capacity and attainment of formal education. For instance, as the monthly per capita consumption expenditure (MPCE) increases, the number of illiterates go down, and the number of persons going beyond primary schooling goes up, and the number of children being educated beyond primary is lesser (Table 1.1). The condition is worse in case of the girl child.

TABLE 1.1
LEVEL OF EDUCATION OF PERSONS AGED 7 AND ABOVE IN RURAL INDIA
ACCORDING TO MONTHLY PER CAPITA EXPENDITURE (%)

MPCE (Rs.)	Not Literate	Literate	Level of Education Among Literates					
			Below Primary	Primary	Middle	Secondary	Higher Secondary	Graduate & Above
0–225	65.1	34.9	52.1	24.6	16.3	4.9	1.4	0.6
225–255	60.4	39.6	50.0	26.3	16.2	4.8	2.3	0.8
255–300	57.3	42.7	48.0	26.0	16.6	6.3	2.1	0.9
300–340	52.9	47.1	44.6	24.2	19.7	7.6	2.5	1.1
340–380	49.2	50.8	42.3	25.6	20.1	7.9	2.8	1.6
380–420	46.8	53.2	39.8	24.6	21.4	9.0	3.6	1.5
420–470	43.0	57.0	37.0	25.8	22.3	9.6	3.7	1.6
470–525	40.5	59.5	33.1	25.2	23.7	11.3	4.7	2.0
525–615	37.2	62.8	30.9	24.4	24.2	12.6	5.4	2.7
615–775	32.2	67.8	25.2	23.6	25.2	14.7	6.9	4.3
775–950	27.6	72.4	21.7	20.9	24.9	18.4	8.1	5.9
950+	21.0	79.0	15.9	18.2	22.3	20.5	12.2	11.0
All	44.0	56.0	34.6	24.1	22.0	11.4	5.0	3.0

Source: Based on (NSSO 2001).

The economic incapacity to spend on education affects girl children and Dalits more (Table 1.2). Girls become the obvious choice in a patriarchal set-up to be taken out of education compared to boys. This is true in urban centres as well. NSSO data shows that much fewer girls belonging to poor households (households spending less) complete primary schooling (NSSO 2001). Similarly, there are relatively few Dalits who are able to obtain even the secondary education. And within Dalits girl children remains further deprived.

TABLE 1.2
LEVEL OF EDUCATION OF PERSONS AGED 7 AND ABOVE ACCORDING TO SEX AND SOCIAL GROUP (%)

Social Group	Not Literate	Literate	Distribution by Level of Education Among Literates					
			Below Primary	Primary	Middle	Higher Secondary	Secondary	Graduate & Above
Rural								
Male								
Scheduled Tribe	46.2	53.8	40.9	24.9	20.1	8.2	3.7	2.2
Scheduled Caste	41.2	58.8	38.6	24.5	21.1	9.5	4.3	2.2
Other Backward Class	32.2	67.8	33.5	23.2	23.2	11.5	5.5	3.1
Others	21.9	78.1	26.9	20.9	23.3	15.9	7.4	5.6
Not recorded	34.9	65.1	25.0	28.9	26.4	13.4	1.5	4.8
All	32.2	67.8	32.6	22.7	22.6	12.5	5.9	3.8
Female								
Scheduled Tribe	69.9	30.1	46.2	25.9	18.6	6.0	2.3	0.7
Scheduled Caste	66.4	33.6	46.4	27.1	17.3	6.6	1.8	0.9
Other Backward Class	58.9	41.1	38.9	26.8	20.9	8.8	3.2	1.5
Others	43.3	56.7	32.8	25.8	22.2	12.0	4.8	2.5
Not recorded	61.5	38.5	50.9	20.3	27.3	0.8	0.5	0.3
All	56.6	43.4	38.0	26.3	20.7	9.5	3.5	1.8

(*Table 1.2 continued*)

(*Table 1.2 continued*)

Social Group	Not Literate	Literate	Distribution by Level of Education Among Literates				Higher Secondary	Graduate & Above
			Below Primary	Primary	Middle	Secondary		
Urban								
Male								
Scheduled Tribe	21.9	78.1	25.7	17.5	21.8	12.9	10.5	11.7
Scheduled Caste	24.0	76.0	28.2	22.9	22.5	13.4	7.5	5.4
Other Backward Class	16.5	83.5	21.7	20.1	23.4	17.3	9.1	8.5
Others	8.6	91.4	15.2	14.6	18.4	18.7	13.1	19.9
Not recorded	13.6	86.4	23.5	11.1	20.4	17.5	15.7	11.8
All	13.5	86.5	19.0	17.2	20.5	17.5	11.2	14.7
Female								
Scheduled Tribe	38.8	61.2	28.8	20.8	22.1	12.8	8.0	7.7
Scheduled Caste	44.3	55.7	31.4	25.0	23.5	10.4	6.1	3.6
Other Backward Class	33.6	66.4	25.3	23.3	22.7	15.2	8.0	5.6
Others	19.0	81.0	17.9	17.2	19.9	17.9	11.5	15.7
Not recorded	34.3	65.7	25.9	11.9	18.0	29.4	6.5	8.4
All	27.7	72.3	21.7	19.8	21.2	16.2	9.8	11.3

Source: Based on NSSO (2001).

It is not only Dalits who are deprived of educational benefits, but also tribal populations. They lag behind Dalits when it comes to availing educational facilities as indicated by Table 1.2. This happens despite recommendations of the education policy to educate them on a priority basis as early as 1986. The 1986 National Policy on Education specifically laid down that opening of primary schools in tribal areas will be undertaken as priority. It also emphasised on the need to develop instructional material in tribal languages at the initial stages in order to create propitious conditions for their smooth

shift to regional language education. Despite such recommendations, we are still to find their reflection in tribal areas. Not much
effort has gone into preparing textbooks in tribal languages. Neither
has their educational status shown much improvement.

Another problem that grapples the education debate is the retention of children in school systems. Even when children are enrolled
in schools they drop out at very early stages. Many studies have tried
to identify the reasons for this absence of retention. The drop-out
rate put forth by the government indicates that 39.7 per cent boys
drop out in classes I to V, whereas the figure for girls is 41.9 per
cent. Fifty per cent of boys and 57.7 per cent of girls drop out by
class VIII. The trend continues to go up as we move up (Government of India 2002c: 68). The drop-out rate for girls in some states
is staggeringly higher compared to the national average. What has
concerned educationists is the lack of serious intervention on this
front. The reasons for dropping out are many, but disinterest in
studies, 'inability' to cope academically, and financial constraints are
the major reasons.

TABLE 1.3
MAIN REASONS FOR NOT ATTENDING SCHOOL (%)

Reasons	Male	Female
Not interested in studies	25.8	15.8
Costs too much	26.2	24.5
Others	17.6	13.4

Source: IIPS and ORC Macro (2000).

That the education system in India favours those who have the
capacity to spend becomes obvious also in light of the nature of
the predominant socio-economic system we live in—a commodified social relation characterises this system. Once something is
commodified and its value determined, it can be used by only those
who can spend. Hence, the demand for making education a State
responsibility also entails a demand for an end to the commodification of education. Apart from this economic discrimination, there
are other forms of difficulties that characterise the education system.

Being part of the social system and a reflection of its character, education is discriminatory across caste and gender lines as well.

Discrimination in the system is aggravated when there emerges a notion of government schools being inferior to their private counterparts. Though the question of inequality needs a bigger space of debate, it is relevant to point out that the formal schooling system in India has suffered because it has been consistently ignored by the State. Statistics even today speak starkly of that. We are at such a juncture that many states are experiencing decrease in enrolment in government schools. The NCERT (2002: Table FS38) reports in its Seventh Survey that, in comparison to its Sixth Survey in 1993, states like Goa (–15.76 per cent), Kerala (–14.52 per cent) and Punjab (–10.57 per cent) have experienced decreases in enrolment in classes I to V. This negative growth is also a reflection of the increasing commodification of education. Government schools are considered inferior and students are shifting to private schools as these have come to denote 'quality education' according to the popular notion. This notion is so rampant that even the sections of the populace incapable of affording such 'extravagant education' prefer to send their children to private schools. This notion, nevertheless, is not completely unfounded. There is neglect of infrastructural facilities as well and there are 16,777 primary schools without buildings (ibid.: Table FS10). The pupil–teacher ratio (PTR) is 1:42 at an all-India level, with states like Bihar, Uttar Pradesh and West Bengal having PTR above 1:50 (ibid.: Table FS56). There are 8,465 primary schools without any teachers, 97,670 with one teacher, 281,278 with two teachers, 108,228 with three teachers, 57,538 with four teachers, and only 39,224 schools with five teachers (ibid.: Table FS55). Therefore, there are 553,179 primary schools having less than five teachers, thus implying that many schools do not even have a teacher for every class.

CARRYING THE DEBATE FORWARD

Emerging from this scenario is a range of debates that sharpened in the post-liberalisation era. After the 86th Amendment was passed by the Parliament making education a fundamental right, a clear-cut construction of mainstream discourse in favour of the Act, not ready to make any scathing criticism, can be seen. However, the truth remains that there are many educationists and activists who see 'abdication by the state' of its responsibilities to make education of good quality accessible to all children. It is being argued by activists and academicians that the State in the wake of liberalisation has further neglected the social sector, and hence, education. Under pressure from the World Bank and international aid agencies, seen as carriers of the neo-liberal agenda, the Indian State has institution-alised discrimination by ignoring all prior recommendations of various government-appointed committees. Instead of enforcing equal access to quality education to all through formal schooling, it is initiating new schemes of non-formal education for the vast masses of the poor, Dalits and girl children. The chapters in this volume address the multiple dimensions of inequity embedded in our educational debates, planning and implementation. As a common concern they highlight, though in different vein, the systemic issues confronting elementary education in India today. Vasudha Dhagamwar and Anil Sadgopal in their respective chapters look into the validity of constitutional amendments in their historicity and question the State's agenda post-86th Amendment. Vasudha Dhagamwar opens her essay by questioning the motive of the State at not including education in Part III (Fundamental Rights) of the Constitution but in Part IV (Directive Principles of State Policy). She also raises concerns about the way the government has failed to implement many national and international provisions already existing. Girl children, SCs and STs are still educationally the most backward sections. The government, instead of tackling problems head on, launched adult literacy and many other non-formal literacy programmes. She criticises the Indian State for not being able to fulfil the aspirations of Article 45. Though, the Constitution was amended finally with the insertion of Article 21A, she argues, there is the task of filing writ petitions so that the State can spell out the kind of education it desires, which remains ambiguous in the amendment. Much like many of the papers in this volume, she believes that there is a widespread hunger for education. However, parents and children should be duty bound to go to school if NFE is to be challenged at all.

Anil Sadgopal's paper tries to contextualise critically the current educational scenario in the historico-structural context of international and national developments, thereby providing a premise on which to proceed. He goes a step further in his critical appraisal of the Indian State's policies and contends that even the 86th Amendment is a continuance on similar lines of abdication by the State.

After analysing the provisions for education in Indian's Constitution as well as in the international covenants and looking at the commitment of the Indian State towards educating every child, the volume moves towards looking at the how the state has tried to tackle the crisis in elementary education. The issue of formal schooling for all is also challenged on the grounds that the State cannot afford it. If on the one hand there is the argument that the State needs to be welfarist in nature as far as the education sector is concerned, then on the other hand there is a strong opinion that it should be privatised to enhance accessibility. The latter argument not only suggests that the teacher must have a feeling of insecurity to perform (unlike prior government commissions which went to extent of recommending empowerment of teachers associations), but also develops the concept of the 'teacher entrepreneur' (Kumar et al. 2003). Such arguments prepare grounds for non-state funding and creation of entrepreneurial stakes in education. These arguments are based on the opinion that the government faces a resource crunch today, and therefore each and every child cannot be provided formal education. Thus, they raise the issue of the State's economic capacity (ibid.). The issue of systems capability to ensure good-quality education has also been raised. Many believe that 'by and large it is obvious that the government does not have the capacity to work simultaneously on several fronts—access, quality and relevance' (Ramachandran 2003: 959–60). Such an understanding begins from a premise that the government cannot deliver quality education. This lacks the historical-structural approach of looking at how different processes over a period of time have contributed to the current state of formal schooling. If the government can deliver equal educational opportunities in other countries, why not India? More importantly, is there any other possibility that can educate the vast mass of impoverished Indians, especially when 'alternative' education is also not proving very effective and is not without problems (Leclercq 2003).

Amarjeet Sinha's paper deals with these issues of State commitment and resources. He argues that 'the constitutional amendment has created a legal right and space' for better educational opportunities. He is optimistic about the developments taking place in the field of education. The child has come to occupy the centre stage in education policies and the government is gradually striving to change the situation. He looks positively at different kinds of experiments ranging from the DPEP and NGO-based activities to the SSA, and holds formal schooling responsible to a great extent for slowing down the process of change.

In the present day the whole debate in education rests on the triangle of quality, equality and quantity. The concerns emerge from the state of education that we encounter today, as revealed by macro surveys of the government and other institutions as well as micro studies (Karlekar 2004; Rana and Das 2004; Rana et al. 2003). It has been argued that the equity agenda that was conceived in education during the independence struggle has been completely rejected. Sadhna Saxena in her paper argues that in current times there is a stagnation or decline in school participation in many backward districts of the country. The neo-liberal onslaught has led to an increasing trend of privatisation and contractualisation in the education sector. In fact, she argues, contractualisation is a normal follow-up of neo-liberal policies. Hence, what we see is the Indian State talking about the universalisation of elementary education on one hand, while dismantling the system of formal schooling that existed on the other. The smokescreen of quality and pedagogy, that presents engagement with political repercussions, is helping the smooth transition. A new language such as the portrayal of *shiksha karmi*s as change agents and social workers establishes and justifies the decline of an equitable education further. She stresses that the education policies are myopic and, therefore, fail to locate the education of children in their socio-economic realities. The result today is that even where access, enrolment and retention are attained quality of education is very poor.

An improvement in the situation can be acknowledged only if there are evidences of discrimination not being practised in the delivery of education and when a child gets education up to a certain common level. The data and the social reality around us paint a completely different picture. The NFHS-2 survey (IIPS and ORC Macro 2000) puts the male household population, in the age group of 6 to 14 years, attending school at 83.1 per cent against 73.7 per cent female attendance. In case of states like Rajasthan (55.6 per cent), Madhya Pradesh (62.8 per cent), UP (61.4 per cent), Bihar (50.5 per cent) and Andhra Pradesh (61.5 per cent) the attendance of female was much lower (ibid.: 33). It has been observed that there is a gender bias in choice of schools by parents. They send girls to government schools and boys to private schools, which are considered better (Ramachandran and Saihjee 2002: 1604). Hence, the issue of access to schools remains a major problem. 'The democratisation of access to schools is ironically being accompanied by a reification of a child's caste, community and gender in defining which school he or she attends' (ibid.: 1606). Even the much-hyped DPEP could not address these prejudices.

Scholars have raised concerns about whether girls will get equitable education even if their enrolment increases (Nambissan 2004: 41). The gendered dimension of education, especially at the elementary level, is multifaceted. Studies have shown absence of parental enthusiasm to educate girls, gender-biased perception of teachers who stereotype tasks for girls in schools or attend to girls differently in classrooms, and so on. Even the textbooks reflect an overwhelming male-centric approach. Though gender identity is acquired 'prior to their entering schools', schools further crystallise them (ibid.: 42).

Of late there has been an apparent emphasis on girls' education in government policies, but they 'are mainly directed towards increasing access to education and encouraging parents to send girls to schools rather than with the quality of learning experience for children in general and girls in particular' (ibid.: 41). The increasing significance of non-formal centres in government policies further exacerbates the problem. The targets of such policies are those sections that have been left out of the system—that is, girls and other deprived sections at the margins of the educational scenario.

It is in such a context of educational deprivation of the girl child that Karuna Chanana's paper argues that social reality plays an important role in the education of the girl child. For instance, the concern to protect female sexuality keeps girls away from schools. She stresses on the need to question the nature of social relations and structure. 'It is critical to have an understanding of the nature and functioning of familial socialisation as the process of gender construction and its impact on the education of the girl child,' she says. Girls will remain excluded from education till schools remain as sites maintaining gender identity and inequality. The condition has further worsened in the post-liberalisation phase.

The issue of educational marginalisation will be incomplete without dwelling on the issues of Dalit children. The data cited clearly show their educational marginalisation. This is demonstrated in macro data as their low enrolment or high drop-out rates and is explained in detail if one looks at the micro picture. The question of equal educational opportunity for Dalits is closely related to the State's policies. This relation is more important because it is Dalits who go to government schools because they cannot afford the private education system. Hence, the emphasis on improving the condition of formal government schools and expanding their reach is extremely important if at all Dalit children are to be educated (Nambissan 1995). Somewhere, the demand for education of Dalit children also becomes a struggle for social equality in the sense that upward mobility in terms of any variable of development that has not been traditionally allowed to them becomes a challenge to the entrenched classes and castes in local societies. Hence, apart from the physical deficiencies of schools, social accessibility is also a problem that is generally not measured (Nambissan 2002).

Geetha Nambissan in her paper looks at 'the 'institutional framework' that has come into place in the wake of policy initiatives for universalisation of elementary education, more specifically on the increasing stratification in schools on the one hand and the setting in place of decentralised and participative structures for public participation in and academic support for education on the other. She views inclusion as a far more complex process than just reflected in enrolment, attendance or retention. It should 'position social groups differently in relation-valued resources: knowledge, skills and cultural attributes, future opportunities and life chances, sense of dignity, self-worth and social respect'. This notion of inclusion becomes important in today's context when Dalits are *included* in schools at the point of entry, but the terms of their *inclusion* in relation to institutional structures and processes are discriminatory.

Education has no doubt led to upward mobility among Dalits, but only a small section has reaped the benefits of formal education. Retention in schools remains a major problem. There are a variety of factors, apart from social discrimination, responsible for inequitable access to schools, such as location of their hamlets, economic condition, migration, the condition of schools, 'curriculum transaction' and attitude of teachers. In this context the 86th Amendment has been enacted, finally, making education a fundamental right, but the draft legislation suffers from unclear pedagogical norms and facilities and excessive bureaucratisation. Given the larger landscape, only an equitable elementary education can provide a critical base for expansion of opportunities for Dalits, especially after the new amendment.

The debate on marginalisation is further carried forward by the paper on disabled children by Madan Mohan Jha. He argues that inclusive education can best be addressed as part of the regular schooling system. The notion of 'charity' and 'benevolence' cannot address the concern of disabled children. There have been many provisions stated by the United Nations conventions on making education of the disabled a part of the mainstream system rather than a distinct category of 'special schools' as has been the practice in our country. The Salamanca Declaration (1994) was a major watershed in this direction. The Indian education policy has seldom argued on lines of making the disabled a part of the mainstream education system, and it is at this juncture that he calls for critically examining even the much-lauded Kothari Commission and later committees. Non-formal education has done much damage to the education of the disabled and the latest constitutional amendment furthers this system of inferior educational facilities. Only a common schooling system on the lines of the Kothari Commission, but with certain modifications, can make any effective change in the lives of disabled children.

The volume ends with Ravi Kumar's paper based on a village study done among one of the most backward Dalit castes in Bihar—the Mushars. Their educational condition is such that their literacy rate did not go beyond 5 per cent till 1991. They view education as a source of upward mobility, apart from its utility in daily life, like the other sections of society. Despite this perception they remain educationally backward. The paper tries to explore the reasons behind this. The cultural notions created around the community, the paper argues, appear to reproduce the existing social structure and hence retain their educational backwardness. Their economic condition also impedes their participation in the education process, which is present in the form of an ill-equipped formal school. In such a context, it will be difficult for the new constitutional amendment to go beyond and try to address the structural processes that reproduce socio-economic and educational inequality.

The volume bases itself in a context of acute educational crisis emanating out of systemic problems and taking the form of inequality and extreme marginalisation. It tries to address the different challenges in education, which becomes more relevant after the enactment of 86th Amendment making education a fundamental right.

Notes

1. In 1942, the Indian capitalists set up the 'Post-War Economic Development Committee' as a part of their effort to wage an ideological war against the communists. G.D. Birla, one of the leading industrialists of India, in 1936, had already expressed concern at Nehru's tilt towards the Left and called for giving concessions to the Right-wing Nationalists. However, the strong undercurrent of socialism that was present in the Indian political scenario forced the Indian capitalists to evolve a strategy to adjust to the then strong socialist movement, all the while ensuring that their interests remained unscathed. In order to safeguard their interests, this

Committee drafted what came to be known as the Bombay Plan. This document cited reforms as the 'most effective remedy against violent social upheavals'. It also, among many things, called on the State to help those Indian capitalists who had poor resources and take over heavy industries, mobilise surplus resources, etc., with their own vested interests in mind. State ownership was to operate at two levels: (a) 'where the Indian capitalist class was itself unable to make headway because of foreign competition and the large resources required'; and (b) 'to take over certain existing key sectors where foreign capital dominated' (Mukherjee 2002: 49–50 and 357–360).

2. UN Declaration on Human Rights (adopted by the UN General Assembly Resolution 217A [III] of 10 December 1948). Text available on http://www.knesset.gov.il/docs/eng/un_dec_eng.htm.

3. Declaration of the Rights of the Child proclaimed by General Assembly Resolution 1386 (XIV) of 20 November 1959. Text available at the Web site of the Office of High Commissioner of Human Rights (UNCHR), http://www.unhchr.ch/html/menu3/b/25.htm.

4. International Covenant on Economic, Social and Cultural Rights, adopted and opened for signature, ratification and accession by General Assembly Resolution 2200A (XXI) of 16 December 1966, entry into force 3 January 1976, in accordance with Article 27. Text available at http://www.unhchr.ch/html/menu3/b/a_cescr. htm.

5. The Convention on the Rights of the Child was adopted and opened for signature, ratification and accession by General Assembly resolution 44/25 of 20 November 1989. It entered into force on 2 September 1990, in accordance with Article 49. Text available at http://www.unicef.org/crc/crc.htm.

6. Asia and Pacific Regional Framework for Action: Education for All—Guiding Principles, Specific Goals and Targets for 2015 was adopted by the Asia-Pacific Conference on EFA 2000 at Bangkok, Thailand, on 17–20 January 2000. Text available at http://www.unesco.org/education/efa/wef_2000/regional_frameworks/frame_asia_pacific.shtml.

7. Please see the Dakar Framework for Action Education for All: Meeting Our Collective Commitments (2000), Adopted by the World Education Forum, Dakar, Senegal, 26–28 April.

References

Acharya, Poromesh. 1997. 'Educational Ideals of Tagore and Gandhi: A Comparative Study', *Economic and Political Weekly*, 32(12): 601–6.

Allman, Paula. 2001. 'Critical Education Against Global Capitalism: Karl Marx and Revolutionary Critical Education'. In Henry A. Giroux (series ed.), *Critical Studies in Education and Culture Series*. Connecticut: Begin & Garvey.

Bhattacharyya, N. 2000. 'Public Sector Units: Privatisation or Economic Destruction?', *Revolutionary Democracy*, 6(1). Available at http://www.resolutionarydemocracy.org/rdv6n1/psus.htm, accessed in January 2005.

Biswas, A. and S.P. Aggarwal. 1994. *Development of Education in India: A Historical Survey of Educational Documents Before and After Independence*. Delhi: Concept Publishing.

Dreze, Jean and Amartya Sen. 1995. *India: Economic Development and Social Opportunity*. New Delhi: Oxford University Press.

Giroux, Henry. 1998, 'Education Incorporated', *Educational Leadership*, 56(2): 12–17.

Goldstein, Harvey. 2004. 'Education for All: The Globalization of Learning Targets', *Comparative Education*, 40(1): 7–14.

Government of India. 1944. *Post-War Educational Development in India: Report by the Central Advisory Board of Education*. Simla: Government of India Press.

————. 1966. *Education and National Development: Report of the Education Commission*. New Delhi: Ministry of Education.

————. 1967. *Report of the Committee of Members of Parliament on Education*. New Delhi: Ministry of Education.

————. 1986. *National Education Policy, 1986, and Programme of Action*. Calcutta: AIFUCTO Publication.

————. 1990. *Towards and Enlightened and Humane Society: Report of the Committee for Review of National Policy on Education, 1986* [i.e., National Policy on Education Review Committee Report (NPERC) or Acharya Ramamurti Committee Report], Department of Education, Ministry of Human Resource Development. New Delhi: Government of India.

————. 1992. *Report of the CABE Committee on Policy*. New Delhi: Department of Education, Ministry of Human Resource Development.

————. 1998. *Evaluation Study on Impact of Non-formal Education*. New Delhi: Programme Evaluation Organisation, Planning Commission, Government of India.

————. 2001a. *Approach Paper to the Tenth Five Year Plan (2002–07)*. New Delhi: Planning Commission, Government of India.

————. 2001b. *The Tenth Five Year Plan* (Volume 2). New Delhi: Planning Commission, Government of India.

————. 2001c. *India as Knowledge Superpower: Strategy for Transformation* (Task Force Report). New Delhi: Planning Commission, Government of India.

————. 2002a. *National Human Development Report, 2001*. New Delhi: Planning Commission, Government of India.

————. 2002b. *Report of the Committee on India Vision 2020*. New Delhi: Planning Commission, Government of India.

————. 2002c. *Selected Educational Statistics 2000–2001*. New Delhi: Planning, Monitoring and Statistics Division, Department of Secondary and Higher Education, Ministry of Human Resource Development.

International Institute for Population Sciences (IIPS) and ORC Macro. 2000. *National Family Health Survey (NFHS-2), 1998–99*. Mumbai: IIPS.

Karlekar, Malavika. 2004. 'The Total Literacy Campaign: An Overview'. In Malavika Karlekar (ed.), *Paradigms of Learning: The Total Literacy Campaign in India*. New Delhi: Sage Publications.

Kaura, Sanjiv. 2004. 'How Should the State Fund Education?', *Economic Times*, 24 February.

Kumar, Krishna, Manish Priyam and Sadhna Saxena. 2001a. 'Looking Beyond the Smokescreen: DPEP and Primary Education in India', *Economic and Political Weekly*, 36(7): 560–8.

———. 2001b, 'The Trouble with Para-teachers', *Frontline*, 18(22). Available at http://www.frontlineonnet.com/fl1822/18220930.htm, accessed in December 2004.

Kumar, Sanjay, B.J. Koppar and S. Balasubramanian. 2003. 'Primary Education in Rural Areas: An Alternative Model', *Economic and Political Weekly*, 38(34): 3533–35

Leclercq, Francois. 2003. 'Education Guarantee Scheme and Primary Schooling in Madhya Pradesh', *Economic and Political Weekly*, 38(19): 1855–69.

Mukherjee, Aditya. 2002. *Imperialism, Nationalism and the Making of the Indian Capitalist Class 1920–1947*. New Delhi: Sage Publications.

Nambissan, Geetha B. 1995. 'Human Rights Education and Dalit Children', *PUCL Bulletin*. Available at http://www.pucl.org/from-archives/Dalit-tribal education.htm, accessed in January 2005.

———. 2002. 'Equity in Education? The Schooling of Dalit Children'. In Ghanshyam Shah (ed.), *Dalits and the State*. Delhi: Concept Publishing.

———. 2004. 'Integrating Gender Concerns', *Seminar*, 536, April: 44–5.

National Council of Educational Research and Training (NCERT). 2002. *Seventh Educational Survey*. Available at http://www.7thsurvey.ncert.nic.in, accessed in March 2005.

National Sample Survey Organisation (NSSO). 2001. *Literacy and Levels of Education in India, July 1999–2000* (NSS 55th Round, Report No. 473). New Delhi: Ministry of Statistics and Programme Implementation, Government of India.

Nehru, Jawaharlal. 1998. *The Discovery of India*. New Delhi: Jawaharlal Nehru Memorial Fund and Oxford University Press.

Pathak, Avijit. 2002. *Social Implications of Schooling: Knowledge, Pedagogy and Consciousness*. Delhi: Rainbow Publishers.

Ramachandran, Vimla. 2003. 'Backward and Forward Linkages that Strengthen Primary Education', *Economic and Political Weekly*, 38(10): 959–68.

Ramachandran, Vimla and Aarti Saihjee. 2002. 'The New Segregation: Reflections on Gender and Equity in Primary Education', *Economic and Political Weekly*, 37(17): 1600–13.

Rana, Kumar and Samantak Das, 2004. 'Primary Education in Jharkhand', *Economic and Political Weekly*, 39(11): 1171–78.

Rana, Kumar, Samantak Das, Amrita Sengupta and Abdur Rafique. 2003. 'State of Primary Education in West Bengal', *Economic and Political Weekly*, 38(22): 2159–64.

Rikowski, Glenn. 2002. 'Globalisation and Education', www.ieps.org.uk.cwc.net/rikowski2002d.pdf, accessed on 19 January 2005.

Sadgopal, Anil. 2001. 'Political Economy of the Ninety Third Amendment Bill', *Mainstream*, 22 December: 43–50.

———. 2003, 'Education for Too Few', *Frontline*, 20(24). Available at http://www.frontlineonnet.com/fl2024/stories/20031205002809700.htm, accessed in January 2005.

Saxena, Sadhna. 2004. 'Revisiting Ajmer Total Campaign'. In Malavika Karlekar (ed.), *Paradigms of Learning: The Total Literacy Campaign in India*. New Delhi: Sage Publications.

Swaminathan, Padmini. 2002. 'The Violence of Gender-based Development: Going Beyond Social and Demographic Indicators'. In Karin Kapadia (ed.), *The Violence of Development: The Politics of Identity, Gender and Social Inequalities in India*. London & New York: Zed Books.

Tilak, J.B.G. 2003. 'Public Expenditure on Education in India: A Review of Trends & Emerging Issues'. In J.B.G Tilak (ed.), *Financing Education in India*. New Delhi: NIEPA.

UNESCO. 1997. *Challenges of EDUCATION FOR ALL in Asia and the Pacific and the APPEAL Response*. Bangkok: Principle Regional Office for Asia and the Pacific.

———. 2000. *World Education Report: The Right to Education—Towards Education for All Throughout Life*. Paris: UNESCO Publishing.

Wadhwa, Soma. 2004. 'Pencil Erasure'. *Outlook*, 1 March: 58–62.

2

CHILD RIGHTS TO ELEMENTARY EDUCATION

NATIONAL AND INTERNATIONAL PROVISIONS

Vasudha Dhagamwar

The Indian child's right to education has many spokespersons, but no champions. In 2005, the President of India regretted the fact that only 4 per cent of the GDP was spent on education. Yet, the framers of India's Constitution had not forgotten the schoolgoing child and its right to education. Unfortunately, this was not put into Part III, which enshrines the fundamental rights. There it would have emerged as a right. Instead, it was placed in Part IV, which contains the Directive Principles of State Policy. Perhaps this was done on account of the expenditure involved. The Directive Principles of State Policy (DPSP) are virtually the blueprint of a new India. DPSP (Articles 36–51) are only directives to the state. This is where they differ from fundamental rights. No one may approach the courts for enforcement of any of the Directive Principles of State Policy. In legal terminology, while fundamental rights are justiciable, directive principles are not. It is up to the government of the day to decide when to act upon them.

Part III of the Constitution spells out fundamental rights (Articles 13–35). These rights cover almost all aspects of one's life. They breathe life into the aspirations and rights of the ordinary people of India. A most important right is guaranteed by Article 32, the right to petition the Supreme Court directly if any fundamental rights are violated. Without this the Constitution would remain a jumble of pretty words. In various writ petitions the Supreme Court of India has widened the scope of the right to life to mean right to live with dignity, (judgement delivered in the *Bandhua Mukti Morcha vs Union of India* case, AIR 1984 SC 802), even in jail (as pronounced in the *Sunil Batra vs Delhi Administration* case, AIR 1980 SC 1579) and outside it with a living wage (as shown by the judgement delivered in the *People's Union of Democratic Rights vs Union of India* case, AIR 1982 SC 1473). *The fact that the right to elementary education was not included is a reflection on the absence of petitions by civil society for schools.*

Article 45 of the Directive Principles of State Policy deals with the education of children up to the age of 14. Though amended now it originally read:

Provision of free and compulsory education for children: The State shall endeavour to provide, within a period of ten years from the commencement of the Constitution, for free and compulsory education for all children until they complete the age of fourteen years.

Education was to be *free, compulsory* and *universal.* The Constitution commenced on 26 January 1950, so the grace period ended on Republic Day of 1960. During this period the government was not entirely inactive on either the national or the international front.

INTERNATIONAL INSTRUMENTS RATIFIED BY THE GOVERNMENT OF INDIA

The government became signatory to a number of international instruments that mentioned education as a child's right. The first was the Universal Declaration of Human Rights (UDHR) of 1948.[1]

Article 26 of UDHR laid down:

Everyone has the right to education. Education shall be free at least in the elementary and fundamental stages. Elementary education shall be free and compulsory. Technical and secondary education shall be accessible and higher education shall be available on basis of merit.

India is also a signatory to the Convention of the Rights of the Child (CRC) adopted by the UN General Assembly in 1989. India ratified this convention only on 10 December 1992, which is the International Human Rights Day. Principle 7 of the Convention of the Rights of the Child proclaimed:[2]

> The child is entitled to receive education, which shall be free and compulsory at least in the elementary stages. He shall be given an education which promotes his general culture and enable him, on a basis of equal opportunity, to develop his abilities, his individual judgement and his sense of moral and social responsibility and become a useful member of society.
>
> The child shall have full opportunity for play and recreation, which should be directed to the same purposes as education; society and the public authorities, should endeavor to promote the enjoyment of this right.

Secondary and higher education was to be made available and accessible to all. It should be noted, however, that the state was not required to make post-primary education either compulsory or free. Article 28 of CRC also asked states to take steps to encourage regular attendance at school and reduce drop-out rates.

Article 13(2) of the International Covenant on Economic Social and Cultural Rights (ICESCR) also says categorically that primary education shall be compulsory and available free to all, and that it is the responsibility of the state parties to achieve this objective. While the UDHR mentioned elementary education, the CRC as well as ICESCR talked of primary education. None of these instruments, however, mentioned any age for commencement of education, nor specified an upper age limit.

Successive UN meetings and World Summits formulated resolutions that furthered the aims of the UDHR and CRC. In 1990, the World Summit for Children pointed out that 100 million children throughout the world were without basic schooling and out of them two-thirds were girls. The Summit concluded that the provision of basic education and literacy were among the most important contributions that could be made to the development of children throughout the world.

The Convention for Elimination of Discrimination Against Women (CEDAW) of 1979 was ratified by India as late as on 29 June 1993. The Convention only speaks of education in general terms, without making any mention of primary education. A committee was set up to receive reports from state parties on implementation of CEDAW by them. In its first report in 2000, the committee identified making of primary and secondary education compulsory as one of the goals for state parties (Government of India 2003: 2).

National Initiatives

Even before Independence, primary education in *government* schools had been free. In other words, no fees had to be paid, although books and stationery were not free. On the other hand, there were fewer books and hardly any stationery needed. For the first few years children went to school with one slate and one book. The slate was the writing equipment, wiped and written on over and over again. One book did service for all subjects: it contained stories with a moral, history lessons in the shape of biographies of great men and women, and even concepts of geography could be taught from it, using prominent landmarks of one's town or village. That one book served to teach reading and writing. Arithmetic was taught from the blackboard. Much of it was oral learning, through recitation of multiplication tables and poems. Apart from the inevitable and frequent breakage of slates there was hardly any expense. Only in the class IV exams were children permitted to write with a pencil. There was no uniform. While a uniform has many benefits—it is a great social leveller for it prevents open display of wealth—but poor parents initially resist it as it looks like an extra expense. They later realise that the uniform is a substitute for, and not an addition to, everyday clothes.

After Independence, government schools continued to provide free primary education. The question has never been of charging fees in government schools. It has been of making it available to all and of making it compulsory. In the old Bombay province, the Bombay Education Act (1923) had also made it compulsory. It provided for a fine of Rs. 5.50 on guardians for not sending children to school. In Baroda state, Sayaji Rao Gaikwad had also made it compulsory. An old woman who was in domestic service told this author that the school peon would call at the home of the absent child to ask why she or he was not in school. Perhaps the princely states of Mysore and Aundh had similar policies. After the states merged into the Indian Union, this rule fell into abeyance. The old woman from Baroda was literate; her granddaughter was not. Such is the power of compulsion until sending children to school becomes second nature.

The question then, as now, is not of making primary education free: it is of making it universal and compulsory. It is also of making it good quality. If for the first the government is responsible, the civil society is responsible for eroding the quality of government schools. Anyone who can afford it has steadily withdrawn from State schools, giving preference to private ones. State schools have become synonymous with low-quality education, only for poor people. Even those, as we shall see, are preferred over non-formal education centres. And for university education we return to the State. By that time the competition for higher education seats is all but over because children from State schools, especially in rural areas, rarely make it to the portals of colleges, leave alone professional institutions.

To go back to the legal scenario, the Constitution divides the responsibility for a given subject into three groups. The subjects that devolve on the government of India are on the Union List. Some are on the State List. The third list is of items on which both state and central governments can legislate, with central legislation having priority. Residual subjects belong to the central government.

Some central universities such as the Universities of Delhi, Aligarh and Benares were on the Union List. Institutions imparting technical education of excellence could also be added to that list. That is how the Indian Institutes of Technology and Indian Institutes of Management, which came into existence much later, found

themselves placed in the Union List. Other tertiary or higher educational institutions were on the Concurrent List. School education
was on the State List. This arrangement in itself tells us volumes
about the importance given to school education. In 1977, by the
42nd Amendment, all education was transferred to the Concurrent
List. However, the items on the Union List were left untouched.

Even while school education was a state subject, the education
ministry of the central government had some responsibility for
schools. The Government of India allocated some funds from the
central budget to schools as well as for freeships to Scheduled Caste
(SC) and Scheduled Tribe (ST) children, and girls from almost all
communities. Both state and central governments crafted their own
laws for primary education.

EDUCATION COMMITTEES

The Government of India appointed several committees to look
into the status of primary education and make their reports on the
subject. Two such early reports were by eminent educationists,
notably, D.S. Kothari (Government of India 1971) and J.P. Naik
(ICSSR 1975). Between them we can get a fair idea about the state
of primary education for the first three-quarters of the 20th century,
while Vimala Ramachandran completes the picture with
information for the last two decades.

The numbers for children in school from 1950 to 1974 are given
by the Naik Committee (ibid.: 9). By 1950–51 the enrolment of
children in primary schools had certainly increased. At that time
19.2 million 6- to 11-year-old children were enrolled in classes I to V.
Of them, 13.8 million were boys and 5.4 million were girls. Girls
were about 39 per cent of children in school. In terms of percentages to total population, as many as 60.8 per cent boys in the
6 to 11 age group were in primary school. However, only 24.9 per
cent girls and 42.6 per cent of the total number of children between
6 to 11 were with them. *At no time does the sex ratio account demographically
for the low school enrolment of 6- to 11-year-old girls. Such figures also disprove
any theory that gives poverty as the reason for not sending children to school.*

Even this low figure slumped for children between 12 to 14 years. In absolute numbers, only 3.1 million children were enrolled in classes VI to VIII or upper primary school. Of them girls were only 0.5 million *in the entire country*. In terms of percentages to the total population of children between 12 to 14 years, only 12.9 per cent children in this age group were in school. Of them a mere 4.3 per cent were girls.

By 1955, enrolment of 6- to 9-year-olds had crossed the 50 per cent mark (52.8 per cent). The number of girls had also gone up. Nearly a third of the total numbers of girls were in school (32.8 per cent). As usual, boys far exceeded girls—72 per cent or nearly three-fourths the total numbers of boys were going to primary school.

In 1960–61, children in primary school had almost doubled, and 35 million were in classes I to V. Of them 23.6 million were boys, an increase of 10 million in a decade. The figure for girls had doubled to 11.4 million. Now the girls in school were just under half the number of boys or about 48 per cent. Of boys of the same age group, 82.6 per cent were in school as compared to only 41.4 per cent of girls. Of the total 12- to 14-year old children in India, only 22.5 per cent were in school. 32.2 per cent of the boys, and 11.3 per cent of the girls, in this age group were in school.

But the same sad story was repeated in upper primary school. There were still only 6.7 million children in classes VI to VIII, although admittedly it was double the number from 1951. Of them a mere 1.6 million were girls and as many as 5.1 million were boys. Even that is a very low figure. In terms of the total population of 12- to 14-year-olds, 32.2 per cent boys and 11.3 per cent girls and 22.5 per cent of the total were in upper primary school. In 1965–66 the figures rose to show that 96.3 per cent boys, 56.5 per cent girls and 76 per cent of total children were in primary school.

The Naik Committee found that in 1968–69, of 6- to 11-year-olds, 95.6 per cent boys and 59.6 per cent girls were in lower primary school. The total came to 78.1 per cent (32.2 million boys, 20.2 million girls, and total of 54.4 million children). But among 12- to 14-year-olds, only 33.5 per cent were in upper primary school. Forty-seven per cent boys and only 19.3 per cent of all girls were in school, which was a huge gap compared to absolute figures (9 million boys, 3.5 million girls).

This upward trend continued and the Naik Committee records that in 1974 the enrolment of boys in classes I to V had reached 100 per cent, and 66 per cent girls were similarly in school. Eighty-four per cent of the total children between 6 to 11 years of age were in primary school. In absolute numbers, 39.4 million boys, 24.4 million girls (making a total of 63.8 million) were going to primary school. The gap between girls and boys had narrowed further.

Enrolment in *upper* primary school continued to be low, although the numbers had risen. 10.5 million boys, 4.5 million girls (total of 15.0 million) were in classes VI to VIII. But only 48 per cent boys, 22 per cent girls and 36 per cent of the children who should have been in upper primary schools were actually there. It also meant that girls were still less than half the number of boys.

The data undoubtedly shows that enrolment in classes I to VIII was increasing steadily during the century. But the gap remains more or less the same. If we draw a chart, the line of enrolment to classes VI to VIII over a given period will rise every year. But it will also be nearly parallel and below that for classes I to V. *This looks as if the target now has to be to increase all children in upper primary school and of girls throughout primary school.*

This is not the only problem. The Naik Committee talked only of children in primary and upper primary schools without breaking down the data any further. The older Kothari Committee report had analysed the data *within* the primary schools. It noted that even in the age group of 6 to 11 there were wide variations. The number of children in school peaked at the age of 6 to 7 years; then it began to fall and went on falling. Even in 1911–12, 20.6 per cent of the 5- to 6-year-olds were in school. Their number peaked to show that as many as 24.6 per cent children between 6 and 7 years were in school. But it fell to only 21.2 per cent for 7- to 8-year-olds and went on falling. Among the 8- to 9-year-olds only 11.8 per cent were in school in 1911–12. Even in 1950–51, a similar bell curve was obtained. From 19.9 per cent for children who were 5 to 6 years old, it rose to 32.1 per cent for 6- to 7-year-olds, and then fell to 25.7 per cent for 7- to 8-year-olds. Then it fell even more steeply, to 12.5 per cent for 8- to 9-year-old children. In 1961–62 the story was the same. Only 18.4 per cent of 5- to 6-year-olds went to school. The figure rose for 6- to 7-year-olds to 31.7 per cent, and then fell to 25.7 per cent for 7- to 8-year-olds. It was just 12.5 per cent of 8- to 9-year-old children. One can guess the figures were even lower for girls.

These figures tell us that the largest number of school attendees were 6- to 7-year-olds.

From Vimala Ramachandran's data (Ramachandran, 2004a: 54) we can locate figures for 1981 and 1991 (Table 2.1). She adds two other factors to enrolment data: actual attendance and acquisition of literacy. Here, we discover that half the children who are enrolled drop out of school. The drop-out rate is so high that one cannot draw any comfort from the increasing enrolment figures. Even fewer children report that they are literate. *So even among those children who do stay on all are not literate.* As may be expected, more girls than boys in any category will drop out of school.

TABLE 2.1
CHILDREN ENROLLED IN SCHOOL (6 TO 10 YEARS)
ACCORDING TO THE 1981 AND 1991 CENSUSES (%)

	Enrolled	Reported as Literate	Attending School
1981			
All areas			
Boys	95.8	38.1	50.6
Girls	64.1	27.9	31.4
Rural			
Boys	N.A.	33.2	38.3
Girls	N.A.	21.6	25.1
1991			
All areas			
Boys	112.8	65.2	50.6
Girls	86.9	51.9	45.4
Rural			
Boys	98.6	60.3	52.3
Girls	81.8	44.8	39.3

Source: Ramachandran (2004a: 54).[3]

When we look at another requirement—all children must go to school, they must stay there, and they must be taught what they are supposed to learn; they must then continue in the upper primary school—then we find that this does not happen.

We also run into another statistical riddle. In 1973–74, 100 per cent boys were shown to be enrolled in primary school. This in itself stretches the bounds of disbelief. The figure is simply not credible. But there is more to come. From 1979 onwards, from time to time the data shows more than 100 per cent boys in the age group of 6–10 as being enrolled in classes I to V. As many as 118 per cent boys were shown to be enrolled in primary school in 1991.

The answer is that children over 11 years who have joined primary school are also counted in the age group of 6 to 11. This in turn means that even when the data showed less than 100 per cent children, a part of that number belonged to the upper primary level. Many 6- to 11-year-old children who should have been in school are not even enrolled. Second, the need of older children for bridge courses is kept concealed. What applies to boys will, of course, be true of girls, although experience dictates that girls who were kept back at a younger age are even less likely to be sent to school when they are older.

The problem of the high rate of drop-outs and low rate of acquired literacy skills is even more acute for SC and ST children. The problem of older children in primary classes apply to them as well and are even more true of them (Table 2.2).

TABLE 2.2
CHILDREN ATTENDING SCHOOL BY SEX AND CASTE ACCORDING
TO THE 1981 AND 1991 CENSUSES (%)

	SC	ST	Total Population
All-India rural males			
1981	41.6	35.3	50.6
1991	–	–	52.3
All-India rural females			
1981	20.5	17.3	31.4
1991	–	–	39.3

Source: Ramachandran (2004a: 56).

In fact, ST children lag even further behind SC children. Fewer schools, greater distance from urban habitations, and language difficulties may be some of the reasons for which they are not in school. As usual, girls suffer even more; data is not even available for them in 1991.

As we have seen, the situation was pretty bad in 1950. Instead of tackling the problem head on, beginning from 1950s the government launched a number of adult literacy programmes. Adult literacy was fine, but it should not have competed with children's education for scarce resources. *Most important, this programme was not even distantly related with the directive of Article 45.* This gap or lack of connection was unwittingly underlined by a young rural housewife way back in the 1950s when a social worker was trying to enrol her in one such class.[4] The busy mother wanted her children to be taken to school instead. When the social worker said that the school was not for children, in all innocence she asked, 'Will my boys grow up like this, and then will you take them to your school?'

Since the last quarter of the 20th century, a new model has found favour with the government. It is of non-formal, part-time education. Both models assumed that poor children would not be able to stop working as poor families could not afford full-time education for their children, particularly for girls. Either they learnt in part-time schools or they grew up to attend adult literacy classes. None of these programmes had achieved the goal of Article 45.

SUPREME COURT JUDGEMENTS ON PRIMARY EDUCATION

Mohini Jain vs The State of Karnataka[5]

In 1991, a young woman named Mohini Jain was asked to pay capitation fees in a private medical college in Karnataka. She filed a writ petition before the Supreme Court saying that this infringed her right to life, which had been long interpreted as the right to live with dignity. The Supreme Court accepted the argument and declared that higher education was a fundamental right. Please remember, such a right is neither enjoined by the DPSP nor by the numerous UN conventions India has signed. Higher education has to be made available within the economic capacity of the state; it need not even be cheap, leave alone free.

Unnikrishnan vs The State of Andhra Pradesh[6]

Soon thereafter, the subject matter was mentioned in Supreme Court in another public interest petition. In 1993, in the justly celebrated case of *Unnikrishnan vs The State of Andhra Pradesh*, the Supreme Court struck down the Mohini Jain ruling and held that the right to education up to the age of 14 years was a fundamental right. The Court argued that this right flowed from Article 21, which guaranteed the fundamental right to life. In 1950, the Constitution had set a time limit of 10 years in which the right was to be given effect. But as this goal had not been met, 'we think that the Court should step in'. That is what the Court did; they declared that every child had a right to free education till the age of 14 years. Forty-five years had passed since the Constitution had become the supreme law of the land.

In his long judgement Justice Jeevan Reddy referred to distinguished educationists such as D.S. Kothari and J.P. Naik, and also to the noted scholar Gunnar Myrdal.

To quote:

Higher education calls heavily on national economic resources. The right to it must necessarily be limited in any given country by its economic and social circumstances. The State's obligation to provide it is, therefore, not absolute and immediate but relative and progressive.... [B]y holding education as a fundamental right upto the age of 14 years this Court is not determining the priorities. On the contrary, reminding it of the solemn endeavour, it has to take, under Article 45, within a prescribed time, which time limit has expired long ago.

Later the Court said:

> *It is noteworthy that among the several articles in part IV, only Article 45 speaks of a time-limit; no other article does. Has it no significance?* Is it a mere pious wish even after 44 years of the Constitution? Can the State flout the said direction even after 44 years on the ground that the article merely calls upon it to 'endeavour to provide' the same and on the further ground that the said article is not enforceable by virtue of the declaration in Article 37. Does not the passage of 44 years—more than four times the period stipulated in Article 45—convert the obligation created by the article into an enforceable right? In this context, *we feel constrained to say that allocation of available funds to different sectors of education in India discloses an inversion of priorities indicated by the Constitution.* The Constitution contemplated a crash programme being undertaken by the State to achieve the goal set out in Article 45. It is relevant to notice that Article 45 does not speak of the 'limits of its economic capacity and development' as does Article 41, which inter alia speaks of right to education.[7] *What has actually happened is more money is spent and more attention is directed to higher education than to—and at the cost of primary education.* By primary education, we mean the education, which a normal child receives by the time he completes 14 years of age. Neglected more so are the rural sectors, and the weaker sections of the society referred to in Article 46.[8]

The Court noted that this 'inversion of priorities' has been commented upon adversely by both the educationists and economists. Thus, Gunnar Myrdal (1972: 335) observed in his *Asian Drama*:

> Although the declared purpose was to give priority to the increase of elementary schooling in order to raise the rate of literacy in the population, what has actually happened is that secondary schooling has been rising much faster and tertiary schooling has increased still more rapidly. *There is a fairly general tendency for planned targets of increased primary schooling not to be not reached, whereas targets are over-reached, sometimes substantially, as regards increase in secondary and, particularly, tertiary schooling. This has all happened in spite of the fact that secondary schooling seems to be three to five times more expensive than primary schooling, and schooling at the tertiary level five to seven times more expensive than at the secondary level.*
>
> *What we see functioning here is the distortion of development from planned targets under the influence of the pressure from parents and pupils in the upper strata who everywhere are politically powerful.* Even more remarkable is the fact that *this tendency to distortion form the point of view of the planning objectives is more accentuated in the poorest countries,* Pakistan, India, Burma and Indonesia, which started out with far fewer

children in primary schools and which should therefore have the strongest reasons to carry out the programme of giving primary schooling the highest priority. *It is generally the poorest countries that are spending least, even relatively, on primary education, and that are permitting the largest distortions from the planned targets in favour of secondary and tertiary education.* (Emphasis added)

The Supreme Court also cited the opinion of J.P. Naik, 'whose report of the Education Commission, 1966 is still considered to be the most authoritative study of education scene in India [that] educational development ... is benefiting the "haves" more than the "have-nots"'.

The Court pointed out that in *Challenge of Education: a Policy Perspective*" (Government of India 1985), it was stated that:

Considering the constitutional imperative regarding the universalisation of elementary education it was to be expected that the share of this sector would be protected from attribution. Facts, however, point in the opposite direction. *From a share of 56 per cent in the First Plan, it declined to 35 per cent in the Second Plan, to 34 per cent in the Third Plan, to 30 per cent in the Fourth Plan. It started going up again only in the Fifth Plan, when it was at the level of 32 per cent, increasing in Sixth Plan to 36 per cent, still 20 per cent below the First Plan level. On the other hand, between the First and the Sixth Five Year Plans, the share of university education went up from 9 per cent to 16 per cent.*

The Court then added:

Be that as it may, we must say that at least know the State should honour the command of Article 45. It must be made a reality—at least now. *Indeed, the 'National Education Policy—1986' says that the promise of Article 45 will be redeemed before the end of this century. Be that as it may, we hold that a child (citizen) has a fundamental right to free education up to the age of 14 years.*

This does not however mean that this obligation can be performed only through the State schools. It can also be done by permitting, recognising and aiding voluntary non-governmental organisations, who are prepared to import free education to children. This does not also mean that unaided private schools cannot continue. They can continue. Indeed, they too have a role to play. They meet the demand of that segment of [the] population who may not wish to have their children educated in State-run schools. They have necessarily to charge fees from the students. In this judgment, however, we do not wish to say anything about such schools....

Before proceeding further, we think it right to say this: We are aware that "Education is the second highest sector of budgeted expenditure after the defence. A little more than three per cent of the Gross National Product is spent in education," as pointed out in para 2.31 of 'Challenge of Education'. But this very publication says that "in comparison to many countries, India spends much less on education in terms of the proportion of Gross National Product"—and further "in spite of the fact that educational expenditure continues to be the highest item of expenditure next only to Defence the resource gap for educational needs is one of the major problems. Most of the current expenditure is only in the form of salary payment. It hardly needs to be stated that additional capital expenditure would greatly augment teacher productivity because in the absence of expenditure on other heads even the utilisation of staff remains low". We do realise that ultimately it is a question of resources and resources-wise this country is not in a happy position. All we are saying is that while allocating the available resources, due regard should be had to the wise words of Founding Fathers in Articles 45 and 46. Not that we are not aware of the importance and significance of higher education. What may perhaps be required is a proper balancing of the various sectors of education.

This was a hard-hitting, well-reasoned landmark judgement. The judges knew all the facts, all the arguments, and dealt with them. Now the need of the hour was action on all fronts by government, civil society and NGOs. A spate of writ petitions invoking *Unnikrishnan* would have done the trick. But there was total silence. Despite the Court holding out a promise, no one came forward to take advantage of it. Indeed, speaking to a group of lawyers and judges seven years later, in 2001, the then Chief Justice of India (he had written the dissenting judgement in *Unnikrishnan*) wondered aloud what would have happened if thousands of petitions had flooded the court. We shall never know. But one thing was made clear by another judgement dated 1997 in another public interest litigation, that child labour was still consuming our schoolgoing children.

M.C. Mehta vs The State of Tamil Nadu[9]

The plight of the children working in the Siva Kasi fireworks factories had been known since 1979 when a bus carrying children, who were virtually toddlers, to the factories fell into a dry river bed, killing most of them. This petition arose over the situation of the same children. In their judgement the Supreme Court highlighted data about child labour throughout India, and noted the following statistics: In the 1971 Census, out of all children between the ages of 5 and 14, 10.7 million or 4.68 per cent were child labourers. These figures may not include girls, who mostly work at home without any wages.

In 1973, the NSS 27th Round gave the figure of 16.3 million child workers. The 1981 Census gave 11.16 million child workers. In 1983 the Planning Commission said that 17.36 million children between the ages of 5 to 10 years were child workers. It also mentioned 15.7 million children between the ages of 10 and 14 were child workers. The 1985 NSS showed 17.58 million children workers. NGO assessment for child labourers ranges from 40 to 100 million children.

In its judgement the Supreme Court said:

> Our Constitution makers, wise and sagacious as they were, had known that [the] India of their vision would not be a reality if the children of the country are not nurtured and educated. For this, their exploitation by different profit makers for their personal gain had to be first indicated. It is this need, which has found manifestation in Article 24, which is one of the two provisions in part IV of our Constitution on the fundamental right against exploitation. *The framers were aware that this prohibition alone would not permit the child to contribute its mite to the nation building work unless it receives at least basic education. Article 45 was therefore inserted in our paramount parchment casting a duty on the state to endeavour to provide free and compulsory education to children (after the decision by a Constitution Bench of this Court in Unnikrishnan, 1993–1 SCC 645, this provision in Part IV of our Constitution has acquired the status of a fundamental right).*

This is the other link we have been ignoring: the existence of child labour opposes and denies all possibility of universal primary education. Conversely, if free and compulsory education is implemented, then child labour will be eradicated in no time at all. Myron Wiener (1994a: 83–86) has noted that no country has successfully ended child labour without first making education compulsory.

Despite such landmark judgements our children still remained out of school. In 2002 the government finally amended the Constitution (86th Amendment to the Constitution in 2002) to insert Article 21A. It reads:

> The State shall provide free and compulsory education to all children of the age of six to fourteen years in such manner as the State may, by law, decide.

There has not been a single writ petition filed after this momentous amendment. Unless that happens we shall not find out what kind of education the State may decide to give, for we do not know what the following words mean: *in such manner as the state may, by law, determine.* One thing, however, is sure. Article 45 had only spoken about children up to the age of 14 years, whereas Article 21A specifies a lower age limit of 6 years. Now the state cannot be compelled to look after children from 0 to 6 years. This looks as though pre-primary education could be at the discretion of the State, unless political compulsions dictate otherwise. That in turn will depend on voters being alert, aware and vigilant.

Over the years, this author has heard it said that after the CRC no legal change was needed. However, this is not true. The ratification of UN instruments makes it mandatory for a state party to pass suitable national legislation. The same people argue that after the CRC, Supreme Court judgements and the constitutional amendment were all superfluous. This, too, is not true. All these instruments are to be used only in the Supreme Court and high courts. We even need a local education Act that can be used in district courts.

Meanwhile, let us go back to our unanswered questions about children not completing school. Admittedly, there has been increased activity in the area of elementary education since the 1980s, as Ramachandran's data shows. But this good news is followed by bad news; the drop-out rate is high and the rate of learning basic skills of literacy is low. This could be one of the reasons why children and their parents consider school a poor use of time.

From Table 2.3 it appears that 75 per cent rural girls attend primary school and 63.6 per cent are literate. The enrolment figures

TABLE 2.3
CHILDREN ENROLLED IN SCHOOL (6 TO 10 YEARS) (%)

	Enrolled	Reported as Literate	Attending School
NFHS-I (1992–93)			
All Areas			
Boys	118.1	64.0	75.0
Girls	92.7	53.6	45.4
Rural			
Boys	N.A.	60.3	52.3
Girls	N.A.	44.8	39.3
NSS 50th Round (1993–94)			
All areas			
Boys	115.3	68.5	75.0
Girls	92.9	62.1	61.3
Rural			
Boys	N.A.	60.1	66.4
Girls	N.A.	50.2	56.0
NSS 52nd Round (1995–96)			
All areas			
Boys	98.6	N.A.	73.0
Girls	81.8	N.A.	63.0
Rural			
Boys	N.A.	N.A.	71.0
Girls	N.A.	N.A.	58.0
NFHS-2 (1998–99)			
All areas			
Boys	N.A.	73.1	85.2
Girls	N.A.	67.4	78.3
Rural			
Boys	N.A.	70.0	83.2
Girls	N.A.	63.6	75.1

Source: Ramachandran (2004a).

are not available, but they will be higher. We have not segregated data for SC and ST children.

Recent figures from a government Web site on education says that 142 million children (82 per cent) were enrolled in primary schools in 2002. But select educational statistics also reveal that in 2002 as many as 59 million children in the 6 to 14 age group were still out of school (Ramachandran 2004b: 14–17). How many stayed on? How many learnt anything? We can only guess as there are only some indicators (Table 2.4 and Table 2.5). For example, Ramachandran tells us that there are regional variations (Table 2.4).

TABLE 2.4
SOME STATE-WISE VARIATIONS IN ATTENDANCE IN PRIMARY SCHOOLS (%)

State	Attendance
Himachal Pradesh	90
Kerala	90
Bihar	< 60

Source: Ramachandran (2004b).

It comes as no surprise that Ramachandran found that in higher classes everywhere fewer girls attend school, and that this is so almost all over the country, not just in the backward states of Madhya Pradesh, Uttar Pradesh, Bihar and Rajasthan, but also in the advanced states of Gujarat, Tamil Nadu and Karnataka. This was particularly the case in urban slums, tribal areas and in habitations of the lower social strata.

TABLE 2.5
SOME STATE-WISE VARIATIONS IN COMPLETION OF PRIMARY SCHOOL OF ENROLLED CHILDREN (%)

State	Completion Rate
Kerala	100
Tamil Nadu	86
Maharashtra	82
Bihar	28
Rajasthan	30
West Bengal	26

Source: Ramachandran (2004a).

Ramachandran noted that children did not seem to learn anything. This is especially true of rural one- or two-teacher schools. Teaching may occur for as few as 140 days in a year, and it may be for as little as 25 minutes in a day! In Karnataka, Rajasthan, Uttar Pradesh and Andhra Pradesh children in classes III and IV were not able to read fluently. 'He cannot read a postcard', complained one father. Note, the father wanted his child to read; he was not looking at the job potential of the child.

Echoing George Orwell, 'All animals are equal, some animals are more equal than others', some government schools are better than others. There are different levels of municipal schools or government schools. Some are very good, like the Central Schools (Kendriya Vidyalaya) or army schools. Navyug/NDMC schools in New Delhi are also good. Class III and IV government servants, particularly, send their children to these schools. Children of Class I and II government servants will go to successively more expensive schools. In rural schools the number of students per teacher is very high, the building dilapidated, and the equipment poor or non-existent. In many schools there is not enough space for children to sit. In one school in Uttar Pradesh, the headmaster told this author that he could accommodate the children only because a certain percentage remained absent every day. But as children from CREDA's (Centre for Rural Education and Development Action) bridge courses[10] came every day there was a problem (UNDP 2003)!

Scholars and NGOs have noticed a great hunger for education. That is why Ramachandran calls it 'the best of times'. It has led to a virtual mushrooming of private schools in educationally backward areas of Bihar and Uttar Pradesh to make up for poor-quality government schools or no schools. Even the poor try to find money for their children's education. Research undertaken by MARG (Multiple Action Research Group) also found this to be true in Ferozabad district of Uttar Pradesh. But the really poor cannot afford these schools.

Ramachandran says that till a few decades ago even in schools run by private agencies, education was nearly free. The latter included Ramakrishna Mission schools, Dayananda Anglo-Vedic or DAV schools, church schools, and private schools by educationists like Dr Karve and Karmaveer Bhau Patil in western Maharashtra, and by innumerable regional and even local educational trusts and societies. They charged little by way of fees. A 35-year-old woman said that her primary school in Ludhiana charged only 10 paise every month. Education has become a lucrative business since then. It is another indicator of the hunger for good education.

Children do not stay in school because they do not find it interesting. Schools have no buildings, teachers, equipment or books. Thus, Operation Blackboard had to be launched in 1987 to provide at least two teachers and some equipment to schools! The children leave or their guardians withdraw them because they learn nothing. There is not enough money in the budget to give them education in schools.

THERE ARE NOT ENOUGH TEACHERS

The M. Venkatarangaiya Foundation (MVF) in Andhra Pradesh and CREDA in Uttar Pradesh, the two NGOs who run bridge courses for child labourers, have started providing volunteer teachers to government schools in their vicinity. That is the only way their children can get some teaching. Many schools rely upon their help to conduct classes. The state governments do not employ sufficient number of teachers. There are not even two teachers in many schools. Even with two teachers, four classes cannot be handled with any success. In Mirzapur, Uttar Pradesh, one headmaster also said that the CREDA staff did not have other duties that occupied his teachers. He was referring to their various non-teaching duties from the census to polio eradication campaign. The headmasters also asked CREDA for equipment such as *durry* strips for children to sit on.

After the Fifth Pay Commission in the early 1990s, the impact on the teaching profession has been shatteringly adverse. All government servants were meant to gain from large income hikes. Government administrative staff from Classes I to IV certainly gained. Their salaries skyrocketed. No government can dare to displease its administrative staff. But what of the teachers? Did they benefit? The answer is no.

In at least three states as widely separated by distance and social advancement as Maharashtra, Uttar Pradesh and Andhra Pradesh, this author learnt that the recruitment of full-time teachers has been badly affected, if not halted altogether. The district education officer (DEO) in one district of Uttar Pradesh said quite frankly that the government could not afford the high salaries that would have to be paid to teachers. This was when a headmaster retired at Rs 10,000 a month. Instead, the government employed part-time teachers who would be glorified as *shiksha mitras*; para-teachers or some other such name. They would be engaged at Rs 2,500 only and they would be dismissed every summer vacation. A school would have one or two such part-timers. The DEO did not deny that this arrangement would give the head-master unfair control over the teachers who would be recruited if he recommended them. From experience one can tell how the position could be misused; it could culminate into undue demands for free goods or services, or even a share of the salary. With such service conditions, teachers are called by praiseworthy nomenclatures such as *acharya*s in the Education Guarantee Scheme and they would be paid a fixed salary of Rs 1,000. CREDA pays its teachers only Rs 1,300 per month, while MVF pays even less.

When Naik suggested hiring voluntary teachers to reduce the cost of teachers' salaries, he surely did not envisage that the increased burden of the Fifth Pay Commission would actually cut down the number of regular teachers.

THE NON-MYSTERY OF THE MISSING CHILDREN IN UPPER PRIMARY SCHOOLS

Another question we ask is about the large number of children who never enrol in upper primary schools after class V. The simple truth is that *children do not go to upper primary school because they do not have access to one.* In 1993, in the *Unnikrishnan* judgement, the Supreme Court quoted the following figures as regards the number of institutions:

1. 1950–51

   • Primary schools (class I–V): 210,558
   • Upper primary schools: 13,146
   • Total: 223,704

2. 1990–91

   • Primary schools: 5,381,636
   • Upper primary schools: 361,059
   • Total: 6,242,695

This means, in 1950–51 one upper primary school had to accommodate children from 16 primary schools. By 1990 the ratio had improved infinitesimally. Children from 14.9 primary schools had to compete for place in one upper primary school.

As we saw, in 2002 there were 142 million children in school, although 59 million children were still out of school. For them there were 664,000 primary schools (Ramachandran 2004b), which was not much of an increase. There were also 219,000 upper primary schools and 139,000 high schools (ibid.). This is steep increase over 1991, but it was not enough. These figures mean that for children from *three* primary schools, one upper primary school is provided. Students from three upper primary schools are supposed to be accommodated in 1.6 high schools. That is to say, for students of five primary schools there is one high school. The figure would be even lower for higher secondary schools, except for one fact: many rural children do not pass their class X exams. It is too tough, too urban-child-oriented. The headmaster of a higher secondary school in Uttar Pradesh said he had enough seats vacant in class XI as hardly anyone passed class X. This author also remembers a poor student in tribal Maharashtra who said that as no one in the entire *taluka* had passed, he could not get any class X second-hand books.

All this goes to show that in government planning there is still no expectation that children will complete elementary education.

Many upper primary schools also contain primary schools; similarly many high schools already have their own primary, upper primary and secondary school sections. The headmasters of high schools in Mirzapur district said they give preference to their own students. Only if they have spare seats left do they take in outsiders. Indeed, this is the practice everywhere, even in elite schools. In most fee-charging schools, classes range from nursery to class XII. Admission in between is very difficult if not impossible. Parents may prefer a local nursery school for their 3-year-old, but they are obliged to send them long distances to a school where they would like the child to go when it is older. Families relocating to another city have a very difficult time getting admission for children who have already started school. If the child is in a school going up all the way to high school, it is more likely to continue than if it has to change schools. Second, the change has strong psychological repercussions on family decisions. If the child is a first-generation schoolgoer and if it is a girl, other questions also come up.

Budget Allocation

The world moves around money and so it is important to look at the budget allocation for elementary education. In this paper we look at this aspect only briefly. In 1975, the Naik Committee had said that universal education would cost the state 3 per cent of its GNP (ICSSR 1975: 69–70). At that time he conceded that it was prohibitively high and suggested some alternatives, which we shall mention later.

In its judgement in the *Unnikrishnan* case, the Supreme Court had pointed out that allocation for education had lost its priorities. More was spent on successively higher stages of education. Elementary education got the smallest portion of the cake, yet, according to Article 41 as well as according to UN Instruments, higher education is to be made available only within the economic capacities of the government. For primary education there was no such condition.

In its Web site[11] the education ministry (http://www.education. nic.in) records that the goal as stated in the resolution on the National Policy for Education (NPE) in 1968 was that 6 per cent of the total national income should be set aside for education. The goal was to be attained gradually.

What is the Definition of Gradual?

In 1951–52 it was 0.8 per cent of GNP, in 1992–93 it rose to 3.3 per cent of GNP, and by the Eighth Plan it was to be 6 per cent. We are now in the 10th Plan. In 2004 the expenditure has reduced to 4 per cent of GNP. In 1975, 3 per cent would have been enough, but it was considered too high a call on the national income. From 1990–91 to 1998–99, on an average 13.6 per cent of the expenditure on elementary education was funded by external aid. Eighty-five per cent of the cost of the District Primary Education Programme is raised through external loans. (HAQ 2001: 31).

SCHEMES AND PROGRAMMES

The 1980s and 1990s saw a marked increase in government efforts to promote primary education. One of the oldest programmes is the non-formal education programme or NFE, which was started in 1979–80 'to support full-time schooling'. It worked in 10 states. The government honoured the NFE as its *flagship programme for universalising elementary education*. Since then it has made its appearance in various guises. The Government of India Web site says without any self-consciousness, that the resolution for preparing the National Policy on Education (NPE) was dated 1968, and the NPE was actually formulated in 1986. The NPE also recognised that:

> School could not reach all children.... A large and systematic programme of non formal education would be required for school dropouts, for children

from habitations without schools, working children, and girls who could not attend day schools.

The Plan of Action (POA) on the NPE was prepared only in 1992. All this is an indication of how seriously elementary education is being taken by the government. Second, the government could not bring itself to give up its obsession with part-time schooling, which would of course be for poor children. The POA strengthened the NFE. According to the government statement, NPE was 'a plan of action by which every child would regularly attend school or *NFE centre*'. The government statement mentioned the two options in one breath. Clearly, it was in no mind to give unrelenting priority to formal full-time schools.

The systematic programmes of non-formal education are not one but many. They are called, diversely, the District Primary Education Programme, Sarva Shiksha Abhiyan, Education Guarantee Scheme, Alternative and Innovative Education, National Programme for Education of Girls at Elementary Level, and so on. This is essentially because the Government of India and state governments of every ideological persuasion are still not able to make up their minds on the continuation of child labour. The official way of thinking seems to be that 'we don't like it on principle but in practice we cannot abolish it'.

Way back in 1975, Professor Naik had suggested some alternatives in order to avoid heavy spending on formal elementary education. His suggestions were to increase the teacher–pupil ratio, introduce two–shift schools, hand out books in classrooms and then circulate them to other children. Naik also suggested getting voluntary teachers and permitting multiple entry points. This meant that older children should be allowed to enter higher classes directly (ICSSR 1975: 69–70) through what we will now call bridge courses. After more than a quarter of a century, we are no nearer to our objective. NFE was revised and extended in 1987–88 to include urban slums, hilly, tribal and desert areas. One wonders how they had been left out the first time. It did not include working children in other Union Territories.

In 1994, the government introduced the District Primary Education Programme (DPEP) with much fanfare. This programme was described as 'a beachhead for overhauling primary education in India'. Yet it suffered from the same fatal flaw. The Government of India Web site for elementary education tells us that 'the basic objectives of DPEP was to provide all children with access to primary education within the formal system *or through the informal education (NFE) programme*'. In 1995, the government launched the National Programme of Nutritional Support for Primary Education, better known as the midday meal scheme. *This was not available to NFE schools.*

Then we come to the Sarva Shiksha Abhiyan (SSA), which was launched in the 21st century. It is referred to by the Government of India as its 'flagship programme for achievement of Universalisation of Elementary Education in a time bound manner' as mandated by the 86th Amendment', which had made primary education a fundamental right. This statement mentions that 192 million children have to be in school in 1.1 million habitations.

The SSA was to strengthen existing schools by providing drinking water, toilets, teachers and even buildings, it would upgrade existing teachers by giving them extensive training. It had a special focus on girls and children with special needs. The objectives of the SSA spell out the nitty-gritty of the programme. The very first one is: all children in school, education guarantee centre, alternative school or back-to-school camp by 2003. Except the first one, all are NFE options. Through this programme the government aimed to have all children to complete five years of schooling by 2007 and eight years of elementary schooling by 2010. The deadline has already been extended to 2015.[12]

In addition to the SSA the government introduced the National Programme for Education of Girls at Elementary Level (NPEGEL). It is not a school but a level. Even the pretense of sending children to school is dropped. The Education Guarantee Scheme and alternative and innovative education were both meant for out-of-school children. The SSA made one addition; it aspires to decentralise education and give greater say to states and to smaller units right up to village education councils, in management. By 2003, NFE had been extended to 25 states, working with state governments and over 800 voluntary agencies.

Government data say that NFE had 138,000 primary schools and 6,800 upper primary centres; 7.4 million children were covered. In other words, at least 7.4 million children were still out of formal schools. Community participation was low. Government servants would not give up control.

The central government's own evaluation of alternative and innovative education has been discouraging. It found that alternate education was popularly regarded as inferior education. Completion rates for primary schools were poor. Very few children entered formal schools. The programme was not successful with girls.

One word here about the *anganwadi* (AW) which is run under the Integrated Child Development Scheme (ICDS). According to the Government of India Web site on education, there are 5,614 projects. At least in Maharashtra the rule is that a project has a minimum of 100 AWs under one supervisor, who can have a maximum of 250 AWs under her/him. It is likely that tribal or hilly areas may have fewer than 100. An *anganwadi* may serve just one village or more depending on population as well as the distance to other villages. It is difficult to tell from this information how many children can access pre-school education. One function of the AW is to provide pre-school education (PSE) to children between 3 and 6 years of age. (In Maharashtra this is done by a separate institution called the *balwadi*, which has specially trained staff, but there will be either a *balwadi* or an *anganwadi* in any given village.) The government found that of the 6- to 14-year-old children currently in school, 85 per cent in ICDS areas and only 15 per cent in non-ICDS areas had received pre-school education.

Eighty-nine per cent of children with PSE were sent by parents to primary school. But only 52 to 60 per cent children without PSE did so. The never-enrolled category had fewer children from PSEs. The overall finding was that PSE plays a large role in promoting enrolment, reducing drop-out rate and promoting greater retention in school. Pre-school education is routine with middle-class children. There is no reason to deny it to everyone else. But after the 86th Amendment no child can claim a right to PSE or an *anganwadi.* Incidentally, the document notes that children could count up to 50 and could recognise upto five objects. This means they learnt numbers without understanding them! We have a shining example of how children may be motivated to go to school without any force, we have seen that parents have no problem in sending children to *anganwadis,* and later they are quite willing to send them to primary school. Thus, if children go to pre-school it becomes easier to motivate them to go to primary school. And this shows that it is not always compulsion that is required to send children to school. The pre-school experience will make it unnecessary to use compulsion for all but a few hard cases. But, unfortunately, now the 0- to 6-year-olds have not been included in the safety net of fundamental rights.

It is now well accepted among certain sections of NGOs and others who are involved in education that keeping children out of school is not necessarily a function of poverty. It is often the result of negative attitudes or of different priorities. This is especially true of girls. Even well-off households may consider household skills more important for them.

It is not just the government that is confused on the issue of full-time education. Even NGOs and intellectuals are confused. The Bill to revamp the Child Labour (Regulation and Prohibition) Act was produced by an NGO. Many people weep buckets over the plight of the poor widow whose son is her sole breadwinner. But economists will tell us and the MVF has proved that when children are withdrawn from the labour force, adults get the jobs *at higher wages.* Child labour leads to adult unemployment and lower wages. Children do not work because they are poor. They are poor because they work.

The point about quality education and relevant education has been misused to discourage education. Children who carry more books than their own weight also do not receive quality education. Another point is that the education is not relevant because it is not vocational—nor any good for earning a living. For a 5-year-old no education is 'relevant'. Till a child completes the age of 14 there is no point in asking for relevant education. Going to school itself is education. It is even more so for children who have been kept out of school for centuries. Asking that education should be of a certain quality or have relevance before going to school is like learning to swim before getting into the pool. That will come about when children and parents begin to experience education.

However, relevance has a strong place in making education intelligible and interesting. A textbook that speaks of traffic jams and flats in high-rise buildings has nothing to offer the rural child. This is especially true of Adivasi children. They need education in their own language, using familiar objects and ideas. For example, the post office and the bus stop are landmarks for an urban person. The rural child will mention trees we do not even recognise. S/he needs to learn in a way that honours and keeps alive the tribes' knowledge systems (Lawrence et al. 2004: 30). I had found Salim Ali's *Book of Indian Birds* the entry into many a village. Then they begin to talk of so many things they had assumed we considered below our educated notice. The culmination came for me in the planning of a report for a dam in Madhya Pradesh. It declared that there were no animals in the forest. How could that be? The bureaucratic writers meant there were no elephants, tigers, bears or deer. The smaller creatures did not matter. They would have found out much more about the flora and fauna if they had asked the tribal people. But they were illiterate, so they had to be ignorant and stupid. This is exactly how our educational system treats their knowledge base.

Relevance for us in the city and village so often comes down to getting jobs. *Why educate them if our boys do not get jobs?* It is one thing to hear villagers say it. At a pinch we can take it from grassroots NGOs. But when educated academics start using the argument one is truly appalled at this understanding of education in their own lives. In the British period when there were not enough educated persons to be *babu*s, every father expected his son to pass high school and get a job. For a peon's job even a class VII certificate was enough. We have spent the last 40 years battling this expectation. Primary education is not about getting a job, it is about getting basic skills and confidence to live one's day-to-day life. It seems that this is something that people who take education for granted simply fail to understand. To be able to read a receipt or a bill, to read the destination on a bus, to be able to write a letter knowing that only the recipient will read it, signing a document only after reading it, to be able to distinguish advertisements from the 7/12 extract[13] and rent receipts—the list is endless. We understand the benefits of our children learning about computers long before a job is in sight; but for poor children only a job will make education relevant. It is a sad commentary on the plastic towers that are our academia. Having spent six years with Bhils, Santals and Pahadiyas as a legal activist, I am left with an intense and unshakable conviction that the basic ability to read and write is essential for every human being. It opens many more worlds than we can think of. When anyone asks what use education is, I am reminded of Edison's conversation with a visitor who came to his exhibition to see the 0 watt lightbulb. When she asked what use it was. Edison replied, 'Madam what use is a newborn baby?'

In the same context, there is some debate on the necessity for having fully trained teachers in every school. The argument is based on the legitimate premise of equality. We want to give the same education to all children, rich and poor, metropolitan and rustic. But well-qualified men and women do not exist in large enough numbers in villages. When they do get training, they set their eyes on cities and better career prospects. The most urgent need of young first-time schoolgoers is to feel comfortable in school. They often do not feel comfortable with those who are too different from them in appearance and speech. This is particularly true of the Adivasi child, with most teachers teaching in Adivasi schools being non-Adivasis and who view their culture and language as inferior to their own. This has a strong negative impact on the children and leads to their dropping out of school (Lawrence et al. 2004: 8).

Debates have also emerged regarding the need to have trained teachers in order to provide better education to children. But is it really the most important factor? In fact, instead of training what is more important is empathy towards children who go to a completely new world when they start school. For instance, the assistants provided by the MV Foundation in Hyderabad are not all armed with class XII and B.Ed certificates, but they make the children feel good. Surely there is no need to insist on all these qualifications for at least the first couple of classes. Let the child feel happy in school before we start loading her/him with much else. But as we are unable to help our own children in posh private schools, bent under piles of homework, forced to learn English before they learn their mother tongue, perhaps we do not see the need for any of this. A housewife's saying in Marathi scoffs at our mentality that makes us say 'either we shall eat with *ghee* or we shall go hungry'.

All this debate distracts us from more serious problems. We are not even aware that NFE really provides poor-quality, irrelevant education. We pay no attention to the fact that 14 is no age to stop education, especially as the school leaver cannot enter the job market till s/he is 18 years old. We do not ask about the dearth of upper primary schools and too few teachers. Over five decades after the Constitution came into force, over a decade after *Unnikrishnan*, and over two years after the 86th Amendment, we are not much further down the road except that the popular desire for education has soared.

There is bitter opposition from liberals to making education compulsory. They are afraid that the police will abuse their powers to persecute, beat and even imprison poor parents. It is worth asking what compulsion has meant in other countries and in the pre-Independence princely state of Baroda. We must remember that a right confers no obligation to act. But if I have a duty then I must perform it.

Things have become so ridiculously one-sided that the Delhi government is planning mobile schools to go around slums because those children do not come to school (*Indian Express*, 10 September 2004: 1). The news item showed a mobile van with a blackboard and a teacher standing before a few students seated on a *durry*. What is to make them stay on till the end of the class? They only have a right to have a school; they have no duty to go to one! Second, why should any one take the NFE camp seriously when the government itself takes education so lightly? Is that how children are meant to be taught?

Myron Wiener, a well-known student of child labour in India, noted that many countries that had made education compulsory, like Japan in 1872, the two Koreas, Taiwan and the Peoples Republic of China, all after World War II, were poor. He then remarked:

Education should not be regarded as a right granted by the state, but as duty imposed by the state. When education is made a duty, parents, irrespective of their economic circumstances and beliefs are required by law to send their children to school. It is the legal obligation of the state to provide an adequate number of schools, appropriately situated and to ensure that no child fails to attend school. (1994a: 87)

In another article Wiener noted:

Modern states regard education as a legal duty, not merely as a right: parents are required to send their children to school, children are required to attend school and the state is obliged to enforce compulsory education.... [T]he state thus stands as the ultimate guardian of children, protecting them against both parents and would be employers (1994b).

We rebel against such statements because we would rather see parents as the paramount authority. Yet the law has changed in many ways to put the interests of the child over and above those of the parents. This is notably so in cases of custody of children. We even want the state to interfere when parents give dowry. Yet when the child is not sent to school, we still do not want to compel parents.

Despite the widespread hunger for education, there are people who do not believe in education at all, especially for girls. The parent must be duty bound to send the child to school, regardless of any pressing need to make cowdung cakes, graze the cow, or attend a wedding or to a guest. Finally, the child must have a duty to go to school, however much s/he may prefer to play cricket or skip rope. Only then there will be an outcry against NFE schools, which get away right now by giving little or no education. Only when all this is put into place will we get full-time schools that spend on educating the child in the real sense of the word.

Notes

1. This was passed in the UN General Assembly vide resolution No. 217A (III) on 10 December 1948.
2. Convention of the Rights of the Child was passed in UN General Assembly through Resolution No.1386(XIV) of 20th November 1989, ratified by India on 10 December 1992.
3. Vimala Ramachandran (ed.) *Gender and Social Equity in Primary Education*. Sage Publications, New Delhi, 2004, p. 54.
4. Experience of Smt. Geeta Sane, narrated in a Marathi article on primary education, reference not available.
5. 1992 (5) SLR 1 (SC).
6. AIR 1993 SC 2178.
7. But that was within the economic capacity of the state and coupled with the right to work.
8. Article 46 was about the educational and economic rights of the SC and ST communities.
9. AIR 1997 SC 699.
10. This information has been brought out in an unpublished CREDA report for UNDP in 2003.
11. Please see the Web site of Ministry of Human Resource Development for details—http://www.education.nic.in
12. 'The Problem', *Seminar*, 536, April 2004, p. 12–13.
13. '7/12 extract' refers to the property register card of a property. It contains such details as the Survey numbers, area and date from which the current owner's name was registered as the owner. The 7/12 extract is issued by the *tehsildar* or concerned land authority.

References

Government of India. 1971. *Education and National Development: Report of the Education Commission 1964–66* (Kothari Commission Report), Department of Women and Children, Ministry of Human Resource Development. New Delhi: Government of India.

———. 1985. *The Challenge of Education: A Policy Perspective*, Ministry of Education. New Delhi: Government of India.

———. 2003. 'Agenda Papers for National Workshop on CEDAW', Department of Women and Children, Ministry of Human Resource Development. New Delhi: Government of India.

———. 2005. Web site on 'Educational Schemes and Policies', http://www.education. nic.in/htmlweb/natpol.htm, accessed in March 2005.

HAQ. 2001. *Elementary Education: India's Children and the Education Budget*. New Delhi: Centre for Child Rights.

Indian Express (*Express Newsline*, Delhi Edition), 10 September 2004.

Naik, J.P. 1975. *Elementary Education in India* (Naik Committee Report). New Delhi: Indian Council of Social Science Research (ICSSR).

Lawrence, Surendra, Kikkeri Narayan and Ritambhara Hebber. 2004. *Adivasis of India and Development Strategies*. Bangalore: HIVOS.

Myrdal, Gunnar. 1972. *Asian Drama* (abridged edition). London: Allen Lane.

Ramachandran, Vimala (ed.). 2004a. *Gender and Social Equity in Primary Education*. New Delhi: Sage Publications.

Ramachandran, Vimala. 2004b. 'The Best of Times, The Worst of Times'. *Seminar*, 536(April): 14–17.

UNDP. 2003. CREDA Report for UNDP (unpublished).

Wiener, Myron. 1994a. 'India's Case Against Compulsory Education', *Seminar*, 413(January): 83–86.

———. 1994b. 'The Right to be a Child'. Background Paper, UNICEF India.

3

DILUTION, DISTORTION AND DIVERSION

A POST-JOMTIEN REFLECTION ON THE EDUCATION POLICY*

Anil Sadgopal

INTRODUCTION

The following news item appeared on International Literacy Day, 2004:

> Facing a shortage of students, the Directorate of Education has decided to close down 53 government schools, many of which are in old Delhi. This is in addition to [the] 55 schools already closed . . . . 'We have seen a steady decline in enrollment in government schools.' (*Hindustan Times* 2004)

*This paper is an updated version of an earlier paper by this author (Sadgopal 2003d). This paper is essentially based on three chapters of a book being written by this author on education policy in India and methods of policy analysis. The three chapters that were compressed in this paper deal with: (*a*) non-formal education; (*b*) constitutional amendment to purportedly make education a fundamental right; and (*c*) impact of structural adjustment and external aid on education policy. This work is part of author's research as Senior Fellow, Nehru Memorial Museum and Library, New Delhi.

Instead of showing concern and taking steps to improve the functioning of the government school system, the authorities seemed to be celebrating. They declared: 'The closure of the schools helps the Directorate in two ways. First, the teachers can be posted in schools having few teachers. Second, there is saving on annual expenditure of maintenance and repairs' (ibid.).

Government schools in Delhi cater to almost 70 per cent of schoolgoing children of the metropolis. Close all of them and the Directorate will be helped maximally. It will save its entire annual expenditure!

This is not the first time that India has witnessed such a phenomenon. In 1999–2000, 30 government schools in the city of Indore were closed down and their campuses, located on prime lands in the heart of the city, were either converted into police stations or handed over to private interests for developing commercial complexes. The district collector, in his report to the chief minister, proudly called it a process of 'rationalisation'! No one cared to know where all the children went. All of them had joined the rapidly mushrooming low-fee school shops in the neighbourhood of the erstwhile government schools.

Almost at the same time, the Ahmedabad city corporation closed down one of its primary schools and handed over its campus along with the buildings to a French-sponsored society to provide education to the well-off sections of society on a 'French pattern'. The poor people in the neighbourhood protested, but no one cared.

Few would believe that the above events were not random happenings taking place due to some local aberrations or some inefficient education officers. These represented the outcome of a well-designed deliberate policy of allowing the government school system to gradually deteriorate until it is replaced by the fee-charging private schools. This is precisely what global market forces, led by powerful international financial institutions and funding agencies, have been working for. This paper is aimed at analysing and exposing this complex phenomenon so that it can be resisted by the people whose children are being denied education.

Look at Another Happening

On 28 November 2001, the Lok Sabha was debating the 93rd Amendment Bill (2001) of the Constitution, introduced by the Government of India, purportedly to make education a fundamental right. As the debate progressed, about 40,000 people from different parts of India held a rally a few kilometres away in the Ramlila Grounds to protest against the Bill. They were contending that it violated the principle of equality enshrined in the Constitution and essentially amounted to snatching away the fundamental right to education that had become available to the people as a consequence of Supreme Court's historic Unnikrishnan judgement (1993).[1] They were demanding, '*Sub ko shiksha, samaan shiksha*' (equality in education for all). In effect, the rally was reminding the government and all political parties of the commitment made *thrice* to the nation: first, through a cabinet resolution in 1968 in the form of a national policy, and twice by the Parliament again through a national policy (in 1986 and 1992) to evolve the common school system for all children as the National System of Education, as recommended by the Education Commission (1964–66). They also knew that the Bill would allow the state to withdraw from its constitutional obligation under the original Article 45 of ensuring free and compulsory education for all children until they complete the age of 14 years by excluding the children below 6 years of age and by shifting, in measured steps, its obligation to the parents and the community in the name of making it their fundamental duty. The rally's demands basically reflected two major concerns that had by then begun to have an impact on the public discourse on education in India, especially due to what happened during the 1990s. These concerns were: (*a*) increasing abdication by the state of its constitutional obligation towards elementary education (that is, a minimum of *eight* years of education from class I to VIII); and (*b*) the steady dilution of policies and programmes relating to 'free education of *equitable* quality' for all children (Bharat Jan Vigyan Jatha 1995; Sadgopal 1994, 2000, 2001d, 2002b, 2003a). Ignoring a nationwide public protest, negating three significant amendment motions moved in Lok Sabha, and turning a deaf ear to critical speeches by several MPs, the Bill was pushed through both Houses of the Parliament. Curiously, there was not a single dissenting vote in either House, despite articulation of severe criticism. The Bill was eventually signed by the president in December 2002. We shall return to this matter later.

In order to comprehend the roots of people's concerns, it is necessary to refer to two sets of critical policy-related documents, one national and the other international. First, the National Policy on Education (henceforth NPE) (1986) and its companion document called Programme of Action (henceforth as POA) (1986), both approved by the Parliament in May 1986 and November 1986 respectively (Government of India 1986).[2] Both the NPE (1986) and POA (1986) were revised by Parliament in 1992 and, as a result, are known as NPE (1986) (as modified in 1992) and POA (1992) respectively (Government of India 1992b, 1992c). Second, the World Declaration on Education for All and its companion document called Framework for Action to Meet Basic Learning Needs adopted by the World Conference on Education for All (EFA): Meeting Basic Learning Needs, held at Jomtien, Thailand, in March 1990 (these documents are referred to as the Jomtien Declaration and Jomtien Framework respectively) (UNDP et al. 1990).

This paper will attempt to establish that the twin trends of gradual abdication of constitutional obligation and steady dilution of policy relating to 'free education of *equitable* quality' that clearly emerged during the 1990s, as also reflected in the 93rd (now called 86th) Constitutional Amendment Bill, had its roots in the policy framework of NPE (1986) and the programme design of POA (1986) (as well as their revised counterparts of 1992). The policy framework will be probed with the aid of policy analysis tools. This will reveal that the policy was designed to basically promote exclusion of millions of children from elementary education and introduce inequality by institutionalising low-quality multiple tracks or parallel streams of education. It was this character of NPE (1986) that provided both the foundation and the necessary socio-political space to international funding agencies, including the World Bank, to exacerbate abdication, accelerate the pace of exclusion, and further marginalise people's aspirations for a Common School System and genuine neighbourhood schools.[3] We begin with NPE (1986).

NON-FORMAL EDUCATION: PROBING THE POLICY FRAMEWORK

The National Policy on Education (1986) marked a watershed as it was the first policy-level acknowledgement since independence that elementary school education of *comparable quality* will *not* become available to all children of India in the 6 to 14 age group. The notion of education of *comparable quality* for all children, irrespective of their class, creed, caste, gender, linguistic or cultural background or physical/mental disability, was clearly implied in the Constitution. Such an implication is seen when the original Article 45 (free and compulsory education for all children up to the age of 14 years)[4] of Part IV (Directive Principles of State Policy) is read in conjunction with Article 14 (equality before law), Article 15 (prohibition of discrimination on grounds of religion, race, caste, sex, place of birth, or any one of them), Article 16 (equality of opportunity in public employment) and Article 21 (protection of life and personal liberty), the latter four Articles belonging to Part III (Fundamental Rights).[5] The concept of equality in *educational opportunities* and *conditions of success* is further strengthened in Part IV of the Constitution by Article 38 (social order with justice and elimination of inequalities in status, facilities and opportunities), Article 39e and f (tender age of children is not abused; children are given opportunities and facilities to develop in a healthy manner and in conditions of freedom and dignity; childhood is protected against exploitation) and Article 46 (promotion with special care the educational and economic interests of the weaker sections of the people, and in particular of the Scheduled Castes and Scheduled Tribes). However, despite such unambiguous Constitutional provisions, the NPE (1986) stated:

A large and systematic programme of non-formal education will be launched for school drop-outs, for children from habitations without schools, *working children* and *girls who cannot attend whole-day schools*. (NPE [1986], Section 5.8; emphasis added)

It further resolved:

This effort [that is, '*ensuring children's retention at school*] will be fully co-ordinated with the network of non-formal education. It shall be ensured that all children who attain the age of about 11 years by 1990 will have had five years *schooling*, or its equivalent through the *non-formal stream*. (NPE [1986], Section 5.12; emphasis added)

As per the Acharya Ramamurti Committee Report (Government of India 1990: Chapter 6, Section 6.2.3, Table 2), out-of-school children were almost half the children of schoolgoing age at the time the NPE (1986) was adopted. The aforementioned component of the NPE (1986) implied that these out-of-school children shall be provided non-formal education, a *parallel* stream to *mainstream* formal school education. Most of the out-of-school children were working children, whether paid wages or not.[6] Indeed, the notion of 'mainstream' emerged in India only because the NPE (1986) gave legitimacy to a parallel stream such as non-formal education, a layer *below* the formal school. Until then, in principle, there was only one officially acknowledged, planned and financially supported stream in Indian education (that is, the government, local body and government-aided schools of comparable quality), the relatively minor streams of private unaided schools (erroneously called public schools) and Kendriya Vidyalayas (or Central Schools) notwith-standing.[7] Recognising this, the Education Commission (1964–66) had strongly recommended the establishment of a *common* school system (often misunderstood as a *uniform* school system) through the instrumentality of neighbourhood schools (Government of India 1996). The Common School System was accepted in the first NPE in 1968 in order to 'equalise educational opportunity' for all children and to promote 'social cohesion and national integration'. In this sense, the policy imperative of non-formal education amounted to violating not only the Constitution and the NPE (1968), but also the NPE (1986) itself, which had made the following commitment:

The concept of a National System of Education implies that, up to a given level, all students, irrespective of caste, creed, location or sex, have access to education of a *comparable* quality. To achieve this, the Government will initiate appropriately funded programmes. Effective measures will be taken in the

direction of the *Common School System recommended in the 1968 policy*. (NPE [1986]),
Section 3.2; also retained in the policy revised in 1992; emphasis added)

Since non-formal education was designed to be provided largely
through evening centres, it was directed particularly at child workers. The POA (1986) was explicit on this point when it stated:

> It has been assumed in the Policy that a large number of out-of-school children
> are unable to avail themselves of the benefit of schooling because they have
> to work to supplement family income or otherwise assist the family. NPE
> proposes taking up of a large and systematic programme of non-formal edu-
> cation for these children and children of habitations without school. (POA
> [1986], II.4)

The policy also had a special provision for afternoon centres for
girls. This implied the willingness of policy makers to adjust with,
rather than challenge, the gender stereotype of the role of girls in
domestic chores and sibling care. In this sense, the NPE [1986]
legitimised both child labour and patriarchy. We shall soon return
to this theme.

UNMASKING THE RATIONALISATION

The rationalisation for setting up alternative and parallel streams
was offered by the POA (1986) as follows: 'The essential characteristics of NFE are organisational flexibility, relevance of curriculum,
diversity in learning activities to relate them to learners' needs,
and decentralisation of management' (POA [1986], II.25).

In the following paragraph (No. II.26) on NFE, the POA (1986)
listed a spectrum of features that were presumed to help in 'maintenance of quality'. These included a learner-centred approach,
instructor as facilitator, emphasis on learning rather than teaching,
enabling learners to progress at their own pace, use of techniques
to ensure fast pace of learning, stress on continuous learner evaluation, participatory learning environment and enjoyable extra-
curricular activities. The next paragraph listed the criteria for
selection of NFE instructors (taking care not to call them teachers).[8]

The criteria for selection of the instructor would include:

- being local,
- being already motivated,
- acceptable to the community,
- preferably from the weaker sections of society, should have given some evidence of work in the community. (POA [1986], II.27)

The POA (1986) went on to add:

Keeping in view the importance of enrolment of girls, and also the fact that NFE has the potentiality of developing into a major programme of women's development, wherever possible women will be appointed as instructors. (POA [1986], II.28)

The notion of NFE was further elaborated in the Government of India's report presented at the Jomtien Conference in March 1990 which stressed the characteristics of NFE in the following words:

In terms of cognitive learning NFE is comparable with the corresponding stage in formal education. Attention is to be paid in NFE to non-cognitive aspects of learning, just as much as we propose in the school system.

It has flexibility to adjust curriculum and textual materials to the needs and interests of the learners.

Its total duration is generally shorter than in formal education.

The programme can be organised at the time convenient for the learners, generally in the afternoon for girls and in the evenings for working children.

It is not dependent on highly paid professional teachers but is organised by local persons who are specially trained for it.

There is the possibility of migration between the formal and non-formal systems. (NIEPA 1990: 53–54)

Let us examine the bizarre logic behind the conception of NFE. Policy makers seem to be essentially telling us that the formal school system *should continue* to be characterised by:

- organisational inflexibility;
- centralised bureaucratic management;

- irrelevant curriculum;
- lack of diversity and flexibility in relating curriculum, textual materials and learning activities to the needs and interests of the learners; and
- school timings that would be inconvenient to almost half of the children, particularly to girls and working children.

Policy makers are further clear that formal schools *will continue* to practice a pedagogy that:

- negates a learner-centred approach;
- refuses to view the 'instructor' as a facilitator for enabling children to learn;
- de-emphasises learning while emphasising *only* teaching;
- rejects the objective of enabling the learners to progress at their own pace;
- ignores techniques for ensuring fast pace of learning;
- disallows continuous learner evaluation (that is, allows only summative evaluation at the end of the year, or worse, at the end of the primary stage);
- opposes participatory learning environment; and
- provides no space for enjoyable extra-curricular activities.

The policy further implies that the formal school system *should* appoint teachers who:

- belong to villages or urban localities far removed from the schools where they are expected to teach;
- are basically unmotivated;
- are unacceptable to the community;
- come from dominant sections of society (that is, who are generally unsympathetic to the weaker sections);
- do not have any record of work in the community; and
- are generally not women, even when it is possible to appoint them.

This is not all. According to policy makers, the formal school system needs neither be concerned with the enrolment of girls nor attempt to evolve into a major programme of women's development, as this gender-sensitive attribute should be the sole preserve of NFE! The formal school system, as policy makers seem to be declaring, is destined (or rather *should be destined*) to be gender-insensitive and anti-women!

Preferring Contradictions (Rather than Resolving them!)

The policy makers had clearly decided that all the desirable features of education must belong to NFE, whereas the formal school system should continue to be afflicted with all the undesirable features! If this was not the case, why would the policy not propose ways and means for incorporating these features into the formal school system itself and, thereby, begin the process of educational reforms for all children? Indeed, this flawed logic is contradicted in the policy itself by the following two perceptions underlying the formulation of the NFE programme:

1. In spite of these superior attributes designed in the policy, NFE shall aspire to be merely *comparable* with the corresponding stage in formal education in terms of both cognitive and non-cognitive development (NPE [1986], Section 5.9; NIEPA 1990: 53–54). This comparability is what will make 'migration between the formal and non-formal systems' possible. One wonders why the superior attributes of NFE would only ensure 'lateral entry' into the formal school, and not entry at a higher stage! The policy is silent on this obvious contradiction.

2. All the desirable features of education—organisational, curricular and pedagogic—as listed in the policy and POA in

relation to NFE, will be introduced by an 'instructor' whose levels of qualifications, teacher training, salary and other service conditions would be of much lower order than those of the regular teacher of the formal school system. Yet, these under-qualified, essentially untrained and underpaid 'instructors' (without any stability in service) will for some magical reason turn out to be, as per NPE [1986] (Section 5.9), 'talented and dedicated young men and women', which, obviously the policy implies, their counterparts in the formal school system cannot be or rather should not be expected to be. Not just this, the NFE instructor, despite these handicaps, is expected by policy makers to have much greater initiative and skills in attracting the presumably 'unwilling' and hitherto out-of-school children, particularly girls and working children, to NFE centres and then ensuring their effective, enjoyable and, more importantly, relevant learning—something the formal school teacher is not expected to do! All this will be achieved by the 'miraculous' instructor by holding NFE classes for merely two to three hours per day (in contrast to the formal school held for four to five hours per day) since the policy states that NFE's 'total duration is generally shorter than in formal education' (NIEPA 1990: 53). The expectations of policy makers from NFE instructors do not end here. Since no provision for even thatched huts (let alone buildings) or teaching aids available under the Operation Blackboard Scheme (meant only for formal schools) is made for NFE, the instructor is expected to use her/his 'genius' to arrange for all these from the community, failing which what she/he is supposed to do the policy prefers not to specify.

This entirely flawed logic and internal contradictions in the policy and POA relating to NFE were noticed and debated by the NPE Review Committee (1990) (Government of India 1990)[9] which observed:

The above listed highly desirable features of NFE are indeed relevant to formal schools as well and they are also the essence of the child-centred approach mentioned by NPE. The criteria mentioned by POA for selection of NFE instructors—being local, being already motivated, acceptable to the community, being preferably from the weaker sections in society, having given some evidence of work in the community—are the criteria relevant to the selection of formal school teachers also. Therefore, it is unclear why the policy has advocated NFE, in effect, as a parallel system. (Government of India 1990, Section 6.4.6)

Based upon this logic, the NPERC recommended that the formal school system be itself 'non-formalised' to include all the desirable features of NFE instead of setting up two parallel systems, one for the children from relatively better-off sections of society and the other for poor girls and working children (ibid.: 169–72).[10] The NPERC proposed specific policy changes and a detailed programme design for building up a responsive and relevant formal school system that can not only reach out to the children from marginalised social segments and remote habitations, but also be much more socially and pedagogically meaningful to the children from the middle class and even the elite sections than the prevailing formal school. In effect, the NPERC seemed to be raising an uncomfortable question for the ruling Indian elite: whom is the formal school system designed for if it is both inaccessible and unsuitable for almost half of India's children? The NPERC, therefore, advocated the necessity of transforming the formal school system itself in such manner that all children, irrespective of their socio-economic status, can socialise and learn together in consonance with the vision of the common school system (ibid.: 92–93, 169–72, 182–84).

THE POLICY'S VISION OF SOCIAL ENGINEERING

Both the NPE (1986) (Section 5.9) and POA (1986) (Chapter II, Section 25) insisted that NFE was designed in order to fulfil the policy's overriding assumption that 'NFE can result in provision of education comparable in quality with formal schooling'. It is indeed ironical that the policy first creates a layer of lower quality below the formal school, mainly for poor girls and child labour, and then claims to design features in it to make it 'comparable with formal schooling'. It prefers not to take any radical measures to transform the social and pedagogic character of the mainstream formal school system such that it will be able to attract child labour as well as children from remote habitations, particularly girls, while ensuring that they enjoy learning and receive education that is relevant to their lives along with the rest of the children in their neighbourhood. Policy makers offer the following lame excuse for not taking radical measures for transforming the formal school system:

> Given the present condition of the schools in general, the challenges before the school system are many, e.g., enrolling and retaining children who cannot afford to attend school regularly; a harmonious interaction with the community around; improving the infrastructure, quality and learning environment; and ensuring that every student acquires minimum levels of learning. *These challenges are daunting enough* and it *does not seem desirable to overload the school system* with yet another formidable challenge of meeting the educational needs of children with severe para educational constraints. (Government of India 1992a: Section 9.13; emphasis added)

Three contradictions need to be noted in the statement. One, policy makers do not regard the 'daunting challenges' to be the central task of the formal school system, if not the very *raison d'être* for its existence. Two, these 'daunting challenges' do not seem to constitute 'the educational needs of children with severe para educational constraints'. One wonders what will. Also, the policy erroneously assumes that it is the child, rather than the school system, that is handicapped by 'severe para educational constraints'. Is this excuse offered because of the lack of policy makers' interest in either abolishing child labour or changing the role of girls from poor families in domestic chores and sibling care? This is obvious since the timings of NFE centres were adjusted to evenings for child labour and afternoons for girls, instead of ensuring that they come to a regular *daytime* formal school, thereby challenging the socio-cultural constraints operating on their lives, as has been successfully demonstrated by MV Foundation in Andhra Pradesh and advocated by Sinha (2000). The fact is that the policy conceived of a parallel stream like NFE, which, instead of helping eliminate the practice of child labour and resist patriarchy, ended up adjusting with and legitimising it.

The policy makers were determined to institutionalise the newly emerging principle of social engineering through parallel layers of so-called educational facilities (not schools). The National Policy on Education Review Committee's (NPERC) recommendation, therefore, to transform the infrastructural, social and pedagogic character of the formal school system did not find favour with the CABE Committee on Policy (Government of India 1992a: Sections 9.7–9.13), which reiterated the same flawed logic critiqued earlier.[11] The NPE (1986) (as modified in 1992) accordingly retained the parallel NFE stream for millions of working children (two-thirds of them being girls), without providing a feasible design in the modified POA (1992) for radically transforming or improving the formal school system. Extending this spurious logic, it was only natural for the CABE Committee on Policy to also reject the NPERC's recommendation for building a common school system (Government of India 1992a, Sections 6.1–6.6). This retrogressive stand of the CABE Committee on Policy with regard to NFE and the common school system at least followed an internally consistent logic and thus enabled the state to clear the path, as we shall see later, for the structural adjustment programme being then imposed on the Indian economy by the IMF and World Bank.

CAMOUFLAGE

We may recall the laborious rationalisation that policy makers preferred to indulge in, which amounted to somehow deluding oneself to trust the rhetoric about the superior attributes of NFE (in comparison to formal schools) designed in the policy. However, there is substantial evidence that none of this indulgence had its genesis in genuine concern for deprived girls engaged in domestic chores and sibling care, working children or children living in remote habitations, but in the perception of policy makers about the lack of financial resources available for elementary education. An insight into the mindset of the state is provided by the perspective document entitled, *Challenge of Education: A Policy Perspective* released as a prelude to the NPE (1986), in the following words:

> Now, *faced with other constraints*, Non-Formal Education is being assigned a very large responsibility in relation to the achievement of Universalisation of Elementary Education by 1990. It is expected that of the additional 64 million children coming up for elementary education, nearly 39 million will be educated entirely through this system. (Government of India 1985: Section 3.13; emphasis added)

This brings out three undeniable facts.

1. Policy makers had made up their mind about institutionalising non-formal education for the marginalised sections of society as a parallel layer to the formal school system *well before* the draft NPE (1986) was circulated all over the country for the much-hyped debate amongst the people of India. Does it not imply that the so-called public debate on the draft was a mere eyewash, if not a complete farce? Or maybe it was a means of necessary legitimisation in a democracy!

2. The non-formal stream was not designed as a minor stream. It was expected to be bigger than even the formal stream— for almost 60.9 per cent of the additional children 'coming up for elementary education' (that is, 39 million out of 64 million children).

3. The government was 'faced with other constraints' that persuaded it to substitute the vision of the Common School System with the policy of 'parallel layers'. Having done this, policy makers indulged in the rhetoric of NFE having organisational, curricular and pedagogic attributes that were supposedly superior to the formal school system.

It is almost scary to realise how policies are formulated. Contrary to public perception, policies are made without any objective basis or scientific evaluation. Let us see what does the *Challenge of Education* document has to say on this issue:

> To-date, no systematic study of the effectiveness of Non-Formal Education is available. It is being argued by some educational planners that this may not be a viable alternative to school education. There are difficulties in the effective monitoring and evaluation of its implementation. These arguments have to be balanced against the necessity of using some mechanism to reach children outside the formal education system. (Government of India 1985: Section 3.14)

What were these constraints faced by the government in 1985 that persuaded it to violate the common school vision of the NPE (1968) (and later also of NPE [1986])? What were those compulsions against which the sound logic of the educational planners had to be balanced against? Answers to such questions is provided by the same *Challenge of Education* document:

> Any substantial improvement in educational coverage as well as retention, which constitutes the core of universalisation of elementary education efforts, will not only require significant increase in educational expenditure on elementary education *but will also have a multiplier effect on the total education budget through increased enrolments in the secondary and higher education.* Hence, policy deliberations vis-a-vis universalisation of elementary education need to be matched with hard financial decisions. . . .
>   Alternatively, other educational approaches, such as non-formal/distance education, and vocationalisation have to be worked out in detail for a large scale implementation and replication. (ibid.: Sections 4.64 and 4.65; emphasis added)

It is then clear that policy makers were not persuaded by the superior attributes conceived by them for NFE, but by perceived financial constraints. Since 'policy deliberations vis-a-vis universalisation of elementary education need[ed] to be matched with hard financial decisions', the NPE (1986) saw in NFE a way out of the dilemma of providing education to 60.9 per cent of children in the relevant age group. It did not matter much even if 'no systematic study of the effectiveness of Non-Formal Education [was] available' or if some educational planners did not see in this 'a viable alternative to school education'. After all, NFE was meant only for marginalised children, not for the children of middle-class families or those of the ruling elite! However, in a democracy like India, one needed to exercise abundant caution. The camouflage of attaching the rhetoric of superior attributes to NFE was, therefore, cleverly designed and incorporated in the policy statement as well as the POA (1986). The Government of India had no hesitation in presenting even the Jomtien Conference held in March 1990 with the same camouflage. International funding agencies might have even welcomed this camouflage since, as we shall see in the next section, the Jomtien Conference was organised precisely for preparing the groundwork for imposing the structural adjustment programme of the IMF and World Bank requiring developing countries like India to minimise their expenditure on the social sector. One of the most significant victims of this requirement in the next few years was going to be elementary education. It is a moot point whether NFE was an outcome of the financial constraints as perceived by the Indian policy makers or of a lack of commitment on their part to push forward the vision of egalitarian education inherent in the common school system. Or maybe it was designed to fit in the framework of the structural adjustment programme that might have been quietly operational in India well before it was publicly declared as an inevitable part of the New Economic Policy from July 1991 onwards. Whatever may be the compulsions, it is now understood retrospectively that NFE provided the foundation for institutionalising a range of parallel layers of low-quality streams of educational facilities for different social segments in the wake of the neo-liberal agenda.

Post-Jomtien Phase of Indian Education

The Jomtien Conference was jointly convened by the UNDP, UNESCO, UNICEF and the World Bank.[12] These international agencies continued to hold follow-up conferences at both regional and global levels during the 1990s.[13] The decadal follow-up of the Jomtien Conference was held at Dakar, Senegal, in April 2000, wherein the progress made by the various nations to achieve EFA goals as set out by the Jomtien Declaration was reviewed. Just as the Jomtien Declaration guided educational planning throughout the 1990s, the Dakar Framework of Action (World Education Forum 2000) has now become the new policy-level international guide post for the first 15 years of the 21st century.[14]

The Jomtien Conference proved to be a turning point in the history of education in India. The Government of India gave a hasty concurrence to the Jomtien Declaration (UNDP et al. 1990), without even consulting Parliament on its major constitutional and policy implications. This marked the beginning of a phase of steady erosion of Parliament's role in policy formulation in education as well as of the Planning Commission and the Ministry of Human Resource Development in formulating the agenda of Indian education and setting its priorities. As provided for in the Jomtien Declaration (Article 10) and Jomtien Framework (Section 3.3), external aid from a host of international funding agencies, operating under the World Bank umbrella, was systematically allowed in the primary education sector *as a matter of policy* for the first time in post-independence India.[15] This policy departure coincided with the beginning of the New Economic Policy in July 1991 in India. With this, it became necessary for the government to accept the IMF–World Bank's structural adjustment programme. The launching of the first World Bank-sponsored comprehensive District Primary Education Programme (DPEP) in 1993–94 was part of this requirement and its attendant Social Safety Net provided under the IMF–World Bank design (Government of India 1993: 88). The serious implication of this new situation was recognised by the government. The Central Advisory Board of Education (CABE) at its 46th meeting in March 1991 formulated a set of guidelines for externally aided projects, which were reiterated at the 47th meeting in May 1992. These guidelines sought to ensure that 'external assistance does not lead to a dependency syndrome' and remains 'an additionality to the [national] resources for education' while being in 'total conformity with the national policies, strategies and programmes' (ibid.: 89).

Yet a series of policy-related documents were issued during the following years, each having impacts upon the policy in a significant manner. This includes Education For All (Government of India 1993), DPEP (ibid.: 1995, 1998), Education Guarantee Scheme (Government of Madhya Pradesh 1998: 9–12), Para Teachers Scheme (Ed. CIL 2000; Government of India 2001a), Ambani–Birla Report (Government of India 2000), National Curriculum Framework for School Education (NCERT 2000), and Education Guarantee Scheme, and Alternative and Innovative Education (Government of India 2001a). The minimum norms for school infrastructure and strength of teachers in a primary school, as specified in Operation Blockboard of NPE (1986) (as modified in 1992), were diluted for the Sarva Shiksha Abhiyan and EFA—National Plan of Action (Government of India 2002, 2003a; Sadgopal 2003c; Tilak 2003). Similarly, the policy relating to women's education stands diluted—from empowering women to merely enrolling girls in school registers—in line with the Jomtien and Dakar Frameworks, as also reinforced by the monitoring parameters (for example, the gender parity index, an index based on enrolment ratios) formulated by UNESCO (Sadgopal 2003c). For none of these was it considered necessary to take the approval of Parliament, even when they contradicted elements of the education policy approved by Parliament.

During the post-Jomtien phase, the Indian education policy was diluted in the following significant ways, whether directly as part of the externally aided projects (for example, the DPEP) or otherwise (for example, the Sarva Shiksha Abhiyan):

1. **Trivialisation of educational aims:** Education being made synonymous with literacy (Sadgopal 1994); competency-based market-oriented narrow framework of minimum levels of learning (MLL) imposed on curricular planning and assessment (Dhankar 2002; Sadgopal 2002b: 118–20); education of girls viewed in terms of only reducing their fertility rates, slowing population growth or increasing their productivity (World Bank 1997: 1, 39, 53); and basically education being viewed in a behavioural paradigm.

2. **Fragmentation of knowledge:** The 'world of work' separated from the 'world of knowledge', thereby reinforcing

the brahminical-cum-colonial character of Indian education;[16] cognitive domain viewed in isolation of the affective domain and psychomotor skills (for example, in MLL); primary education delinked from upper primary stage, ignoring the concept of integrated elementary education of eight years.[17]

3. **Withdrawal from policy commitment to build a common school system:** As discussed earlier in this paper, the issue of improvement (or transformation, if necessary) of quality and relevance of the formal school system in order to build a common school system for all children was gradually defocused after NPE (1986), particularly during the post-Jomtien phase. Instead, institutionalisation of multiple or parallel tracks of low-quality 'educational' facilities replaced the common school policy as the key strategy for providing so-called education to millions of out-of-school children belonging to Dalit and tribal sections of society, several segments of other backward classes, cultural and linguistic minorities, and physically and mentally disabled. Two-thirds of each of these sections, facing educational discrimination, comprised girl children. Apart from continuing with NFE during the post-Jomtien phase, the following multiple tracks or parallel streams were introduced: accommodating the 9 to 14 age group in adult literacy classes (Government of India 1993: 51),[18] alternative schools (ibid.: 1998: 18), Education Guarantee Scheme (EGS) centres (Government of Madhya Pradesh 1998: 9–12; Government of India 2001a, 2001b; Section 3.2.2.2), multi-grade/multi-level teaching (Government of India 1995: 10, 16; ibid.: 1998: 18), bridge courses and back-to-school camps (ibid.: 2001b: Section 3.2.2.2, 2002: 11), and correspondence courses for the 6 to 14 age group (ibid.: 2001b: Section 3.4.18; ibid.: 2003a: 44; ibid.: 2003b, 2003c: Schedule A; NCERT 2000: 22–23).

Four sets of observations will be made here to reveal the ruthlessness with which the State has pursued its agenda of promoting and institutionalising inequality in education:

i. The EGS has no provision whatsoever for any infrastructure (not even for a tent or thatched roof); its supposedly chief beneficiaries, namely, Dalit or tribal communities are expected, as per the EGS design, to arrange for some space for the centre (Government of India 2001a)!

ii. In externally aided DPEP, multi-grade/multi-level teaching has meant nothing other than one/two teacher(s) being trained to teach five classes simultaneously out of sheer necessity. In spite of the confused rhetoric by DPEP authorities, it is not designed to be the progressive pedagogy of 'grade-less teaching', as is the case at Digantar (experimental schools practising grade-less teaching) near Jaipur, Rajasthan. The DPEP has thus violated the Operation Blackboard norms of NPE (1986) (as modified in 1992) for providing at least three teachers and three classrooms to every primary school. Dhankar (2002: 8–9) analyses this DPEP policy aptly:

> The need and rationale for multi-grade teaching is either socio-political or managerial; and *pedagogical considerations are only grafted on to it.* . . . The real solution to the problem is to appoint more teachers. . . . But appointing more teachers costs money. Since most children in these schools belong to the weaker sections of society, easier and less expensive solutions are sought. Therefore, a pedagogical solution for this socio-economic problem is devised in the name of multi-grade teaching strategies. . . . As the [conventional] grade was used to manage children, now in a changed situation the idea of multi-grade is used for the same purpose . . . claiming that [it] is an effort for quality improvement, is *nothing more than making a virtue out of an ugly necessity*—ugly because the children who bear the brunt belong to the weaker sections of the society. (Emphasis mine)

The policy (Section 5.7) had stated that 'Operation Blackboard will be enlarged to provide *three reasonably large rooms* that are usable in all weather and .... [a range of teaching aids]' and 'at least *three teachers* should work in every school, the *number increasing, as early as possible, to one teacher per class* ... at least 50 per cent of teachers recruited in future should be women' (emphasis added). To be sure, these norms were approved by Parliament in May 1992. Through multi-grade/multi-level teaching, the DPEP has cynically attempted to justify the single-teacher and two-teacher schools (almost two-thirds of all primary schools), instead of building up political pressure or legislative action, or catalysing community demand for the fulfilment of Operation Blackboard commitments. This violation during the late 1990s, touted as an interim strategy, apparently opened the doors at the beginning of this century for institutionalising the dilution of Operation Blackboard norms from three teachers/three classrooms per primary school to two teachers/two classrooms per primary school in the Sarva Shiksha Abhiyan, Tenth Five-Year Plan (2002–07) and EFA—National Plan of Action (2003). This dilution is now the basis of financial allocations (Government of India 2003a, Table 9.3, p. 92). It also explains, at least partly, how the government managed to reduce the Tapas Majumdar Committee's estimates by 30 per cent for the Financial Memorandum attached to the 86th Amendment Bill.

iii. The NCERT (2000: 22–23) recommended correspondence courses (euphemised as open schooling or open learning system) for the 6 to 14 age group without any basis in educational research or experience whatsoever. Again, this proposal is in violation of NPE (1986) (as modified in 1992), which had restricted the role of the so-called 'open learning system' to secondary and higher education (Section 5.37). Yet, such a farcical pedagogic notion is already a part of the 10th Five-Year Plan (Government of India 2001b: Section 3.4.18) and EFA—National Plan of Action (Government of India 2003a: 44), and will be shortly presented to Parliament for legitimisation (Government of India 2003b, 2003c: Schedule A). Apart from legitimising child labour, the introduction of correspondence courses for the 6 to 14 age group, most of them being first-generation learners, implies that the girl child will be *officially* denied the *relatively* more liberating atmosphere offered by school than what she is likely to get at home, bound by patriarchal traditions (Sadgopal 2003c).

iv. Whenever faced with criticism throughout the 1990s, policy makers claimed that these multiple tracks or parallel streams are merely *interim* or *transitional* arrangements in order to *eventually* mainstream all children to reach regular formal schools. This is precisely what the nation was told about non-formal education in the wake of NPE (1986) and in the years following NPE (1986) (as modified in 1992), which promised that the NFE scheme 'will be strengthened and enlarged' (Section 5.8). The EFA again assured that 'many measures are being adopted to further strengthen this scheme' (Government of India 1993: 51). In 1995, the externally aided DPEP asserted that it would 'strive for the development of an effective NFE system which can meet the diverse educational needs of children' (ibid.: 1995: Chapter II, Section 17). In 1998, the DPEP declared that 'every state is deciding to set up different forms of alternative schools to ensure participation of working children, street children, children of migrating communities, drop-outs etc.' (ibid.: 1998: 18). To be sure, all the categories of out-of-school children mentioned in the DPEP of 1998 are same as those mentioned in NFE scheme of the 1986 policy. Sarva Shiksha Abhiyan informs that:

> Studies on the Non-Formal Education scheme have pointed out the lack of flexibility which impedes effective implementation across different States. Efforts to provide for a diversity of interventions have been made in the revised scheme that has been approved recently such as setting up of Education Guarantee Schools, Alternative Schooling facilities, Balika Shikshan Shivirs, 'Back-to-School' camps etc. (ibid.: 2002: Chapter III, Section 3.5, p. 35)

We should be prepared for yet another revision of the scheme in the near future since the target of Sarva Shiksha Abhiyan of 'providing universal enrolment by the year 2003' is far from being met. This policy analysis shows that these multiple tracks or parallel streams are there to stay with us for as long as the policy makers refuse to: (*a*) focus on transforming the mainstream formal school system; (*b*) build a common school system; and (*c*) reprioritise the national economy to ensure adequate resources for this central nation-building task. Otherwise, the promise of making these multiple tracks into 'transitional schools'—the latest name for the range of NFE schemes—will remain an elusive dream.

4. **Lowering the status of the school teacher:** In unabashed violation of Sections 9.1 to 9.3 of NPE (1986) (as modified in 1992), which call for raising the status of teachers, the post-Jomtien *operating* policy has been to replace the teacher with under-qualified, untrained (or under-trained) and underpaid persons appointed on short-term contracts, to be called para-teachers (Ed. CIL 2000; Government of India 2001a; Kumar et al. 2001; Sadgopal 2002b: 118, 2003a: 15). The para-teacher is known by a variety of euphemisms in different states—*guruji, lok shikshak, shiksha karmi, lok mitra, vidya upasak, vidya volunteer*, etc.—but care is taken not to call her/him a teacher. This policy of para-teacher is now being rapidly extended to secondary and higher education as well, clearly to facilitate privatisation and commercialisation of education.

5. **Erosion of women's education policy:** The NPE (1986) (as modified in 1992) provided for a sharp perspective on 'Education for Women's Equality' (Sections 4.2 and 4.3) as follows:

> Education will be used as an agent of basic change in the status of women. In order to neutralise the accumulated distortions of the past, there will be a well-conceived edge in favour of women. The National Education System will play a positive, interventionist role in the empowerment of women. It will foster the development of new values. . . . This will be an act of faith. . . .'

The entire credit for this progressive stance must go to India's own women's movement, which persuaded even the policy makers to move away from conventional notions. The only programme that was designed to reflect this policy insight was the Mahila Samakhya. Its objective was to enhance the self-esteem and self-confidence of women; build their positive image by recognising their contribution to society, polity and the economy; develop their ability to think critically; enable them to make informed choices in areas like education, employment and health, especially reproductive health; and ensure equal participation in developmental processes (POA [1992], Chapter 1, Section 1.5.1). However, the Mahila Samakhya remained marginal throughout the 1990s. For every Rs. 100 allocated for elementary education in the Union Budget, hardly 25 paise were given to it. In due course of time, even this miniscule programme lost its basic direction.

The Jomtien–Dakar Framework does not even refer to patriarchy as an issue and essentially reduces girls' education to merely enrolling them in school registers and giving them literacy skills. This is exactly what happened when the World Bank-sponsored DPEP adopted Mahila Samakhya. The focus on collective reflection and socio-cultural action by organised women's groups, as advocated by the policy, was abandoned. It became a *mere girl child enrolment* programme. Critical issues such as girls' participation in schools, gender sensitisation of learning material, and teacher education and holistic educational aims were ignored. Unfortunately, the notion of gender parity (ratio of enrolment of girls and boys) in the *EFA Global Monitoring Report 2003–4* (UNESCO 2003) also reinforces this confusion. Further, the World Bank diluted the goal of women's education to just raising their literacy levels and productivity (rather than educating or empowering them), and turning them into mere transmitters of fertility control, health or nutritional messages (World Bank 1997). The Dakar Framework has now added the ambiguous notion of life skills that seems to be yet another mechanism for social manipulation and market control of the adolescent mindset, particularly girls. India unfortunately gave up its progressive policy on women's education in favour of the international framework that was guided more by considerations of the market than by women's socio-cultural and political rights.

6. **Increasing abdication by the state:** We will only briefly touch upon this alarming post-Jomtien trend here since it has been referred to elsewhere as well as reflected in the various aspects of policy dilution listed earlier. What is needed is recognition of the relationship between these trends and the IMF–World Bank's structural adjustment programme that is accelerating Indian education towards privatisation and commercialisation, as proposed by the Ambani–Birla report (Government of India 2000). However, we need to advance our understanding beyond the Ambani–Birla formulations, which gave the false impression that it called for privatisation only in higher education and partly in secondary education—the report seemed to be saying that elementary education must be entirely a state responsibility. The post-Jomtien policy measures adopted by Indian policy makers have evidently enabled the state to rapidly withdraw even from the elementary education sector. This is reflected in the ever-reducing financial commitment for this sector, as discussed in detail later in the context of the 93rd (now called 86th) Amendment. There is mounting evidence that the state is not ready to re-prioritise the national economy in favour of education of the deprived sections of society, and has become dependent on external aid as it seems to be refusing to provide for even the diluted policy measures and for the much reduced financial requirement.[19] This official stance is in clear violation of the CABE guidelines against 'dependency syndrome' and policy dilutions in relation to external aid (Government of India 1993: 89).

The following observation by Tomasevski (2001), the Special Rapporteur on the right to education to United Nations Commission on Human Rights, on the Jomtien Declaration and Framework will provide the necessary perspective for comprehending the adverse changes in Indian education during the post-Jomtien phase:

> The language of the final document adopted by the Jomtien Conference merged human needs and market forces, moved education from governmental to social responsibility, made no reference to the international legal requirement that primary education be free-of-charge, introduced the term 'basic education' which confused conceptual and statistical categories. The language elaborated at Jomtien was different from the language of international human rights law.

Taking an early cue from the Jomtien Declaration and foreseeing the political, historical and educational significance of this turning point, this author proposed to view the post-Independence history of education in India in two separate phases for the purpose of policy analysis, namely, pre-Jomtien and post-Jomtien phases (Sadgopal 1994).

TAMPERING WITH THE CONSTITUTION

Back to the 93rd (now called 86th) Amendment debate in Lok Sabha, the Bill suffered from the following four major lacunae:

1. The Bill sought to exclude almost 170 million children up to 6 years of age, from the provision of the fundamental right to *free* early childhood care and pre-school education. This was in contravention of NPE (1986) (as modified in 1992), which considered this support during childhood as being crucial for child development and preparation for elementary education (Sections 5.1 to 5.4). The implication was clear: early childhood care and pre-school education will

be denied to not less than 40 per cent of the children in this age group, two-thirds of them being girls, whose parents barely manage to earn minimum wages. This will also prevent girls in the 6 to 14 age group belonging to the same sections of society from receiving elementary education as they will be engaged in sibling care.

2. The Bill made the provision of fundamental right to education even for the 6 to 14 age group children conditional by introducing the phrase '*as the State may, by law, determine*' in the new Article 21A. The implications of this phrase will be discussed below.

3. The Bill shifted the constitutional obligation towards 'free and compulsory education' from the state to the parents or guardians by making it a fundamental duty of the latter under Article 51A (k) to '*provide opportunities for education*' to their children in the 6 to 14 age group. This purpose is now sought to be achieved by promoting and legitimising 'community participation' in raising resources for elementary education (Government of India 2003b, 2003c), yet another measure of abdication by the state.

4. The Financial Memorandum attached to the Bill provided for only Rs. 98 billion per annum (that is, 0.44 per cent of the GDP in 2002–3) over a 10-year period for implementing the provisions under the Bill. This commitment was far from being adequate, as it was 30 per cent less than what was estimated by the Tapas Majumdar Committee in 1999 to provide elementary education to all out-of-school children through *regular formal schools*. This lower estimate was made possible by depending on low-quality parallel tracks of education and lowering several other critically important infrastructural and pedagogic norms for deprived sections of society (Sadgopal 2003c; Tilak 2003).

Detailed critiques of the 93rd Amendment Bill contended that the lacunae were deliberate rather than being a result of an oversight (see Sadgopal 2001a, 2001b, 2001c, 2001d and 2002a; Swaminathan 2001). The amendment was being made, these writings sought to establish, not to make elementary education a fundamental right, but to fulfil the dictates of the IMF–World Bank's structural adjustment programme that demanded reduction in public expenditure on the social sector. The lack of guarantee of free early childhood care and pre-school education will not only result in underdevelopment of deprived children during childhood, but will also adversely affect their learning capacity during school education.

In particular, the critiques focused upon the implications of the phrase '*as the State may, by law, determine*'. No such conditionality existed in the original Article 45. It is contended that the phrase was introduced in order to legitimise the low-budget low-quality multiple and parallel tracks of so-called educational facilities for poor children as well as other forms of policy dilutions discussed. This phrase also legitimises the increasing abdication by the state of its constitutional obligation towards ensuring elementary education of *equitable* quality for all children.

To the agitated MPs from various political parties who criticised the Bill in both Houses of Parliament, an assurance was repeatedly given by the minister that the lacunae in the Bill will be taken care of by enacting a new law. How would a law take care of the lacunae introduced in the Constitution through an amendment? If the government intended to rectify the lacunae later through a law, why was it bent upon introducing these in the Constitution in the first place? The leadership of various political parties neither raised nor pursued such uncomfortable questions in Parliament. The assurance of a law to be enacted later seemed to have led to a curious consensus on what is now termed the 86th Amendment, in spite of its unambiguous bias against millions of children (girl children in particular) belonging to various deprived sections of society (Sadgopal 2001d, 2002a) and violations of several provisions in the Constitution relating to Parts III and IV.

The Free and Compulsory Education Bill, 2004

Let me also briefly examine the draft Free and Compulsory Education Bill, 2004 (Government of India 2004). This is the law that was promised by the previous NDA government in Parliament, presumably to take care of the lacunae in the 86th Amendment Bill. Ironically, a careful scrutiny reveals that, instead of 'taking care of the lacunae', the draft Bill increases them in several ways. It would suffice to refer to Schedules I and II of the Bill, which together provide for *three types* of centres for 'imparting education', specifying their respective minimum norms. The draft Bill thus is an unabashed attempt to legitimise parallel streams of education of differential quality, namely, regular schools, EGS centres and alternative schools, already institutionalised in *operating* policy and programmes (for example, Sarva Shiksha Abhiyan) for the deprived sections of society. This will also legitimise the undesirable sociological principle of 'a separate educational stream for each social strata.'

The draft Bill is both ambiguous and weak on the inclusion of physically and mentally disabled children in regular approved schools. Its provisions will encourage as well as facilitate violation of the policy commitment for inclusive education, which is integral to the fulfilment of constitutional obligation for equality in education and for building up the common school system (Jha 2003). As noted by Jha (ibid.), the Bill might even promote privatisation and commercialisation of education of the disabled.

A detailed and holistic analysis was presented by me at two consultations organised by the MV Foundation and CACL in Hyderabad and Bhubaneswar respectively (Sadgopal 2004a), and some other aspects documented elsewhere (Sadgopal 2004b). This established that the draft Bill attempted to: (*a*) legitimise low-quality educational streams for underprivileged sections of society; (*b*) provide legitimate

space for extra-constitutional authorities to introduce their ideological agenda in school education while keeping them outside the
purview of the constitutional framework; (c) negate the role of *panchayati raj* institutions; (d) promote privatisation and 'corpor-
atisation' of school education; (e) franchise parts or whole districts
to NGOs, corporate or religious bodies for running elementary
schools; (f) shift the state's constitutional obligation towards elementary education to the parents and local communities; (g) promote
'special schools' for disabled children at the cost of inclusive education; and (h) introduce a range of other distortions.

In a sense, the draft Bill carries forward the process of abdication
by the state of its constitutional obligation for which a legitimised
space was created by the 86th Constitutional Amendment by attaching the conditionality, '*as the State may, by law, determine*', to the guarantee of right to free and compulsory education for children in the
6 to 14 age group. The draft Bill is designed to fully protect and
also 'guarantee' the exclusion and discrimination institutionalised
by the Sarva Shiksha Abhiyan in its following statement: 'All children in school, Education Guarantee Scheme (EGS) centre, alternate school, "back-to-school camp" by 2003' (Government of India
2003a: 27).

With this guarantee for protection, the state is continuing to persist in its refusal to reprioritise the national economy and pursue its
campaign for seeking increased external aid, thereby further sub-
jugating the nation's education system and policies to the control
of the global market.

RESOURCES, NATIONAL ECONOMY
AND EXTERNAL AID

The externally assisted DPEP started in 1993–94, and by the year
2000 it had spread to 275 odd districts in 18 states—almost half
the country. The Government of India's *Education For All* document

(1993), while reproducing the CABE guidelines for externally aided projects, partly also cited earlier, stated:

> It would be fair to say that while external funding would be an interim contribution to meet the resource gap, there is *no alternative other than augmenting domestic resources* to achieve the objective of EFA. Economic liberalisation and the consequent financial restructuring can be *expected to facilitate greater resource flow* to elementary education. (p. 90; emphasis added)

External aid has had an adverse impact on the political will to re-prioritise the national economy for mobilising public resources for the universalisation of elementary education. Soon after the 1986 policy, we saw an upswing in national effort to mobilise public resources for education. By 1989–90, almost 4 per cent of the GDP was being spent on education, with little less than half on elementary education. Ironically, with the onset of external aid in primary education in the 1990s, the investment in education (including in elementary education) started declining steadily and was as low as 3.49 per cent of the GDP in 1997–98, the same level as in 1985–86, just before the 1986 policy. Clearly, the political will to mobilise resources for elementary education weakened following the entry of external aid. It is only around the years 1998–2000 that there has been some improvement, followed by a declining trend again in 2001–2, though the level of external aid was twice than that of 1997–98.

In January 2004, the government signed yet another agreement with the World Bank for a loan of Rs. 47.1 billion for Sarva Shiksha Abhiyan for 2004–7, that is, Rs. 15.7 billion per year (World Bank 2004). At the current level of GDP, this loan amounts to merely 0.06 per cent of GDP, that is, 6 paise out of every Rs. 100 India earned in 2004–5 (the level of total external assistance in this sector since 1993–94 has invariably been much lower than this level)! For this pittance, we entered into conditionalities that will never be made public, as has been the case with externally aided projects since 1993–94.

The official stance is in clear violation of the CABE guidelines against the 'dependency syndrome' and policy dilutions in relation

FIGURE 2.1
EDUCATIONAL EXPENDITURE AS PART OF GDP (%)

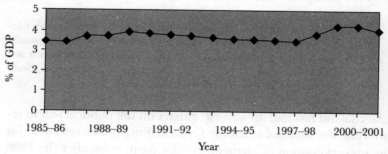

Source: Selected Educational Statistics, 2001–2, rectified on the basis of 'Analysis of Budgeted Expenditure on Education' (various years), Ministry of HRD.

to external aid (Government of India 1993: 89). This dependence on external aid in fact implies that *there need not be any change in the priorities of national economy* since additional funds will keep flowing in as long as the Government of India is willing to adjust its educational policy to the conditionalities of international funding agencies. These are matters of great concern for those of us who have been consistently questioning the role of external aid in elementary education. This issue has unfortunately not found any recognition in the Common Minimum Programme (CMP) of the UPA government and is yet to become a part of the political discourse at the national level.

We need to advance our understanding beyond the Ambani–Birla formulations which gave the false impression that it called for privatisation only in higher education and partly in secondary education—the report seemed to be saying that elementary education must entirely be a state responsibility. The post-Jomtien policy measures adopted by Indian policy makers, however, have evidently enabled the state to rapidly withdraw even from the elementary education sector. This is reflected in the ever-reducing financial commitment for this sector, as discussed earlier in the context of the 86th Constitutional Amendment and elsewhere. There is, thus, mounting evidence that the state is not ready to reprioritise the national economy in favour of education of the deprived sections of society, and has become dependent on external aid for this purpose, as it seems to be refusing to provide for even the diluted policy measures and for the much-reduced financial requirement.[20]

Conclusion

This paper has sought to establish that the exclusion and discrimination inherent in the present *operating* education policy (to be distinguished from that passed by Parliament), though considerably exacerbated by the impact of globalisation, has its roots in the national policies formulated well before global market forces gained a dominant position in India. In this we have a significant lesson: as we must deepen our analysis to comprehend the nature and full dimension of the adverse impact of globalisation on Indian education, we cannot exonerate our own policy makers from accepting primary responsibility for the collapse of the Indian education policy since Independence. Indeed, the weaknesses and internal contradictions in our policy provided the necessary political space to the forces of globalisation to intervene in Indian education.

How do you expect the education system to be any better if flawed policies are being implemented? I would rather contend that the State is normally quite efficient (inefficiency is rather deliberate and selectively practised!). The education system is the disaster that it is due to reasonably *efficient implementation of flawed policies*. A corollary, but a critical lesson, is about the significance of evolving and sharpening the tools of policy analysis and applying them for deciphering the mindset of the state as well as global market forces. Also, this enterprise must not be diluted by being lost in the *analysis of implementation* of the policy. Rather, attention must remain focused on the analysis of the *character of the policy* itself and, through this, of the State.

While the State abdicates its obligations and implements such exclusionary and discriminatory education policy for vast sections of Indian society, it promotes, at the same time, privatisation and commercialisation of school education (not to speak of higher education, which is beyond the scope of this paper) to benefit an upward mobile minority. For this purpose, it extends *direct subsidy* to the so-called public schools for the rich and upper middle class by: (*a*) making available prime land in urban areas at highly reduced costs; (*b*) exempting their income as well as donations to their trusts/ societies under the Income Tax Act; (*c*) providing, free of cost, professionally trained teachers who received their diplomas/degrees through publicly subsidised teacher education programmes; and (*d*) giving their institutions and examinations due recognition through government-supported CBSE or state boards of examinations. Yet these directly subsidised private schools are not expected to fulfil any of their constitutional obligations for ensuring *free education of equitable quality* for India's future generations.[21] The recent trend of some of these private schools undertaking patronising measures (often by setting up parallel streams of their own) for a handful of deprived children must not be allowed to confuse the policy discourse. In contrast, the State expresses its desperation regarding lack of resources for fulfilling its constitutional obligations unless external aid is increased, *seemingly* unmindful of the ways in which India's education policy and agenda have been already undermined by globalisation.

Indian education has hardly acknowledged that issues such as disparity, socio-economic stratification and caste hierarchies, patriarchy and gender inequity, conflicts of cultural and ethnic identity, unemployment and disemployment, regional imbalances, a development policy biased against the masses, inappropriate distribution of the economic cake, hegemonic control over natural resources, attrition of values inherited from the freedom struggle, and a cynical attack on democratic institutions have had a decisive impact on the structure and processes of education. The rise of communalism and the consequent attempts to impose monocultural hegemony during the past couple of decades has seriously begun to threaten the multi-ethnic, multicultural and multilingual character of Indian nationhood. We have already witnessed the cynical communal assault on the nature of knowledge inherent in school curriculum (Sadgopal 2004b; SAHMAT 2001). Policy formulation and any realistic planning of education, therefore, call for reviewing the role of education in social change and redesigning the entire education system to deal with these issues. We must also begin to take note of the rapidly emerging linkages, howsoever tenuous these might seem to be at present, between neo-liberal and communal forces. There is no space whatsoever either in the Jomtien Declaration or in the framework of any of the externally aided programmes for building up a meaningful policy discourse on such critical issues.

It is a matter of serious concern that the CMP of the UPA government also continues to suffer from several of the lacunae and contradictions that have afflicted policy formulation since Independence. More significantly, it shows no evidence of consciousness of the challenge posed by neo-liberal forces on the character of our education policies and the system as a whole. A detailed constructive critique of the education component of the CMP has already drawn the attention of the UPA leadership, including the prime minister and the minister for HRD, as well as of the leadership of its left coalition partners to these concerns, and sought reconstruction of the education policy in consonance with the principles enshrined in the Constitution (Bharat Jan Vigyan Jatha 2004).

It would not be an overstatement to assert that this policy of exclusion and discrimination amounts to *denial of knowledge* to almost 60 to 70 per cent of India's people, while also preventing them from participation in its creation as well as control. In this sense, the stance of the state and its collusion with the forces of globalisation needs to be viewed as an assault of epistemic nature on Indian society (Sadgopal 2002b, 2003a, 2004b). The assault is designed to control the access, production and distribution of knowledge across nations and social classes. It is only by regulating, controlling and distorting knowledge that these forces can dictate their neo-liberal agenda to various nations and large sections of the global society. This paper has attempted to reveal some of such processes and mechanisms already instituted in the Indian school system and having adverse impacts on children's right to education. The impact of the neo-liberal assault on the higher education system has been extensively documented by researchers elsewhere. The design for the attrition of the democratic, secular and egalitarian fabric of Indian society is thus almost complete. The process can be reversed only when, and if, a genuine grassroots movement, supported by progressive sections of society and infused with a consciousness of the dangers inherent in this epistemic assault, is built up for redeeming India's freedom and reasserting national sovereignty in policy formulation.

Notes

1. Supreme Court of India (1993), Unnikrishnan, J.P. & Ors. vs State of Andhra Pradesh & Ors., A.I.R. 1993, SC 2178.
2. The NPE (1986) was preceded by the NPE (1968), the first national policy on education, which was in the form of a cabinet resolution adopted by Parliament.
3. The common school system and the concept of neighbourhood schools was recommended by the Education Commission (1964–66); see Sections 1.36–1.38, 10.05, 10.19 and 10.20 (Government of India 1966). While recommending a 'phased implementation of the Common School System within a ten year time frame', the Acharya Ramamurti Committee Report stressed the need for 'essential minimum legislation', a common language policy for all schools and a 'combination of incentives, disincentives and legislation' to bring into its fold the recognised but unaided private schools (Government of India 1990: Chapter 4D, pp. 91–93). The concept was further elaborated and enriched by Sadgopal (2000: 153–63, 2002b: 122–24, 2003a: 23–27).
4. The original Article 45 now stands substituted by a modified but diluted Article 21A as a result of the 93rd (now called 86th) Amendment to the Constitution. Compared to the original Article 45, the dilution is a consequence of: (a) delinking early childhood care and preschool education (ECCE) from elementary education, thereby not viewing education of all children 'until they complete the age of 14 years' as a continuum; (b) withdrawing the Constitutional guarantee for provision of *free* ECCE; and (c) not including a specific time frame for fulfilment of the commitment.
5. Such a harmonious construction of Part IV with Part III of the Constitution was the basis of the historic Unnikrishnan judgement, giving education of children 'until they complete the age of 14 years' the status of fundamental right (Supreme Court of India 1993). In this judgement Article 45 of Part IV was read in conjunction with Article 21 of Part III.
6. It is now widely acknowledged that all those children of school age who are not in school are to be regarded essentially as child labour, even if they are engaged in domestic chores or outside workplaces to help their parents, including sibling care by girl children. This contention has gained credibility as a result of the work of MV Foundation in Ranga Reddy District, Andhra Pradesh, which led to the revealing sociological principle that 'all children out of school are, by definition, child labourers' (Sinha 2000: 168).

7. NPE (1986) (Sections 5.14 and 5.15) also gave birth to Navodaya Vidyalayas—a yet another parallel layer but *above* the formal school. Navodaya Vidyalayas, like non-formal education, also violate the principle of equality in educational planning and allocation of resources, but a discussion on this issue is beyond the scope of this paper.

8. The government used the term 'instructors' in order to avoid litigation. It was aware that the underpaid NFE instructors can seek justice in courts by contending that, in comparison to regular teachers, they are being discriminated, as 'unequal pay for equal work' violates the constitutional principle of right to equality (Ed.CIL 2000: 7).

9. This author was a member of the 17-member NPE Review Committee (NPERC) (1990) and acted as the convenor of its subcommittee on 'Access, Equity and Universalisation'. The subcommittee examined the policy on NFE and recorded in its deliberations this flawed logic as well as these internal contradictions in much detail. However, the final report included a rather diluted version of these deliberations due to the consideration shown to the hostile opposition to this analysis by the then secretary in the Ministry of Human Resource Development.

10. A comment is needed on the choice of the term 'non-formalise' in the NPERC's recommendations for transforming the formal school system. As convenor of the NPERC's subcommittee on 'Access, Equity and Universalisation', this author was under intense pressure from the Ministry not to criticise the NFE component of the policy since it was considered to be the Ministry's 'best foot forward' for achieving UEE. There were by then almost 2.4 million NFE centres (of these 78,000 centres were exclusively for girls). A great deal of media hype had been by then orchestrated, glorifying NFE (as well as adult literacy campaigns) as a panacea for lack of universal access to education (just as it is being done at present for EGS centres and alternative schools of the DPEP). Being keen to convince the policy makers of the need to focus all political attention on the transformation of the formal school system, the author used the expression 'non-formalisation of the formal school system', implying that the so-called desirable but otherwise non-existent features of NFE need to be in the formal system itself. This 'appeasement' did not work since the policy makers, as we shall see later, had made up their mind neither to transform nor to improve the formal school system, most probably under the influence of Jomtien Declaration and structural adjustment programme.

11. In July 1991, the newly elected central government headed by Prime Minister P.V. Narasimha Rao (Arjun Singh was the HRD minister) constituted a committee under the aegis of the Central Advisory Board of Education (CABE) to 'review the implementation of the various parameters of NPE, taking into consideration the report of the Committee for Review of the NPE and other relevant developments since the policy was formulated and to make recommendations regarding modifications to be made in NPE'. This committee, called the CABE Committee on Policy, was chaired by Janardhana Reddy, the Congress chief minister of Andhra Pradesh. The decision to constitute the CABE Committee

to purportedly review the Acharya Ramamurti Committee Report essentially amounted to *not* giving effect to the major policy changes recommended therein. The CABE Committee Report, submitted in January 1992, fulfilled the objective of the government by rejecting all the significant recommendations of the Acharya Ramamurti Committee for policy changes for promoting equity in elementary education and building up a common school system. Thus, the government managed to keep doors open for structural adjustment in the post-Jomtien phase, as will be shown later in this paper. Accordingly, the NPE (1986) was revised by Parliament in 1992 with only minor modifications.

12. The Jomtien Conference was attended by the representatives of 155 national governments (including the Indian government), 20 inter-governmental bodies and 150 NGOs.

13. For instance, a follow-up Education For All Conference of nine high-population countries was held in New Delhi in 1993. These nine countries included Bangladesh, Brazil, China, Egypt, India, Indonesia, Mexico, Nigeria and Pakistan—collectively referred to as the E-9 countries. This group met recently in Cairo in December 2003.

14. As part of the Dakar Framework of Action, UNESCO now regularly monitors the progress made by each nation in the context of the Dakar Goals and issues the *EFA Global Monitoring Report* annually. The 2003–4 report focused on the education of the girl child and was issued just before the EFA Conference held at New Delhi on 10–12 November 2003. The reports released in 2002 and 2003–4 show that *India is amongst those countries which are unlikely to fulfil any of the six Dakar Goals* (only three out of six goals were assessed), *including the goal of gender parity, even by the target year of 2015.* The Union Minister for HRD, Murli Manohar Joshi, took strong exception to this negative assessment in the UNESCO report and claimed that it is based upon outdated data (*Hindustan Times, Indian Express and Pioneer*, 8 November 2003). However, the Minister's claim was unfounded as shown by this author (Sadgopal 2003b, 2003c).

15. Externally aided projects in primary education in Andhra Pradesh (APPEP) and Bihar (BEP) preceded the Jomtien Declaration, but these were envisaged as special pilot projects rather than being a matter of policy. The possibility can not be denied that international funding agencies might have used the Andhra Pradesh and Bihar pilot projects in the pre-Jomtien phase to test political waters in India, that is, the political will of the ruling elite to stand by its constitutional obligations and policy. The Indian political leadership obviously failed the test as the externally aided projects of the post-Jomtien phase led to major violations of the Constitution and dilutions of the policy.

16. The problem is probably inherent in the ambiguous notions of 'basic education' and 'basic learning needs' in both the Jomtien and Dakar Frameworks. The ambiguity of these notions, most likely deliberate, is what allows them to be used for merging of 'human needs and market forces', as noted by Tomasevski (2001). A discussion on this issue is beyond the scope of this paper. It would be sufficient to point out here that the Jomtien notion of 'basic education' must

not be confused with the revolutionary pedagogic concept of basic education (or *buniyadi shiksha*), as evolved by Mahatma Gandhi at the Wardha Education Conference in 1937 as part of the freedom struggle, which was further elaborated by a committee under the chairpersonship of Zakir Hussain as *Nai Taleem*. The almost servile 'parroting' of the Jomtien's narrow notion of 'basic education' by Indian policy makers in the post-Jomtien official discourse amounts to denial of one of the most inspiring features of the heritage of the freedom struggle, apart from further marginalising the possibility of integrating the 'world of work' with the 'world of knowledge' as conceived by Mahatma Gandhi.

17. The concept of 'basic education' in the Jomtien and Dakar Frameworks is limited to primary education of *five* years only. Elementary education of *eight* years, implied by the Indian Constitution under the original Article 45 as well as the amended Article 21A as the minimum guarantee by the state, is non-existent in these frameworks. Interestingly, the Jomtien Framework concedes that 'these targets represent a "floor" (but not a "ceiling")', and parenthetically provides for '(primary education) or whatever higher level of education is considered as basic' by a particular country (Sections 5 and 8 [2] respectively). It is indeed ironic that Indian policy makers, instead of using these spaces in the framework for persisting with India's constitutional and policy imperatives, allowed the international funding agencies to dilute *elementary* education to *primary* education as the dominant framework for educational planning and financing in post-Jomtien India.

18. This scheme to accommodate the 9 to 14 age group in adult literacy classes was announced with great fanfare by the then prime minister of India in his inaugural address at the EFA Conference of E-9 countries held at New Delhi in 1993. Such glorification of this policy measure is an evidence of *education being reduced to literacy*.

19. According to *Education For All: National Plan of Action* (Government of India 2003a), the total 10th Plan requirement for UEE is Rs. 522 billion (centre and state shares combined). This amounted to an average of 0.47 per cent of GDP in 2002–3, including the external aid component. Of the centre's share (Rs. 397 billion), the Planning Commission promised Rs. 212 billion, that is, only 53.5 per cent of the 10th Plan requirement. This leaves a gap of at least Rs. 184 billion. The gap in the state's share is not yet reported. Recent press reports indicate that the Planning Commission has further reduced its allocation to Rs. 170 billion (a mere 0.15 per cent of GDP), thereby increasing the gap. The story does not end here. The Prime Minister made desperate appeals to the international funding agencies at the UNESCO-sponsored Third High Level Group Meeting of EFA held in Delhi in November 2003 for increasing external aid for elementary education (*Indian Express* and *Hindustan Times*, 11 November 2003); the minister of HRD carried forward this appeal at the E-9 Ministerial-level Review Meeting on EFA held in Cairo in December 2003 (*Rashtriya Sahara*, 21 December 2003). The Government of India seems to have got an assurance of additional external aid of Rs. 150 billion for the 10th Plan. However, as per

press reports, the Ministry of Finance has 'asked the HRD Ministry to adjust Rs. 150 billion in the original allocation of Rs. 170 billion' (*Hindustan Times*, 17 December 2003)!

20. In this context, it may be noted that the UPA government's CMP 'pledges to raise public spending in education to *at least* 6% of GDP with *at least half this amount* being spent *on primary and secondary sectors*.' This pledge calls for *four* comments. *First*, this level of 6 per cent of GDP was to be initially achieved by 1986 but the modified 1986 policy stated that the outlay will '*uniformly exceed* 6 per cent of the national income' during 'the Eighth Five Year Plan and onwards'. Since then, practically every major political party has promised to do this in its election manifestos in each general election. The UPA is, therefore, obliged to produce a clear roadmap for *re-prioritisation of national economy* in order to make its pledge credible. *Two*, the UPA needs to be lauded for *at least not diluting* this commitment as the BJP cleverly attempted to do this in its recent manifesto by promising to raise 'the *total spending* on education to 6% of GDP by 2010, with *enlarged public–private partnership*'. This substitution of policy-level commitment to public spending by private resources was also a part of the NDA manifesto, clearly in deference to the neo-liberal agenda. *Three*, the CMP has not acknowledged the urgent need to fulfil the *cumulative gap* that has been building up for the past three decades due to *under-investment* in education. For elementary education, this was estimated by the Tapas Majumdar Committee (1999) as being equal to Rs. 137 billion per year for the next 10 years. which amounts to about 0.6 per cent of the current level of GDP (that is, merely 60 paise out of every Rs. 100 of GDP). The UPA is expected to provide for this additionality, apart from reaching the level of 6 per cent of GDP. A similar estimate of the cumulative gap in secondary and higher education sectors is yet to be made. *Four*, India is already spending almost half of its total educational outlay on elementary education. The UPA's pledge to spend at least half the total expenditure '*on primary and secondary sectors*' has *negative implications*. This is because, in 1998–99, 78.7 per cent of the total expenditure was on elementary and secondary sectors taken together. The UPA formulation implies that the priority to be given to both of these sectors will be *reduced to merely 50 per cent* of the total expenditure! Hopefully, this is a result of the usual, but still alarming, *misconception about the category of 'primary' education* as referred to in the CMP.

21. A note may be taken here of the recent order of the High Court of Delhi to private unaided schools to provide free education to poor children to the extent of 20 to 25 per cent of their strength as per the terms and conditions of the agreement they signed while receiving free or low-cost land. However, the order has only revealed the long-standing collusion between the state authorities (including the political leadership of various parties ruling the state at different times) and the private school lobby, which ensured that the said agreement will be flouted unashamedly for years, if not decades. The High Court order is a tribute neither to the government nor to the school managements but to Social Jurist, a voluntary body that filed the petition and pursued the matter against all odds.

References

Bharat Jan Vigyan Jatha (in collaboration with Maulana Azad Centre for Elementary and Social Education, Department of Education, University of Delhi). 1995. *Lokshala Project for Universalisation of Elementary Education: Demonstrating an Alternative Vision*. New Delhi: Bharat Jan Vigyan Jatha.

Bharat Jan Vigyan Jatha. 2004. *An Agenda for Common Minimum Programme in Education*. New Delhi: Bharat Jan Vigyan Jatha.

Dhankar, Rohit. 2002. 'Seeking Quality Education: In the Arena of Fun and Rhetoric'. In *Seeking Quality Education For All: Experiences from the District Primary Education Programme* (Occasional Paper). New Delhi: The European Commission.

Ed.CIL. 2000. *Para Teachers in Primary Education: A Status Report*. New Delhi: District Primary Education Programme, Department of Elementary Education and Literacy, Ministry of Human Resource Development, Government of India.

Government of India. 1966. *Education and National Development: Report of the Education Commission 1964–66*. New Delhi: Ministry of Education, Government of India.

———. 1985. *Challenge of Education: A Policy Perspective*. New Delhi: Ministry of Education, Government of India.

———. 1986. *National Policy on Education, 1986, and Programme of Action, 1986*. New Delhi: Department of Education, Ministry of Human Resource Development, Government of India.

———. 1990. *Towards an Enlightened and Humane Society: Report of the Committee for Review of National Policy on Education, 1986* (National Policy on Education Review Committee Report [NPERC] or Acharya Ramamurti Committee Report). New Delhi: Department of Education, Ministry of Human Resource Development, Government of India.

———. 1992a. *Report of the CABE Committee on Policy* (Janardhan Reddy Committee Report). New Delhi: Department of Education, Ministry of Human Resource Development, Government of India.

———. 1992b. *National Policy on Education, 1986 (As modified in 1992) with National Policy on Education, 1968*. New Delhi: Department of Education, Ministry of Human Resource Development, Government of India.

———. 1992c. *Programme of Action, 1992*. New Delhi: Department of Education, Ministry of Human Resource Development, Government of India.

———. 1993. *Education For All: The Indian Scene*. New Delhi: Department of Education, Ministry of Human Resource Development, Government of India.

———. 1995. *District Primary Education Programme: Guidelines*. New Delhi: Department of Education, Ministry of Human Resource Development, Government of India.

———. 1998. *DPEP Moves On: Towards Universalising Basic Education*. New Delhi: Department of Education, Ministry of Human Resource Development, Government of India.

———. 2000. *A Policy Framework for Reforms in Education* (Mukesh Ambani and Kumaramangalam Birla). New Delhi: Prime Minister's Council on Trade and Industry, Government of India.

Government of India. 2001a. *Handbook for Education Guarantee Scheme and Alternative & Innovative Education*. New Delhi: Department of Elementary Education and Literacy, Ministry of Human Resource Development, Government of India.

————. 2001b. *Working Group Report on Elementary and Adult Education: Tenth Five Year Plan 2002–2007*. New Delhi: Department of Elementary Education and Literacy, Ministry of Human Resource Development, Government of India.

————. 2002. *Sarva Shiksha Abhiyan: Framework for Implementation*. New Delhi: Department of Elementary Education and Literacy, Ministry of Human Resource Development, Government of India.

————. 2003a. *Education For All: National Plan of Action, India*. New Delhi: Department of Elementary Education and Literacy, Ministry of Human Resource Development, Government of India.

————. 2003b. *The Free and Compulsory Education for Children Bill, 2003*, Draft bill dated 19 September 2003. New Delhi: Ministry of Human Resource Development, Government of India (posted on the Ministry's Web site).

————. 2003c. *The Free and Compulsory Education Bill, 2003*, Draft bill dated 10 December 2003 (as circulated by the Secretary, Department of Education, Ministry of Human Resource Development, at a public discussion organised by NIEPA, New Delhi, on 15 December 2003.

————. 2004. *The Free and Compulsory Education Bill, 2004*. Draft bill dated 8 January 2004 (Draft III) (as circulated by the Secretary, Department of Elementary Education and Literacy, Ministry of Human Resource Development, at a meeting of State/UT Secretaries of the respective Departments of Education, held at New Delhi, 15–16 January 2004).

Government of Madhya Pradesh. 1998. *The Madhya Pradesh Human Development Report 1998*. Bhopal: Government of Madhya Pradesh.

Jha, Madan Mohan. 2003. 'A Note for NIEPA Meeting on Free and Compulsory Education Bill, 2003'. Unpublished Paper.

Kumar, Krishna, Manish Priyam and Sadhna Saxena. 2001. 'The Trouble with Para-Teachers'. *Frontline*, 9 November, 18(22): 93–94.

National Council of Educational Research and Training (NCERT). 2000. *National Curriculum Framework for School Education*. New Delhi: NCERT.

National Institue of Educational Planning and Administration (NIEPA). 1990. *Education for All by 2000: Indian Perspective*. New Delhi: NIEPA.

Sadgopal, Anil. 1994. Report of the Sub-Group on Education (Chair: Prof. Anil Sadgopal). In *National Consultation on Rights of the Child*. New Delhi: Ministry of HRD, Government of India.

————. 2000. *Shiksha Mein Badlav ka Sawaal: Samajik Anubhavon se Neeti Tak*. New Delhi: Granth Shilpi.

————. 2001a. 'Between the Lines: Writes and Wrongs in Education Bill', *Times of India*, 28 November 2001.

————. 2001b. 'Shiksha ka Haq Chhenane Wala Vidheyak', *Rashtriya Sahara*, 28 November 2001.

————. 2001c. 'Is Shiksha Neeti ka Rajneetik Arthshastra', *Rashtriya Sahara*, 8 December 2001.

Sadgopal, Anil. 2001d. 'Political Economy of the Ninety-Third Amendment Bill', *Mainstream*, 22 December 2001: 43–50.

————. 2002a. 'A Convenient Consensus', *Frontline*, 4 January: 107–8.

————. 2002b. 'Politics of Education in the Age of Globalisation'. In Enakshi Ganguly Thukral (ed.), *Children in Globalising India*. New Delhi: HAQ: Centre for Child Rights.

————. 2003a. *Political Economy of Education in the Age of Globalisation*. New Delhi: Bharat Jan Vigyan Jatha.

————. 2003b. 'Goal Posts Shifted', *Hindustan Times*, 11 November 2003.

————. 2003c. 'Education For Too Few', *Frontline*, 5 December: 97–100.

————. 2003d. 'Exclusion and Inequality in Education: The State Policy and Globalisation', *Contemporary India* (Journal of the Nehru Memorial Museum and Library), 2 (3): 1–36.

————. 2004a. 'De-Constructing "The Free And Compulsory Education Bill, 2003": A Concept Paper for an Alternative Framework'. Presented at National Consultations organised by the M.V. Foundation and Campaign Against Child Labour at Hyderabad, January 2004, and Bhubaneswar, April 2004.

————. 2004b. 'Globalisation and Education: Defining the Indian Crisis', XVI Zakir Hussain Memorial Lecture, Zakir Hussain College, University of Delhi, 10 February.

SAHMAT. 2001. *The Saffron Agenda in Education: An Exposé*. New Delhi: Safdar Hashmi Memorial Trust.

Sinha, Shantha. 2000. 'Child Labour and Education'. In Rekha Wazir (ed.), *The Gender Gap in Basic Education: NGOs as Change Agents*. New Delhi: Sage Publications.

Swaminathan, Mina. 2001. 'Delegitimising Childhood', *Hindu*, 7 October.

Tilak, J.B.G. 2003. 'A Study on Financing on Education in India with a Focus on Elementary Education'. Ministerial Level Meeting of the South Asia EFA Forum, Islamabad, Pakistan, 21–23 May.

Tomasevski, K. 2001. *Right to Education Primers No. 1: Removing Obstacles in the Way of the Right to Education*. Lund, Sweden: Raoul Wallenberg Institute.

UNDP, UNESCO, UNICEF and World Bank. 1990. *World Declaration on Education For All and Framework for Action to Meet Basic Learning Needs* (The Jomtien Declaration). Thailand World Conference on Education For All: Meeting Basic Learning Needs, 5–9 March.

UNESCO. 2002. *EFA Global Monitoring Report 2002: Education For All—Is the World on Track?* Paris: UNESCO.

————. 2003. *EFA Global Monitoring Report 2003/4: Gender and Education For All—The Leap to Equality*. Paris: UNESCO.

World Bank. 1997. *Primary Education in India*. Washington, DC: World Bank, and New Delhi: Allied Publishers.

————. 2004. Project Appraisal Document on a Proposed Credit in the amount of SDR 334.9 Million (US $500 Million) to the Republic of India for an Elementary Education Project (Sarva Shiksha Abhiyan), Report No. 27703–IN (Meant for Official Use Only), New Delhi.

World Education Forum. 2000. *The Dakar Framework for Action* (adopted at World Education Forum's conference on 'Education For All: Meeting Our Collective Commitments') Dakar, Senegal, 26–28 April.

Hindustan Times, 8 November 2003.
Hindustan Times, 11 November 2003.
Hindustan Times, 17 December 2003.
Hindustan Times, 8 September 2004.
Indian Express, 8 November 2003.
Indian Express, 11 November 2003.
Pioneer, 8 November 2003.
Rashtriya Sahara, 21 December 2003.

4

OPERATIONALISING THE CONSTITUTIONAL GUARANTEE OF THE RIGHT TO EDUCATION

ISSUES OF RESOURCE CRUNCH AND STATE COMMITMENT

Amarjeet Sinha

THE CONTEXT

This paper is an effort to understand the context of the 86th Constitutional Amendment, 2002, to make elementary education a fundamental right for child in the 6 to 14 age group. It will try and examine the implications of the amendment with respect to the obligations of the State, the State defined as per Article 12 of the Constitution of India as the central, the state and the local governments. The assumption in this paper is that the constitutional amendment has created a legal right and space for its assertion. The effective implementation of this right, in letter and spirit, depends on the way the State responds to the entitlement of every Indian child, the resources it allocates for quality universal elementary education, the reforms it undertakes for communities to be more assertive in the management of schools, the power relations it transforms to make schools more autonomous and locally accountable and, most importantly, the education it imparts to all children. Former education minister M.C. Chagla's presidential address to the Central Advisory Board of Education (CABE) in 1964 summed up the concerns appropriately:

> Our Constitution fathers did not intend when they enacted Article 45 that we just set up hovels or any sort of structures, put students there, give them untrained teachers, give them bad textbooks, no playgrounds and say we have complied with Article 45. The compliance that was intended was a substantial compliance. They meant that real education should be given to our children between the ages of 6 and 14.

The issue of education of children had been a subject of debate and contention even during the days of the freedom movement. There were many critiques of the colonial Macaulayan school system on the grounds that it was not good as a mass system since its focus was on producing a few *babu*s and clerks. Mahatma Gandhi's *buniyadi shiksha*, Zakir Hussain's *nayi talim*, Aurobinda's critique, Rabindranath Tagore's experiments with education, all attempted alternatives that were deeply embedded in the natural, social and philosophical context of the East. They highlighted the need for integrating physical and mental development, and allowing children opportunities at self-development through exploration, innovation and by doing. Many of these innovations were pedagogically very sound. They, however, got absorbed in the mainstream on account of weak linkages with post-basic education and a need for a common school system that had the same curriculum. In many ways the marginalisation of these experiments led to the demise of efforts at 'non-formalising the formal', eventually ending up in a textbook-centric school system. Mahatma Gandhi, deeply influenced as he was by Leo Tolstoy, looked at the State's role in education with deep suspicion, recommending self-reliant schools that could generate their own resources. Tolstoy's comment when asked why the czar did not spend adequately on education, *that education is a matter of enlightenment and no monarch in his senses would like to do that*, had greatly influenced Gandhi's thinking. We have, of course, with a democratic state, assigned the obligation of basic education for all children, to the State itself.

More recent experiments like the Hoshangabad Science Teaching Project, the work of Eklavya, experiments of the Rishi Valley School in cluster schools, Nalli Kali experiments in Karnataka, innovations in the DPEP in Kerala, and the reading experiments of Pratham did try to question textbook-centric thrusts and argued for systems of learning that allow children to move at their own pace. Experiments and innovations in the governmental and the non-governmental sector in the 1980s and 1990s made a strong case that all children can learn if provided an opportunity to do so. The experiments advocated greater flexibility, community involvement and resources at school level in order to ensure that all children learn. The thrust for non-formalising the formal, however, has been weak in spite of these efforts. Heavy curriculum load, textbook-centric approaches and examination-based assessments, continue to exert pressure on children from a very young age. The heavy curriculum load, with the inability of poor parents to buy tuition time and reference books, further confounds the inequity of our school system.

Article 45 of the Constitution of India declares that 'the State shall endeavour to provide free and compulsory education for all children up to the age of fourteen years, within ten years of the Constitution'. Though a Directive Principle of State Policy, it was expected that this would be a guiding principle of State-led development. The arguments for free and compulsory education gained from the debates on compulsory education in other developed countries like the UK, and this had even led to Gopal Krishna Gokhale tabling a Bill on compulsory education much before India became independent. Various education commissions continued to make a case for elementary education of satisfactory quality, and the need to make at least 6 per cent GDP public investment in education was forcefully made by the Kothari Commission in 1966. The National Policy of Education, 1986, as revised in 1992, provided for universal elementary education of satisfactory quality by the turn of the century. Other important commissions and committees like the Ramamurti Commission and the Yashpal Committee provided useful suggestions on improving the quality of elementary education and ensuring learning by all children. The 42nd Constitutional Amendment, among other things, made education a concurrent subject instead of a state subject, on the grounds that the centre ought to play an 'equalising role' to ensure that children were not denied basic education even in resource-poor states.

The intervention of the Supreme Court in 1993 in the Unnikrishnan case to declare education of children up to the age of 14 a fundamental right, irrespective of the economic capacity of the State, has to be seen in the light of the broad policy commitments and the seemingly unsatisfactory provision made for universal elementary education in spite of it. While GDP public investments had moved up from 0.5 per cent at the time of Independence to nearly 3.5 per cent in the 1990s, more primary and upper primary schools had been established, and teachers' salaries in government/local body schools had improved remarkably compared to pre-Independence times, all children were neither in school, nor were all children learning.

The 1990s had seen an unprecedented demand for education even from the poorest households, and it was clearly a failure of the State to provide functioning, well-equipped schools to meet this strong community demand. The PROBE (1999) study had highlighted the dismal state of government/local body schools in many of the large Hindi-speaking states. It had also made a case of how Himachal Pradesh had witnessed a schooling revolution, making the point that effective public action can make a difference. The 73rd and 74th Constitutional Amendments for decentralisation and local democracy had created space for participation. Reservation for women, Scheduled Castes, Scheduled Tribes and Other Backward Classes had created a movement for social participation, with all its limitations, reflecting even in a greater demand for schooling. The Total Literacy Campaigns in the 1990s had also highlighted the growing demand for elementary education from the poorest households. The efforts at constitutional reforms have to be seen in this backdrop.

The amendment to make elementary education a fundamental right was an occasion when a lot of debates were generated on what was being attempted. The criticism was mainly on four counts— the 0 to 6 age group was being left out; the commitment of financial resources was far short of the 6 per cent public investment promised by the Kothari Commission; the obligation on parents/guardians was not desirable; and quality would suffer as many low-cost alternatives were now being proposed for alternative education. While all the criticisms appear very serious and well-founded, there is a need to look at issues not merely from ideological positions, but pragmatic ones as well. It is important to realise that government systems rarely make quantum jumps as governments, by definition, make incremental gains. No one questions the ideal; one has also to recognise the real as well, especially at a time when fiscal constraints at the central and state levels were putting pressure on resources. If quality elementary education is a priority that has strong political commitment, that commitment ought to reflect in more financial resources for the sector. As the Tapas Majumdar Committee established so forcefully, additional financial resources required for universalisation of elementary education (UEE) of satisfactory quality was well within the commitment of 6 per cent GDP. Rather than reaching a standstill, the assumption in moving ahead with a programme for UEE guaranteeing minimum learning conditions was to put community pressure for more resources through an intensive habitation based upwards process of planning. The hope was that communities that plan for universalisation shall also, at some point of time, demand resources for it. The legal framework was expected to exert further pressure by making the right justiciable.

It is important to understand the process of policy formation in a developing democracy. Article 45 of the Directive Principles of State Policy regarding free and compulsory education up to the age of 14 years, within 10 years of the Constitution, was not exerting the kind of influence on policy planning as it ought to have. The best indication of this neglect of the only time-bound directive principle is best illustrated by the dismally low school participation rates at the time of the 42nd National Sample Survey, 1986–87. Clearly, the Indian State had failed in its obligation to provide free and compulsory education. The Supreme Court's ruling in the

Bandhua Mukti Morcha case and subsequently in the J.P. Unnikrishnan case, 1993, brought the debate on the right to basic education to the centre stage. The courts ruled that it is inconceivable to provide the right to life, without the right to basic education. It dismissed arguments about the economic capacity of the State as far as education up to the age of 14 years was considered. The Unnikrishnan case was followed by the spirited efforts of Satyapal Anand to hold the Indian State accountable in its obligation to children. The states were directed by the Supreme Court to report on the progress made in making elementary education a fundamental right.

As a response to the Supreme Court's proactive espousal of the fundamental right to elementary education, it entered the manifestos of political parties, and the United Front government included it in its manifesto. This led to the setting up of the Muhi Ram Saikia Committee, with education ministers of states as its members, deliberating on implications of making elementary education a fundamental right. In its report submitted in 1997, it endorsed the demand for a constitutional amendment to make elementary education for the 6 to 14 age group a fundamental right. The 83rd Constitutional Amendment Bill, 1997, introduced by the United Front government in the Rajya Sabha, reflected the views of the Muhi Ram Saikia Committee. As is the case, the draft Bill was scrutinised by a Parliamentary Standing Committee that invited suggestions from civil society. The 165th Report of the Law Commission of India also endorsed the proposed constitutional amendment and placed a draft proposal for a central legislation to enforce.

It was during this period that the influential Public Report on Basic Education was published (1999) and released by Amartya Sen, making a strong case for the fundamental right to elementary education, given the strong demand for education from the poorest households. Organisations of NGOs like the National Alliance for the Right to Education (NAFRE) kept the issue centre stage through a series of national and regional consultations. The Tapas Majumdar Committee, 1999, further emphasised that the resource needed for a norm-based provisioning for elementary education was well within the repeated commitment made by successive prime ministers of 6 per cent public investment in elementary education. The formidable figure of an additional Rs. 1368 billion over a 10-year period given by the Tapas Majumdar Committee did make the Finance Ministry uneasy about the cost implications of making elementary education a fundamental right. The delays in its approval can be explained in the context of these competing claims on public resources.

The financial memorandum for the resubmitted Bill that was subsequently approved indicated a figure of Rs. 980 billion over a 10-year period for elementary education. The requirement of resources was lower than the assessment made by the Tapas Majumdar Committee, only because of teacher deployment at 1:40 instead of 1:30, and the implications it has for school facilities. It was also a pragmatic assessment given the fact that most states now recruit teachers at less than pay scale, at least for some years. Neither was there a major slashing of norms, nor a rejection of engagement of regular fully paid teachers. Nothing in the SSA prevents states from recruiting fully paid teachers. A comparison of the SSA and Tapas Majumdar Committee norms will make the point clearer (Table 4.1).

Certain conclusions can be drawn from Tables 4.2 and 4.3. First, there has been an increase in the allocation of resources for education if we consider the long-term trend since Independence. The increases in the 1990s, however, have not been so significant as yet. While part of it can be explained by the fact that GDP growth itself has been very high, therefore, additional allocations do not reflect as a larger percentage, it must also be borne in mind that the slowing down of expenditures has been on account of the fact that state governments have been reluctant to make expenditures where recurrent liabilities are generated. Since schooling is a permanent arrangement and teachers a necessary requirement for effective learning, the requirement is of higher recurring expenditures. The SSA took into account this reluctance of states to incur expenditure in designing a sustainable financing arrangement for teacher salaries beyond the Five-Year Plan periods. Otherwise, we

Table 4.1
Comparing the Tapas Majumdar Committee and SSA Norms

Provision	Tapas Majumdar Committee	Sarva Shiksha Abhiyan
Overall projection	Resource need of an additional Rs. 1368 billion over 10 years. Assumes full pay scale for all teachers from day one—this is not the practice in many states now. Provided 1:30 teacher–pupil ratio as against the 1:40 national policy commitment. Assumes all schoolroom construction to come out of Education Department resources. Made no concessions for private unaided sector. Even then, the resource requirement is well within the national commitment of 6 per cent GDP public investment.	Projected an additional resource need of about Rs. 600 billion in 10 years. The lower projection was for the following reasons: 1:40 instead of 1:30 teacher–pupil ratio; this has implications for number of classrooms as well when the commitment is a room for every teacher; entire cost of construction is not projected in the SSA as it is expected to converge with other departments' schemes; SSA assumes that 10–15% children will access private unaided institutions; SSA assumes teacher salaries as often being less than full pay scale in many states, though it provides for full salary if that is the state's policy.
Teachers–student ratio	1:30 at primary and upper primary levels, with at least two teachers in a primary school. The requirement worked out to more than 3.5 million new teachers.	1:40 at primary and upper primary school, with at least two teachers in every primary school and three teachers in upper primary schools. The requirement works out to nearly 1.1 million additional teachers, since nearly 500,000 have already been added in the 1990s.
Schools	Primary school within 1 km and one upper primary school for every two primary schools.	Primary school/EGS within 1 km, depending on number of children, and an upper primary school for every two primary schools.
Classrooms	A room for every teacher and a room for the headmaster in the upper primary schools. All	A room for every teacher and a room for the headmaster in upper primary schools. Assumes 33% cost on construction.

(Table 4.1 continued)

(Table 4.1 continued)

Provision	Tapas Majumdar Committee	Sarva Shiksha Abhiyan
	construction costs covered in financial assessment.	Assumes convergence with rural and urban development ministries to access more resources for construction.
School equipment	Rs. 50,000 to uncovered upper primary schools and Rs. 10,000 to every new primary school.	Rs. 50,000 to uncovered upper primary schools and Rs. 10,000 to every new primary school.
Textbooks and Stationery	For all children at primary and upper primary levels.	Free textbook for all girls, SC, ST children at primary and upper primary level.
Scholarships and uniforms	For all children below poverty line.	No provision for scholarships and uniforms as it is expected to come from other programmes of state governments/social justice and empowerment ministries.
Free cooked meals	For poor children.	Midday meal scheme is outside SSA but works closely together.
Establishment of District Institutes of Education and Training (DIET)/ Block Resource Centre (BRC)/ Cluster Resource Centre (CRC)	In uncovered districts, blocks and clusters.	BRCs and CRCs from SSA. DIETs under the revised Teacher Education Scheme of GoI that is outside SSA but works very closely to meet SSA needs.
Provision for school maintenance and replacement of school equipment	Provided.	Provided.
Teacher training	Provided.	Provided.
Coverage of all disabled children	Provided.	Provided.
Private unaided schools	No concessions made in the calculations for private unaided assuming that they all have hidden subsidies.	Assumption that 10–15% children will actually opt for private unaided schools.

had the paradox of state governments not having the resources to invest in elementary education and the Government of India not knowing how to utilise its resources.

TABLE 4.2
EXPENDITURE ON EDUCATION IN INDIA

Year	Total Revenue Expenditure on Education (in Rs. million)	Percentage of Education Expenditure Compared to Expenditure on all Sectors	Education Expenditure as Percentage of GDP
1951–52	644.46	7.92	0.64
1960–61	2,395.6	11.99	1.48
1970–71	8,923.6	10.16	2.11
1980–81	38,842.0	10.67	2.98
1990–91	196,158.5	13.37	3.84
1994–95	326,062.2	12.95	3.56
1999–2000	770,563.0 (revised estimate)	14.61	4.31

Source: Selected Education Statistics, 2000–1, Ministry of Human Resources Development.

TABLE 4.3
PER CAPITA EXPENDITURE ON EDUCATION IN 1997–98
(RS. AT 1981–82 PRICES)

State	Per Capita Expenditure
Himachal Pradesh	191
Kerala	164
Maharashtra	158
Tamil Nadu	144
Gujarat	142
Assam	134
Haryana	134
Karnataka	130
Rajasthan	128
Orissa	102
West Bengal	101
Andhra Pradesh	88
Uttar Pradesh	78
Bihar	76
Madhya Pradesh	73

Source: Bashir (2000).

Second, the per capita expenditure in states with large numbers of out-of-school children continue to be lower than others. There is a strong case for stepping up investments in such states if the Millennium Development Goals are to be attained.

Third, while the SSA is a minimalist norm-based approach, it does provide for the basic minimum learning conditions for effective teaching and learning. Higher utilisation by states will really be the test of its effectiveness in pushing up investments in the elementary education sector. Higher utilisation of resources over 2002–4 of the SSA programme is a testimony of its ability to fill the missing gaps.

Fourth, the District Elementary Education Plans (DEEP) are expected to put pressure for more resources based on actual needs to meet uncovered gaps. Since democracies work through pressure groups, it is hoped that the demand for quality basic education will put pressure for more resources. The Programme Approvals Board under the SSA approves a perspective plan that has a 10-year perspective. The financial approvals are for the 10th Plan period. If we total these approvals, it is far higher than the resources being currently earmarked for elementary education. This is bound to create pressure on democratic governments. The commitments of the Common Minimum Programme of the newly elected government to 6 per cent GDP expenditure, hot cooked meals, wage guarantees for the poor, cess on taxes for education and health, are positive steps. The perspective plans of districts under the SSA for UEE will provide an opportunity for use of the additional resource commitments.

Fifth, increase in GDP spending was also on account of higher salaries in many states in the wake of the Fifth Pay Commission. With retiring fully paid teachers being replaced by para-teachers, salary expenditures have stabilised over the last few years. There is, therefore, a need to go into the effectiveness of the expenditure rather than make conclusions only on the basis of broad expenditure trends. One also has to keep in mind the higher rates of growth in the 1990s, and its implications for GDP-based percentage expenditures.

Clearly the constitutional amendment and the national programme for UEE, the Sarva Shiksha Abhiyan, is a major step forward
as it is for the first time that planning for every child is the basis of
a programme. The commitment to UEE is not only in policy—it
is in a programme, and surely this will put pressure on the State both
for reform and for resources. The District Elementary Education
Plans that are to be the basis of planning for the SSA are likely to
exert pressure for additional resources for elementary education.
It is hoped that ultimately in a democracy the people's will shall
triumph.

Reverting to the main points of criticism regarding the amendment, no one disputes the importance of early childhood care and
education. Given the high levels of malnourishment in the 0 to
3 age group, food security is a very important concern as well. The
question, however, is that at present, even if the ICDS system was
assumed to be working at full capacity (which it does not), the coverage of the 0 to 6 age group will only be 20 to 25 per cent. While
ideologically it should be made a fundamental right, at the present
stage of coverage that will amount to nothing but enacting a farce
as we are not in a position to enforce compliance unless there is a
quantum leap in allocations for the age group. That is why the second best option of explicitly stating early childhood care and education as a Directive Principle of State Policy has been attempted
under the amendment. The Supreme Court's recent ruling on an
ICDS centre in every habitation, if operationalised, can make a
case for early childhood care and education as a fundamental right.
With hot cooked meals in schools, there could be more under-age
children in formal schools, and this may put pressure for establishing a preparatory class prior to Class I to take care of pre-school
education.

On the issue of resources, as mentioned earlier, while there is a
departure from the Tapas Majumdar assessments especially with
regard to teacher–pupil ratio and actual teacher emoluments, there
are no major departures on norms. It is rightly argued that pedagogically a move to the 1:30 ratio, as suggested by the Yashpal

Committee, may be a superior and necessary option, especially for first-generation learners. At a time when states like Uttar Pradesh, Bihar and West Bengal had teacher–pupil ratios of over 80 in more than 20 per cent schools, it was important to first establish the school-specific (and not district- or state-specific) norm of 1:40. On the issue of duty of parents, the amendment clearly places the obligation on the government (local, state and central) and not on the parents. The idea of making it the duty of parents is to make schooling merge as a social norm, irrespective of gender or disability. On the issue of low-cost initiatives, the SSA is primarily about strengthening formal systems through reforms and resources. Its objective is quality education for which a lot of the emphasis is on assuring minimum learning conditions for each child. That is why the norms are worked out for every child, every habitation and every school. The norm-based approach has been adopted to improve transparency and make people know their rights to basic education. With the central legislation on free and compulsory education, communities should be in a position to demand basic learning conditions for their children, deduced on the basis of transparent child-, school- and habitation-specific norms of the SSA. While doing so, care has to be taken to ensure that alternative forms of learning are only seen as an interim measure and not a cost-cutting effort.

The challenge of the constitutional amendment and the SSA programme is to put community pressure for more accountable and well-endowed government and local body schools. It is poor households that are sending their children to these schools and any improvement in the condition of these schools will directly affect the lives of the poor. The amendment facilitates a rights-based approach to meeting the obligation of the State. While it is true that allocation of resources for basic education is always a struggle, it is hoped that planning for all children with community ownership under the SSA will put greater pressure on the political executive to fulfil the obligations of quality basic education. A need-based demand for resources based on meticulous household-based planning is the best way of putting pressure on the democratic State to put more resources in a more accountable basic education system.

WHERE ARE WE ON CONSTITUTIONAL GUARANTEES? ARE ALL CHILDREN IN SCHOOL?

This section examines the progress on basic education since 1986 by looking at a large number of independent studies, evaluation studies, household surveys, etc. It tries to assess where the 6 to 14 age group are, and whether the position has changed since 1986. An effort is made to understand developments in states as well and to see what is keeping children out of schools.

Table 4.4 lists findings on basic education from studies undertaken in the 1986–2003 period. They raise issues around where we are and what is it that explains non-participation.

TABLE 4.4
FINDINGS ON BASIC EDUCATION (1986–2003)

Survey, Year, Sample Size, Coverage	Main Findings
1986–87	
42nd Round National Sample Survey (NSSO)	42.79% males and 69.23% females in rural areas aged 6 and above never enrolled in any educational institution. The comparable figures for urban areas was 17.15 and 36.31 respectively.
49,681 households surveyed all over India	It is somewhat striking to note that 'not interested' is as much a major cause for never getting enrolled in an educational institution as for discontinuance of studies in the middle of a course. While about 50% of men do not go to school for economic reasons, participation in domestic work is a significant reason keeping women away from school.
	In rural areas, 47.61% males and 68.38% females were non-literate. Only 6.52% males and 1.98% females had reached matric (secondary and above) in rural areas.
	Ever-enrolled female SC/ST/others who discontinued at primary level reveal social group-wise levels of drop-out.
	Andhra Pradesh drop-out at primary level in rural areas for ST girls was 100%, for SC girls was 82.81%, and for other girls was 71.63%.

(Table 4.4 continued)

(*Table 4.4 continued*)

Survey, Year, Sample Size, Coverage	Main Findings
	Bihar drop-out at primary level in rural areas for ST girls was 149.64%, for SC girls was 100%, and for other girls was 78.51%.
	Kerala drop-out at primary level for ST girls was 64.16%, for SC girls was 38.50%, and for other girls was 32.27%.
1992–93 NFHS-1 (IIPS and ORC Macro 1995)	67.5% 6 to 14 age children attending schools—75.5% boys and 58.9% girls.
1994 *India: Human Development Report* (NCAER 1999) 33,000 households surveyed over 16 states of India	The enrolment rate for rural India as a whole is 71% with a gender disparity of 0.84, showing a deficit of 16% for girls. Enrolment is generally high in the southern and western states and also low gender disparity. Though the lowest enrolment was found in Bihar (59%), Rajasthan stands out both with regard to low levels of enrolment (61%) and a high level of gender disparity. Landless wage earners, STs, SCs and Muslims, and villages with low development, have very low levels of school enrolment. Enrolment rates were lowest in households in which there was no literate adult male or female: 54% for boys and 36% for girls. Ever enrolment rates for SCs, STs and Muslims was 62%.
1995–96 52nd Round National Sample Survey (NSSO) 43,076 rural households and 29,807 urban households surveyed all over India	27% of the population of age 5–24 years has never attended educational institutions at all. Another 23% in the age group 5 to 24 years are currently not attending educational institutions though they were enrolled in the past. Of them, more than 90% had dropped out before completing schooling, 21% dropping out without completing even the primary level, and another 29% dropping out before completing the middle level. Half of the population of the age group 5 to 24 is currently participating in the formal education system. The average private expenditure per student per annum works out to Rs. 501 at primary level, Rs. 915 at middle level, Rs. 1,577 at secondary/higher secondary level, and Rs. 2,923 at college level.

(*Table 4.4 continued*)

(*Table 4.4 continued*)

Survey, Year, Sample Size, Coverage	Main Findings
	For the population 15 years and above, the overall illiteracy rate is 45.7%. It is 53.6% in rural population, as against 23.0% in urban population. There is also wide disparity between males and females. Among males, illiteracy rate is 32.7% and among females it is 59.3%. Among urban males, the illiteracy rate is 14.3% and among rural females it is 68.3%. The rural–urban, male–female disparities accentuate as one moves up the educational ladder. At the postgraduate level there are 25 persons per 1,000 among urban males, 14 among urban females, 4 among rural males and just 1 among rural females.
	Gross attendance ratio for classes I to V is 85%, and for classes VI to VIII is 65%.
	Age-specific attendance ratio for age 6 to 10 is 69%, and for age 11 to 13 is 72%.
	Net attendance ratio for classes I to V is 66%, and for classes VI to VIII is 43%.
	Of the 5 to 24 age group, 53% students are in primary, 24% in middle, 19% in secondary/higher secondary and only 4% in higher education.
	6.8% students were getting scholarships, 25.6% were getting free or subsidised books, 17.9% were getting midday meals.
	268 persons out of every 1,000 persons of age 5 to 24 years have never been enrolled in any educational institution. In rural areas the number is 315 and in urban areas it is 120. Among males it is 201 and among females it is 342. Among rural females it is as high as 406. When we compare across age groups, we see that as we move from 18 to 24 years to 14 to 17, and further to 11 to 14, there is a decline in the proportion of those never enrolled, which is an encouraging sign. The trend, however, changes when we move to the 6 to 10 age group. This is because of the late entry of children into the education system. Quite a high proportion of children aged 6,7, etc., who are currently not enrolled, do join schools later.

(*Table 4.4 continued*)

(*Table 4.4 continued*)

Survey, Year, Sample Size, Coverage	Main Findings
	Gross attendance ratio is lower than gross enrolment ratio, especially for classes I to V, where the difference is about 20%. It is possible that official enrolment gets overstated when compared to actual attendance.

1996

Public Report on Basic Education in India (1999)

70% of all children aged 6 to 14 in the sample households in the PROBE states (Bihar, Madhya Pradesh, Rajasthan and Uttar Pradesh) are currently enrolled in school. This is an encouraging trend, considering that out-of-school children made up four–fifths of the 5 to 14 age group in the PROBE states as recently as 1986–87. However, this trend has to be read in the light of the fact that: (*a*) 'nominal enrolment' is a common and possibly growing practice; and (*b*) even among genuinely enrolled children, attendance rates are often low.

Covered 1,221 households in 188 villages in Bihar, Madhya Pradesh, Rajasthan and Uttar Pradesh, and 48 villages and 154 households in Himachal Pradesh

The PROBE survey found plenty of evidence of the rapid progress of schooling in Himachal Pradesh. In this state 48 villages (located in seven districts) were surveyed, and 154 households were interviewed. Among 285 children aged 6 to12 in the sample households, only five had never been to school, and the proportion currently attending school was as high as 97% for boys and 95% for girls. The fact that true drop-out rates are, in all likelihood, much lower than the official estimates is good news. However, this finding has to be read in the light of the fact that many schools practise 'automatic promotion' of children from one class to the next. Some of them learn very little in the process.

1998–99

NFHS-2 (IIPS and ORC Macro 1998–99) Covered 90,000 households in 25 states

19% of the population age 6 and above are literate, but have not completed primary school; 27% have completed primary school or middle school, but not high school; and 17% have completed at least high school. Even among the population age 20 to 29, only 31% have completed high school. Delhi, Kerala, Goa and Punjab are the only States where more than one in five females have completed at least high school.

56% boys and 43% girls in the 15 to 19 age group had completed elementary education.

(*Table 4.4 continued*)

(Table 4.4 continued)

Survey, Year, Sample Size, Coverage	Main Findings
	79% of children aged 6 to 14 are attending school. Among children aged 15 to 17, however, the school attendance rate is only 49%, indicating a high rate of school drop-out.
	For both boys and girls the cost of schooling is the most frequently mentioned reason for never attending school, and the child's lack of interest in studies is the most frequently mentioned reason for not currently attending school.
1999 State surveys (Vaidyanathan and Nair 2001)	State-specific findings: Madhya Pradesh and Maharshtra: Households with never-enrolled persons have less land and lower per capita consumption, depend more on labour for their living, and are markedly higher in proportion in case of SCs/STs. Uttaranchal: The educational status of 5- to 14-year-old children varies across occupation groups. Enrolment rates are highest among male children of cultivator households and lowest among labourers. But, somewhat surprisingly, female enrolment ratios are the lowest among cultivators and the highest among labourers. The steady increase in the number of non-enrolled children with increasing number of animals is another noteworthy feature. Enrolment rates among males and females are the lowest among SCs, and their drop-out rates are highest. Gender differentials among SCs, in both respects, are also much more pronounced. The upper castes have come close to achieving universal elementary education. Andhra Pradesh: The proportion of children currently enrolled among the poor, middle and well-to-do families (as judged by investigator's ratings) was 63.6%, 81.2% and 93% respectively. Enrolment ratios across the caste groups are not markedly different.

(Table 4.4 continued)

(*Table 4.4 continued*)

Survey, Year, Sample Size, Coverage	*Main Findings*

Kerala:
Discrimination of the girl child is no longer in evidence; in three of the villages, all of which are Muslim dominated, enrolment ratios and grade attainment rates were higher for girls, and in two villages, drop-out rates for girls were also lower.

Tamil Nadu:
Parental education and household prosperity important in determining school differentials. Differences in educational access on the basis of gender and, to a lesser extent, on the basis of caste are observed.

Uttar Pradesh:
Rampur's educational performance was poorer that Ballia's despite being economically more prosperous. SCs fared better than Muslims and OBCs in Rampur. Crucial importance of public action at the local level.

Orissa:
There are significant differences between social groups in enrolment and completion. The mean literacy rate for population aged 7 years and above ranges from 16% in a Koraput village to 70% in a Puri village in the survey. The mean for the selected villages of Koraput district (31.4%) is almost half that of Puri district (59%).

2001

Study on elementary education (Jhingran and Jha 2002) Carried out in some of the poorest parts of Bihar, Jharkhand, Orissa, Assam, Madhya Pradesh, Uttar Pradesh, Gujarat, Karnataka, Andhra Pradesh and Maharashtra, covering 1,077	Less than two-thirds (64.4%) of children in the age group 6 to 13 are currently enrolled in schools. Only about 65% of the total enrolled children regularly attend school. Regularity relatively high in the southern and south-western parts of the country. Notable inter-village differences exist in both enrolment and regularity in all districts. Although Dalits emerge as one of the most educationally deprived social groups in terms of children's school participation, there exist large intra-group variations within them. At one end, in villages like Karandi in Maharashtra and Doddathupur in Karnataka, more than 90% of Dalit children regularly attend school. At the other, in villages like Sultana in Uttar Pradesh and Doriya

(*Table 4.4 continued*)

(*Table 4.4 continued*)

Survey, Year, Sample Size, Coverage	Main Findings
households, 2,190 children and 87 school in rural and urban areas.	in Bihar, barely 20 to 25% of Dalit children attend school regularly.

2001–2

IIM studies in eight Phase-I DPEP states. Study carried out in Maharashtra, Madhya Pradesh, Chhattisgarh, Karnataka, Haryana, Tamil Nadu, Assam and Kerala, based on 30 villages in two districts of the selected states, and household surveys of all children aged 5 to 13.	State-specific findings:

Maharashtra:

In 2001 there were 2% non-enrolled children, with little social and gender difference. Overall completion rate for children in Aurangabad is close to 80% and in Osmanabad it is 74%. In Aurangabad attendance of ST boys and girls is lower than that of the general category and SC. In Osmanabad all the groups seem to have uniform attendance, higher than 86%.

Karnataka:

The total non-enrolled proportion is negligible and there is absence of social disparities in non-enrolment. Very marginal difference across gender and social groups in completion as well. Repetition rates have fallen, both for boys and girls, over time, in the lower primary classes, and the difference between boys and girls, in either direction appear to be very marginal. Belgaum had 74% completion rate and Mandya 90%.

Tamil Nadu:

Attendance rates have improved and drop-out rates reduced. Most of the drop-outs occurred during the first two grades, accounting for more than 80%. Very few children were identified as-out-of school in the survey covering 2,686 households. Most of the nearly 1% disabled children are also schoolgoing. Attendance rates are in the 80-plus range for all social groups and across gender. Cuddalore had higher than 85% completion rate, while Dharmapuri had over 60% completion.

Assam:

Almost 95% of the Hindu households in the age group 6 to 9 years are enrolled in schools in Morigaon district, and the corresponding figure for Darrang district is

(*Table 4.4 continued*)

(*Table 4.4 continued*)

Survey, Year, Sample Size, Coverage	Main Findings
	about 85%. In the case of Muslim households, the corresponding figures for Morigaon and Darang are about 85% and 82% respectively. Only 21.58% of the original stock completes four grades in four years' time.
	Madhya Pradesh: Household survey revealed that both Betul and Sidhi have 52:48 proportion of boys and girls in the sample villages. Betul and Siddhi have 93.34 and 92.34% children attending schools. Grade completion ratios are in the 60% range. There are no significant gender or social differences.
	Haryana: Grade completion rate is higher for class III than for class V. Gap between boys and girls is more pronounced at class V than at class III level.
	Chhattisgarh: Grade completion ratio is unsatisfactory both for boys and girls as 40% villages have reported 0 for girls and 50% villages have reported 0 for boys.
	Kerala: In a survey of 3,627 families, there were 120 children who were out of school. Attendance rate is more than 90%. The lowest attendance rate was with regard to ST students. The grade completion ratio is a little below 80%.
2001 Census (Registrar General and Census Commissioner of India 2001) Complete enumeration of all households in the country	For the first time the total number of non-literates has come down in absolute numbers—from 328 million to 296 million. Andhra Pradesh, Uttar Pradesh, Maharashtra, Rajasthan, Madhya Pradesh and Tamil Nadu significantly contributed to this decrease. The number of non-literates increased in Bihar. Male literacy in 2001 was 75.85% and female literacy 54.16%. Overall 65.38%. Male–female literacy gap has come down to 21.70% from 24.84 in 1991. Jammu and Kashmir, Rajasthan, Andhra Pradesh, Madhya Pradesh, Chhattisgarh, Uttar Pradesh, Bihar, Jharkhand, Orissa, Arunachal Pradesh, Assam and Meghalaya have literacy rates below the national average.

(*Table 4.4 continued*)

(*Table 4.4 continued*)

Survey, Year, Sample Size, Coverage	Main Findings
	The states that gained more than 15% points in literacy in 1991–2001 are Rajasthan (22.48), Chhattisgarh (22.27), Madhya Pradesh (19.44), Andhra Pradesh (17.02) and Uttar Pradesh (16.65).
2002	
Vimala Ramachandran's (2002) study of three states Based on studies conducted in six villages and six urban settlements in Uttar Pradesh, Andhra Pradesh and Karnataka	The relation between health and education is often perceived as a one-way street, with most discussions focusing on the role education can play in facilitating health awareness and improving the health status of individuals and communities. Usually left out of the debate is the critical and reciprocal link between health and education, specifically in relation to children, whereby poor health and nutrition act as a barrier to attendance and educational attainment/achievement. Children do not receive adequate nutrition. Most children in the surveyed households are enrolled. Many of them are also attending school, with varying degrees of regularity.
	Discussions with children revealed that a great number do not eat anything in the morning, especially girls who have little time, given their morning chores. On most days almost 10 to 15% of children (majority of them being girls) come to school without eating.
	Another significant factor that emerged was of changing social norms with regard to schooling. Discussions in rural Karnataka and Andhra Pradesh revealed that sending children to school has become a community norm. This is yet to emerge fully in Uttar Pradesh.
2003: January to April	
The Future of Mid Day Meals (Dreze and Goyal 2003) Survey of 81 villages in Rajasthan, Chhattisgarh and northern Karnataka.	Only five of 81 sample schools reported occasional gaps in the provision of midday meals. Pupil enrolment in class I rose by 15% in the sample villages after midday meals were introduced. The surge in class I enrolment is twice as large for girls (19%) as for boys (10%). In most of the sample schools children of different social backgrounds happily share a common meal. Frugal lunch menus have severely diluted the nutritional impact of midday meals.

The following conclusions can be arrived at from the assessments in Table 4.4. First, the position with regard to school participation was absolutely abysmal in 1986, at the time of the 42nd Round National Sample Survey. The non-enrolment rate of 42.79 per cent males and as high as 69.23 per cent females never enrolled in any educational institution, and a drop-out rate of 100 per cent for tribal girls in Andhra Pradesh and Dalit girls in Bihar at the primary stage in rural areas is a severe indictment of the efforts made for basic education in the first four decades after independence. Clearly, elementary education, in spite of being a professed Directive Principle of State Policy with a 10-year time frame, did not receive the attention that it deserved in most states. The fact that only 6.52 per cent males and 1.98 per cent females in rural areas had reached matric in 1986–87 confirms the poor completion of primary and upper primary education in rural areas.

Second, there has been a significant decline in the number of out-of-school children in the 1986–2003 period, even though rates of successful completion still leave much to be desired, especially at the upper primary stage. In spite of the decline in the number of out-of-school children, completion rates at primary, upper primary and secondary level indicate large gaps in gender and among social groups in most states. These gaps are larger in states performing not so well in eastern and northern India, and those lower in the better-performing southern and western parts. School participation of girls in general and from the minority community—in particular, Dalit and tribal children—continue to be much lower than for general categories in states like Uttar Pradesh, Andhra Pradesh, Bihar, Madhya Pradesh, Rajasthan and Orissa. Districts like Malkangiri in Orissa, Palamu in Jharkhand, Jhabua in Madhya Pradesh, Banswara in Rajasthan, Kishanganj in Bihar and Sonebhadra in Uttar Pradesh, with their very high incidence of poverty and impoverishment, also have large gender and social gaps in school participation. On the other hand, these gaps, at least on enrolment and school participation, have been significantly bridged in districts like Gadhchiroli in Maharashtra, Bellary in

North Karnataka, Panchmahal in Gujarat, Tirunelveli in Tamil Nadu and Mallapuram in Kerala, among others. Recent efforts to expand access to schools in Madhya Pradesh and Rajasthan have led to increased participation in remote habitations in the schooling process. It is still not clear whether the increased participation will be sustained without incremental improvements in provisioning for the low-cost schools established in these regions.

Third, the gains in enrolment do not still show substantially in grade completion rates, though some improvement is discernible in states like Karnataka, Maharashtra, Tamil Nadu, Kerala, Assam, Madhya Pradesh, Chhattisgarh and Haryana. The policy of no detention in most states masks the real transition from class to class, as it could be a case of children moving on without learning adequately, an issue that will be examined more closely in the next section. The discrepancy between gross enrolment rates published by the Ministry of Human Resource Development, Government of India, and the gross attendance rates brought out by the 52nd Round of the National Sample Survey, 1995–96, highlights the need to take enrolment figures with caution. Jyotsna Jha and Dhir Jhingran's study on the poorest districts also highlights the case of irregular attendance of those who are enrolled. In the light of no detention policies at the primary stage in most states, perhaps the real measure of grade completion will be assessment of achievement rather than a mere transition from class to class.

Fourth, the household surveys bring out the strong community demand for basic education. The poorest of the poor households want quality education for their children and there is ample indication of an aspirations revolution among the poor. What is failing them is an unprepared or under-prepared schooling in meeting the diverse learning needs of all these children. It is the private costs of schooling and non-functional schools that keep children away rather than any large-scale incidences of child labour. Vimala Ramachandran's (2002) study brings out how schooling of boys and girls has become a social norm in states like Karnataka and Andhra Pradesh, but not quite in Uttar Pradesh as yet.

Fifth, states are clearly at different stages in their efforts to provide eight years of elementary schooling to all children. There are states like Kerala, Maharashtra, Tamil Nadu, Karnataka, Mizoram and Kerala, where nearly all the children have reached school and are remaining in school for many years. There are others like Andhra Pradesh, Rajasthan, Madhya Pradesh and West Bengal where most children have started going to class I/II, but it is still not clear whether the low-cost, habitation-specific schooling facility will be able to meet the goal of primary completion. There are still others like Bihar, Orissa and Uttar Pradesh, where, some recent efforts notwithstanding, a very significant number of children continue to be out of school.

Sixth, income, gender and social group continue to matter in terms of school participation and completion, though the scenario is changing very rapidly. A substantial number of children coming to government/local body schools are from the hitherto underprivileged social groups of SCs/STs/OBCs/minorities. It is a different matter that completion rates and participation in higher levels of education indicate a continuing gender and social gap.

Seventh, there seems to be a major gain in the last few years in enrolment in states like Uttar Pradesh, Madhya Pradesh, Rajasthan, Andhra Pradesh, West Bengal, Orissa and even Bihar. Recent studies on Rajasthan, north Karnataka and Chhattisgarh reveal significant improvement in girls' enrolment on account of, among other factors, hot cooked meals. It is also a fact that a large number of initiatives in elementary education are being currently attempted and they too have had an impact on school participation. With elections to *panchayats* granting reservation for women, SCs, STs and OBCs, and the proposed devolution of powers to them, there has been a greater sense of ownership of institutions like the school/alternate schooling facilities by the hitherto underprivileged social groups. There is a social assertion by these groups, reflecting in habitation-specific schools and greater school participation. Table 4.5 tries to capture some of the changes.

TABLE 4.5
IMPROVEMENT IN SCHOOL ATTENDANCE OF GIRLS AGED 6 TO 14

States	Girls Attending Schools in 1992–93 (NFHS-1) (%)	Girls Attending Schools in 1998–99 (NFHS-2) (%)	Difference
Andhra Pradesh	54.8	70.5	15.7
Assam	66.0	75.0	9.0
Bihar	38.3	54.1	15.8
Gujarat	68.4	72.8	4.4
Haryana	74.7	85.5	10.8
Karnataka	64.4	77.6	13.2
Kerala	94.8	97.4	2.6
Madhya Pradesh	54.8	70.8	16.0
Maharashtra	76.6	86.9	10.3
Orissa	62.0	75.1	13.1
Punjab	77.8	90.0	12.2
Rajasthan	40.6	63.2	22.6
Tamil Nadu	78.7	88.5	9.8
Uttar Pradesh	48.2	69.4	21.2
West Bengal	62.9	76.7	13.8

Source: NFHS-1 and NFHS-2 (IIPS and ORC Macro [1995, 2000]).

Are Children Learning?

This section will look at whether children are learning what is expected of them. There could be three ways of making the assessment—findings of achievement studies and classroom assessments, assessing completion rates at various levels, and assessing what percentage move up to higher education. Independent studies by Vimala Ramachandran in Andhra Pradesh, Karnataka and Uttar Pradesh have pointed out how children in class III/IV in many of the schools surveyed could hardly read or write. Pratham's work in urban area schools in Maharashtra, Delhi, Patna, Vadodara, etc. also pointed out the inability of a large number of boys and girls in primary classes to read and write simple sentences. The policy of 'no detention' followed by most state governments at the primary level often conceals the actual progress of pupils as they are promoted irrespective of their achievement. Tables 4.6, 4.7, 4.8 and 4.9 try to capture the real situation.

TABLE 4.6
PERFORMANCE IN CLASS IV/V AND CLASS VII/VIII TESTS *

State	Class IV/V		Class VII/VIII	
	Boys	Girls	Boys	Girls
Andhra Pradesh	59.90	59.12	52.62	54.75
Assam	21.17	18.52	14.72	13.09
Bihar	32.14	31.86	23.87	24.00
Gujarat	53.88	54.29	59.07	63.27
Haryana	29.89	30.11	16.40	17.50
Himachal Pradesh	44.91	46.55	16.98	19.04
Jharkhand	22.89	22.60	19.97	20.19
Karnataka	59.37	60.49	44.26	48.98
Kerala	38.90	42.85	35.92	41.16
Madhya Pradesh	23.73	23.05	18.99	21.96
Maharashtra	63.16	62.38	25.34	26.98
Orissa	10.50	9.52	12.17	11.93
Rajasthan	52.50	51.22	46.97	48.48
Tamil Nadu	44.64	47.63	24.95	26.69
Uttar Pradesh	39.34	38.29	32.56	36.70
Uttaranchal	40.23	36.05	24.22	23.95
West Bengal	40.21	38.40	23.31	21.40

Source: Aggarwal (2002).
Note: *Percentage of boys and girls securing more than 60% marks.

TABLE 4.7
MEAN ACHIEVEMENT SCORES OF CLASS IV STUDENTS

State/district	Mean Achievement Score in Language		Mean Achievement Score in Mathematics	
	Boys	Girls	Boys	Girls
Haryana				
Jind	58.85	55.90	46.82	46.35
Kaithal	45.30	52.66	42.31	48.19
Chhattisgarh				
Bilaspur	53.88	50.52	41.59	38.20
Raigarh	50.12	46.06	33.17	33.93
Madhya Pradesh				
Betul	66.09	67.53	62.09	61.76
Dhar	59.94	59.33	48.13	46.01
Tamil Nadu				
Dharampuri	71.46	69.92	61.50	60.69
Villupuram	68.00	67.56	62.28	62.49

Source: NCERT (2002).

Table 4.8
The Dropping Enrolment Scenario (million)

Class	Boys	Girls	Total
I	17.1	13.4	30.5
II	13.4	10.4	23.8
III	12.2	9.6	21.8
IV	11.0	8.6	19.6
V	10.2	7.8	18.0
VI	9.4	6.6	16.0
VII	8.3	5.9	14.2
VIII	7.6	5.0	12.6
IX	6.2	4.0	10.2
X	5.4	3.4	8.8
XI	2.4	1.6	4.0
XII	2.1	1.4	3.5

Source: Selected Educational Statistics, 2000–1 (as on 30 September 2000).

Table 4.9
Where Do Children Go Post School Education?

Course	Boys	Girls	Total
Teacher training schools	57,000	60,000	117,000
Polytechnic institutes	315,000	80,000	395,000
Technical, industrial, arts and crafts schools	408,000	68,000	476,000
MBBS	88,000	60,000	148,000
B.E./B.Sc./B.Arch.	325,000	93,000	418,000
B.Ed./B.T.	70,000	52,000	112,000

Source: Selected Educational Statistics, 2000–1.

The following conclusions can be drawn from the tables. First, the performance of boys and girls in schools are dismal, considering that a large number of them complete class IV/V with less than 60 per cent marks. While marks are not necessarily the best indicator of children's performance, it does tend to indicate whether learning is taking place in a school or not. Most children completing primary classes with less than 60 per cent marks are unlikely to complete middle/secondary level schooling as the academic load increases considerably at these stages. Low mean achievement scores also indicate serious learning lacunae as most children continue to achieve far below-mastery levels in tests. It indicates major gaps in understanding levels of children. Since knowledge is incremental and depends a lot on clarity of concepts at the primary stage, most of these children are likely to have serious problems in coping with the demands of the school system at higher levels.

Second, the confirmation of children not learning enough is also deduced from the dropping enrolment scenario with there being 30.5 million children in class I and only 3.5 million continuing up to class XII. Even after assuming under-age enrolments in class I, the dropping enrolment is very significant and reflects the low level of learning taking place in the system. Most of the children are not completing the grades for which they enrolled. The 52nd Round of the National Sample Survey (Government of India 1995–96) had pointed out that 27 per cent of the 5 to 24 age group had never attended any educational institution. Another 23 per cent in the same age group were not currently attending, though they had been enrolled in the past. Of them, more than 90 per cent had dropped out before completing schooling, 21 per cent dropping out without completing the primary level and another 29 per cent before completing the middle level. Most people reach the age of 24 having failed at some level of schooling—primary, upper primary, secondary or higher secondary.

Third, even though children are reported to be progressing within the primary classes on account of a policy of no detention, in practice little learning is taking place. The experience of children of classes III and IV not being able to read and write simple sentences has been a finding in many studies, and surely indicative of something being seriously wrong. Many schools do not emphasise on reading skills and this compromises the ability of children to develop mastery in language and mathematics. Besides being proof of effective learning, reading skills are also a very important pedagogic tool in improving understanding for future learning.

Fourth, assessment of the provisions of learning at the post-basic education level, especially for those not able to cope with the rigours of secondary and higher secondary education, seem grossly inadequate. The provision for higher learning seems to be much more in the domain of those who complete higher secondary education successfully rather than those who are declared failures of the system. This explains a lot of the depression among adolescents and the mad craze for tuition shops that promise jobs. The Indian education system allows for individual excellence, but does not seem to meet the needs of mass-level skill formation and development as required.

Fifth, while the issue of relevance of basic education has been debated since colonial times, especially with the Gandhian thrust on *swavalamban* (self-reliance) and *samvaya* (integration of physical and mental development), there is not enough evidence from the states of progress towards a more relevant basic education that allows for improved mastery over nature, learning by observation, learning by doing and, most of all, learning for life. While the Sarva Shiksha Abhiyan makes learning for life a stated objective, it will have to be seen how far it is able to take the debate on education for life—rather than mere literacy and numeracy skills.

Sixth, there appears to be a curriculum load at each level. Children are finding coping with academic load increasingly difficult. It is not at all unusual to see a large number of students at various levels seeking private tutors outside school hours. Private tuition has really emerged as an industry given the high motivation of many parents for individual excellence. High curriculum load works against first- and second-generation learners, as it necessarily requires home support, which is completely absent in a large number of households. The practice of homework, therefore, ends up as one of the most iniquitous arrangements when first- and second-generation children are involved.

Operationalising the Constitutional Guarantee of Right to Education: Issues of Resource Crunch and State Commitment

The 1990s had seen a very strong articulation of a demand for education from the poorest households. Even low-cost local functional initiatives have attracted children in large numbers, in spite of a series of bad rainfall years. Poor parents understand the value of education and are willing to make adjustments to support their children, including girls, in schools. The demand for a basic education facility in every habitation has become a symbol of social assertion with hitherto unprivileged communities demanding a school of their own, however under-funded it may be. Travelling in the remote corners of Madhya Pradesh, Andhra Pradesh, Rajasthan, Orissa and Jharkhand, one is struck by the enthusiasm in the community for local education, low cost, local teacher-run facilities. Tribal girls in a Balika Shikshan Shivir in Baran district of Rajasthan, tribal girls from the KBK districts of Orissa in low-cost hostels, child labour in back-to-school camps of the MV Foundation in Andhra Pradesh, community enthusiasm for special summer camps for reading skills for urban deprived children by Pratham in Mumbai, Delhi and other cities, all tell a tale of community assertion for quality schooling. Is the State responding adequately? Are mindsets changing? Are adequate resources being provided matched with effective decentralisation and school autonomy? Are the demands of poor people for quality education being reflected in national and state level resource allocation? Do poor people really matter?

Despite the increasing demand for education, the formal system is taking a long time to improve its accountability. Education administrators are still grappling with effective and efficient management of schools, very reluctant to shed powers to elected representatives and school committees. Transfer of teachers, deployment of teachers against fake enrolments, and non-accountability of school systems to local people, continue to be in the mystified domain of powerful bureaucracies. Decentralisation is paid lip-service when it comes to shedding powers over teachers and schools. Transparency is shunned and corruption reigns supreme in many states in matters like teacher appointment and deployment. Teachers continue to dodge processes of local accountability and *sarpanch*s manage to keep communities away from exercising greater control over schools. Parent–teacher associations and elected school education committees have stepped in to demand improved schools,

but their voice is often drowned in the fathomless educational bureaucracy. Teacher development and establishment of institutions
of excellence to support this process at cluster, block, district and
state levels is still weak in many states; these institutions often being
seen as a dumping ground for those unwanted as education administrators or preferred options for those teachers not wanting to teach
at remote locations. Will we ever achieve the goals of the SSA if
we do not focus on the reform and decentralisation agenda, school
autonomy and institutional development thrust? The answer is an
emphatic no. But then, this is what the framework of the SSA ex-
pects states to initiate and adopt. The challenge of the SSA is to
change the mindset of education bureaucracies and teachers, to
make them responsible for meeting the learning needs of all children, providing all the resources at their command to do so. The
challenge is to create basic minimum learning conditions for all
children in all schools/learning centres in all habitations.

The apathy of the State reflects in the slow pace of effective decentralisation and community control for local accountability of
the school system. With the proliferation of private unaided schools
and parental preference for these, government-funded schools today
are catering largely to the poor. Any significant improvement in
their performance, therefore, will have very positive consequences
for poverty reduction. The withdrawal of children of the élite from
government schools has also led to their decline as those responsible
for maintaining government schools do not suffer if the school
functions irregularly or ineffectively. Given the political clout of
the teaching community in many states, any effort at making them
locally accountable are resisted fiercely, often with success. The
choice before the political and bureaucratic élite today is whether
to side with an unaccountable school system or to ensure that poor
children get quality education through well-endowed and effectively
managed government schools. The Kendriya Vidyalayas, Navodaya
Vidyalayas and specially-endowed schools in some states are all examples suggesting that government-funded schools can also be well
endowed.

The starting point for the SSA has been an intensive habitation-
based household survey to ascertain the status of under-14 children.

These household survey forms, stitched together, are expected to form the education register, and be available in the local school. This register, prepared in collaboration with local communities, has to be annually updated to record the progress of children in the school system. Community-owned school registers are already being maintained in Madhya Pradesh, with very effective outcomes, under the supervision of the Rajiv Gandhi Mission. Habitation planning is a reality in Andhra Pradesh. Periodic household surveys are the norm under Rajasthan's Shiksha Aapke Dwaar programme. Many chief ministers have expressed a strong political will to honour the right to education through community contact programmes, special interventions and overall support for universal elementary education. The constitutional amendment making elementary education a fundamental right along with the comprehensive SSA programme is an opportunity for states to move towards honouring the right to elementary education. It is not simply a resource issue; it is an equally important reforms issue as well, as no amount of resources can substitute for a fundamental change in the mindset of those who currently control and manage school systems.

There surely are many signs of hope. Involvement of elected representatives of panchayats and parents of children in schools has surely increased in most states. The Supreme Court's intervention for hot cooked meals is having the right impact, with more states complying with its instructions. There are more resources available at the school level to meet the contingent needs of teaching and learning materials, school repairs and maintenance, and petty grants. New textbooks are available to most students, mostly on time. School facilities have improved with the thrust on village education committee-led school construction efforts. Government and local body schools look more attractive these days than ever before on account of the fact that school maintenance support and large-scale low-cost teaching materials have been developed—even though these are not adequately used in many schools—through teacher and school grants. Teacher development programmes have increased and many states and block and cluster resource centres have started functioning effectively for teacher support. Household and school surveys have generated enthusiasm in teaching out-of-school children. A diversity of interventions like residential and non-residential bridge courses for the 9 to 14 age group have made it possible to provide for age-specific mainstreaming of older children who are out of school. EGS schools and other forms of alternative schooling in unserved habitations have led to an access revolution of sorts, however ill-equipped and under-funded the initiative may be.

Large-scale recruitment of locally selected but generally higher secondary-passed teachers at lower than pay scale has become a reality, even in states like Bihar and Uttar Pradesh, even though teacher vacancies continue to be staggering in some of the educationally backward states. While there can be no alternative to a well-paid and well-trained teacher in the long run, the evidence in the short run indicates that low emoluments are not coming in the way of teacher effectiveness. The SSA norms of a teacher for a group of 40 children, primary schools where numbers justify their conversion from alternative forms, upper primary schools as per need, possible interventions for all disabled children, and preparation of 10-year perspective District Elementary Education Plans reflecting the uncovered gaps for universalisation, are all sending very strong messages of the right to elementary education as never before. We live in times of change, times of demand for quality elementary education from the poorest households. While the SSA is a minimalist programme for guaranteeing basic learning conditions, nothing prevents the central government and states from adding on to the framework in the context of special needs. The National Programme for Girls Education in over 2,000 educationally backward blocks and the proposed residential schools for girls in remote regions are examples of how there has been a conscious effort to add on to the norms. The idea of setting up a General Council for Elementary Education under the prime minister, with representation of a few state chief ministers, and with all powers within the budgets allocated for elementary education, was precisely to move norm-based planning to more need-based planning. In many ways a norm-based planning process is a starting point for more effective need-based planning. Even when the bulk of expenditure under the SSA is for improving the formal school, a lot of the criticism is about promoting alternative under-funded learning centres. There are instances where SSA funds are actually being used to strengthen the alternative learning centre and develop it into a well-endowed formal school.

The sobering thought is that we need to move much faster both on reform and resource. The government's own assessment of resources in the financial memorandum to Parliament for the Amendment Bill to make elementary education a fundamental right was Rs. 980 billion over 10 years. Even this commitment is not being honoured in the annual allocations, significant increases notwithstanding, and is a serious cause of concern as Parliament had approved the amendment, including the financial memorandum. All arguments of fiscal constraints vanish into thin air as ultimately it is a matter of priority, a matter of whether elementary education of poor children really matters. It is mostly poor children who throng government/local body schools, and all efforts at their improvement are directly pro-poor. For a nation striving for global eminence, eight years of quality schooling for all is the minimum requirement for sustainable enhancement of human capital and banishing poverty.

There is a strong case for further improving resources for schools to ensure that all children, from diverse backgrounds, get an opportunity to learn. The Yashpal Committee had made a strong argument for one teacher for a group of 30 children. There is clearly a strong argument that the hardest-to-reach children, belonging to the poorest of households, require a stronger commitment of financial resources for their effective participation. The recent emphasis of the Supreme Court on serving hot cooked meals in schools and setting up of ICDS centres in every habitation are steps in the right direction, requiring higher resource commitments for these sectors. In the light of experiences in the field, there could be a case for modification to norms of the SSA. The General Council under the prime minister, approved for the SSA, has all the powers within the budget of the Department of Elementary Education and Literacy to innovate and modify norms. Initiatives for girls in over 2,000 educationally backward blocks and provision for residential schools for girls in remote regions under the Kasturba Gandhi Swantantra Vidyalaya Programme will add to the diversity of interventions to improve participation of poor children.

The Common Minimum Programme of the government is promising, with its emphasis on livelihood and wage guarantees for the poor, hot cooked meals for children in primary and secondary schools, and interventions to improve investments in the basic education and health sector through imposition of a cess on taxes. Creation of basic learning conditions to meet the diverse needs of all children requires greater flexibility for need-based planning. Norm-based initiatives are a first step in moving towards a rights-based perspective. Effective realisation of the goal of UEE of satisfactory quality for all would require even greater diversity of approaches.

Resource alone, however, is only part of the solution. In order to ensure that reforms effectively decentralise down to the school level, it is important to allow for local initiatives, make communities manage the affairs of the school, encourage transparency and social audit, focus on institutional capacity development for quality and excellence and, most of all, develop an accountable public system of schooling. Effective decentralisation is inconceivable without a strong emphasis on microplanning and habitation-based planning. Communities ought to have the right to plan for the educational needs of their children. Broad norms would be acceptable, but denying the community a role in planning interventions and expecting it to play a limited role in execution is not the way in which school autonomy and effective decentralisation can be nurtured. Much greater investment on developing skills among teachers and community leaders for effective management of schools is required for effective decentralised management. Forms of social audit that allow full transparency in maintenance of school records will be needed if schools have to acquire autonomy in real terms. The SSA framework provides space for a lot of such efforts, only if reform is on top of the agenda of states.

The challenge of having all children in school, all children learning and completing eight years of elementary schooling by 2010, is indeed a daunting one. It not only requires more resources; it requires major reforms as well. Reforms necessarily question existing power relations. If schools have to exercise more powers, others above in the chain have to be willing to shed powers. Similarly, for institutions (CRC, BRC, DIET, SCERT [State Council for Educational Research and Training]) to develop as centres of excellence, they have to have transparent selection criteria and clear responsibilities. Large-sized bureaucracies often cover up non-performance as the outcome orientation is weak. The challenge, therefore, is to look at a change in power relations in the school system.

The poor are demanding education. Hungry, malnourished faces thronging schools, both in rural and urban areas in enrolment drives in the month of July, is reason for hope. Not doing enough to keep them in schools will become grounds for despair. Hope never dies in a democracy. Political democracy has really moved in independent India with poor people in very large numbers participating in elections at all levels. Leaders from hitherto unprivileged communities are today in positions of power. It is an opportunity for them to honour their commitment to social justice. Remember, children not in school are from poor families in rural and urban India, mostly girls and children from Dalit, minority and tribal households, eking out livelihoods as agricultural labourers, migrant labourers, construction workers, destitute women, or lowly-paid seasonal labourers. Even they have demanded quality schooling for their children. Let democracy not fail them.

References

Aggarwal, Yash. 2002. *DPEP Universal Access and Retention: Where do We Stand? Elementary Education Report Cards*. New Delhi: NIEPA.

Bashir, Sajitha. 2000. *Government Expenditure on Elementary Education in the Nineties*. Delhi: European Commission.

Chagla, M.C. 1964. 'Presidential Address of the Education Minister to the Central Advisory Board of Education. http://www.education.nic.in/cd50years/g/12/1k/121K0301.htm, accessed on 22 December 2005.

Dreze, Jean and Aparajita Goyal. 2003. *The Future of Mid Day Meals*. New Delhi: Centre for Equity Studies.

Government of India. 1993. *Learning Without Burden: Report of the National Advisory Committee or Yashpal Committee Report*. New Delhi: Ministry of Human Resource Development.

————. 1998. *165th Report of the Law Commission of India on Free and Compulsory Education for Children*. New Delhi: Law Commission of India.

————. 1999. *Tapas Majumdar Expert Committee Report*. New Delhi: Ministry of Human Resource and Development.

————. 2002. *National Human Development Report 2001*. New Delhi: Planning Commission.

Indian Institute of Management Studies. 2001–2.

The reference here is a combination of many studies. Those references are as follows:

Chand, Sherry, P.G. Vijaya. 2002. *External Evaluation of DPEP in Karnataka State*. Ahmedabad: Indian Institute of Management.

Indian Institute of Management. 2002. *External Evaluation of DPEP in Karnataka State*. Bangalore: Indian Institute of Management.

Indian Institute of Management. 2002. *External Evaluation of DPEP in Kerala State*. Government of India (Place not mentioned).

Nayantara, S. and V. Nagadevara. 2002. *External Evaluation of DPEP in Tamil Nadu State*. Bangalore: Indian Institute of Management.

Reddy, V.N. and R. Chattopadhyaya. 2002. *External Evaluation of DPEP in Assam State*. Calcutta: Indian Institute of Management.

Sharma, R. 2002. *External Evaluation of DPEP in Maharashtra State*. Ahmedabad: Indian Institute of Management.

Singh Shailender, K.S. Sridhar and Shivganesh Bhargave. 2002. *External Evaluation of DPEP I in Chhattisgarh State*. Lucknow: Indian Institute of Management.

————. 2002. *External Evaluation of DPEP in Haryana State*. Calcutta: Indian Institute of Management.

————. 2002. *External Evaluation of DPEP I in Madhya Pradesh State*. Lucknow: Indian Institute of Management.

International Institute for Population Sciences (IIPS) and ORC Macro. 1995. *National Family Health Survey (NFHS– 1), 1992–93*. Mumbai: IIPS.

————. 2000. *National Family Health Survey (NFHS– 2), 1998–99*. Mumbai: IIPS.

Jhingran, Dhir and Jyotsna Jha. 2002. *Elementary Education for the Poorest and Other Deprived Groups: The Real Challenge of Universalisation*. New Delhi: Centre for Policy Research.

National Council of Applied Economic Research. 1999. India: *Human Development Report—A Profile of Indian States in the 1990s*. New Delhi: Oxford University Press.

National Council of Educational Research and Training (NCERT). 2002. *Student Achievement under TAS: An Appraisal in Phase I DPEP States*. New Delhi: Ministry of Human Resource Development.

NSSO. 1991. 42nd Round 1986–87, 'Participation in Education', *Sarvekshana*. XIV (3), January–March.

NSSO. 1998. 52nd Round 1995–96, 'Attending an Educational Institution in India: Its level, nature and cost 1995–96', *Report No. 439 (52, 25.2/1)*. New Delhi: Ministry of Statistics and Programme Implementation, Government of India.

Public Report on Basic Education (PROBE). 1999. New Delhi: Oxford University Press.

Ramachandran, Vimala. 2002. *Gender and Social Equity in Primary Education*. New Delhi: European Commission.

Registrar General and Census Commissioner. 2001. *Census of India 2001: Provisional Population Totals—Paper 1 of 2001*. New Delhi: Government of India.

Vaidyanathan, A. and P.R. Gopinathan Nair (eds.). 2001. *Elementary Education in Rural India: A Grassroots View*. New Delhi: Sage Publications.

5

MARGINALISATION OF THE EQUITY AGENDA

Sadhna Saxena

The unprecedented attention that elementary education in India received in the last decade and a half needs to be appraised critically. If the late 1980s and the early 1990s was the era of adult literacy campaigns, the focus shifted entirely to elementary education from 1992 onwards, with international agencies evincing keen interest in funding primary education in the developing countries. It seemed logical too as several adult literacy campaign studies showed that these campaigns created awareness and generated demand for children's education (Karleker 2004; Mukherjee and Duggirala 2002). However, this renewed focus on universalisation of elementary education (UEE) could also be traced to the much-discussed Jomtien Conference of 1990 when the first Education for All (EFA) meet was held. The Jomtien Conference was held in the context of the impoverishing impact of neo-liberal policies, including the squeezing of social sector expenditure, in many developing countries. Though universalisation of elementary education in a modern democracy committed to equity and social justice is a basic right, the issue of social deprivation is intrinsically linked to this right as the countries that underwent reforms in the 1970s and 1980s were clearly showing further marginalisation of the deprived (Graham-Brown 1991; Kumar et al. 2001a).[1] Therefore, the situation demanded an in-depth debate and investigation on such issues during the Jomtien Conference.

The Conference, however, made little attempt to relate the international debt crisis to the broader economic and political context within which education occurs. This crisis, apart from having a distressing impact on the lives of the poor, led to further deterioration of the quality of education, and drop-outs at an early age remained a serious problem (Graham-Brown 1991: 153 and 159). Instead, the Conference focused on the funding of education—offering soft loans to countries undergoing 'stabilisation' and 'reforms', and more importantly, stressing the 'privatising' of funding of education. Graham-Brown states that privatising of funding has taken place, 'not through private schools, but by mobilising private resources for education within the public sector' (the Indian situation will be discussed in later sections of this article). On the basis of extensive case studies in Southern Africa and Central America, it was emphasised that this trend, 'puts considerable pressure on the poorest families, who are also experiencing falling or stagnating income levels' (Saxena 2000: 270).

The dismal state of primary education was highlighted further during the EFA conference held in New Delhi in 1993 for working out strategies to universalise primary education in the *nine most populous* countries of the world, thus clearly indicating that education has a role in reducing fertility rates. Hence, the persistent anxiety and propaganda of the developed world about the population 'explosion' in developing countries being the cause of all the problems were also to be addressed through school education.

BASIC EDUCATION DEBATE

Problematising education of the underprivileged people, which remains a major concern for the State and the civil society, albeit for different reasons, is the primary focus of this paper. It looks at the changes that elementary education has undergone in the past decade and a half, and its long-term implications. For many years educationists have argued and studies have shown that the formal system of education is neither reaching the deprived sections nor is it meaningful. Therefore, in recent times, there have been efforts to revive the debate on 'basic education' and integrate it into the mainstream discourse to address the issue of irrelevance of formal schooling. Basic education was considered 'the most significant dissent from this (the British) system' (Shukla 1979: 2), the 'only major attempt made in our country to move education away from its colonial legacy' (Kumar 1996: 2369), and possibly a relevant one for a primarily agrarian society like India. Critics underline the fact that basic education, the way Gandhi envisaged it, was never integrated in the post-Independence education policies of India and the concept needs to be reconsidered in totality. Taking into account the high drop-out rates and the fact that only 66 per cent of children in the age group of 6 to 10 were attending primary school and only 43 per cent attending the upper primary school, a fresh debate on the fundamental tenets of basic education is urgently warranted.[2]

For planners and the policy makers, however, the appeal of basic education was primarily in its perceived potential of economic self-sustainability (Shukla 1997). The national commitment of providing free and compulsory education to all by 1960 seemed possible only through 'cost-free' basic education (Saxena 2000: 40–41). Since the Indian state is constantly 'struggling' to invent cheaper alternatives for educating its masses, the perceived potential of basic education is significant even now. Therefore, a debate on basic education has to take these two competing and somewhat contradictory object-ives/interpretations—conceptual and economic—into account. A variety of 'cost-efficient' and 'community-dependent' alternatives of elementary education for the 'unreached' masses, was devised with little financial support from the government, and they are already operational in many states, thus making it all the more important. The changes that have been introduced in the past decade draw justification precisely from the fact that the regular school system has not helped in improving drop-out rates in any significant manner. The paper looks at some of these crucial changes and interrogates the justification.

Structure of the Paper

The paper is divided into two main sections. In the first, the author summarizes issues related to targets, achievements and the poverty–education relationship. This is an indicative section, not based on exhaustive data, as the purpose is to highlight the major trends so as to contextualise the arguments of the second section which covers the major changes with policy implications for the universalisation of education. This section also deals with the wider social and political implications of such changes and locates them in the context of neo-liberal policies and underlines the contradiction between the stated goals of educating the masses and the changing reality on the ground, that is, dismantling of the existing system. The paper argues that this new phase indicates a major departure in the history of formal education. Whether it will actually help the deprived sections in accessing meaningful education for their children and help them lead a better life or further marginalise them, remains to be seen and critically reviewed.

SECTION I

The Promise of the DPEP and SSA

All centrally-sponsored programmes for improving elementary education, including the state-specific education projects in Bihar, Rajasthan, UP and Andhra Pradesh, and the ambitious District Primary Education Programme (DPEP) in 248 districts of 18 states are being integrated under one umbrella called Sarva Shiksha Abhiyan (SSA). This programme promises to provide free and compulsory satisfactory quality education to all children in the age group of 6 to 14 years, and carries a clear time frame for universalising elementary education (EE). In the SSA, for universalising elementary education, emphasis is on community ownership. Its aims as stated in the 'Framework for Implementation' are: 'to provide useful and relevant elementary education for all children in the 6 to 14 year age group by 2010', and 'to bridge all social, regional and gender gaps, with the active participation of the community in the management of the schools' (Government of India n.d.:1).

A significant caveat, however, is that relevant education for all children may not be through regular schools but through alternative arrangements, namely education guarantee centres, alternate schools and back-to-school camps. Clearly, the commitment is not to provide 'schools' as formal institutions, but through alternative strategies that are less expensive and more dependent on community resources. It is through such arrangements that the SSA programme is aiming to 'bridge all gender gap and social category gaps at primary stage by 2007 and at elementary stage by the year 2010', and universal retention by 2010 by focusing on 'satisfactory education'.

Indian education history, which is replete with failures in achieving educational goals, surely requires a deeper understanding of the fractured reality. Instead, more targets are set. Compared to SSA, the DPEP was less ambitious and in a limited time period of five years it aimed 'to reduce the differences in enrolment, drop out rate, and learning achievement among boys and girls and between social groups to less than 5 per cent, and overall drop out rates to 10 per cent reducing gender gaps' (Kumar et al. 2001a: 562).

A Brief Appraisal

ACHIEVEMENT LEVELS Despite this renewed thrust and effort, education indicators do not show any dramatic improvement in the ground situation towards achieving these goals. For example, UNESCO, which is monitoring the global progress of Education for All (EFA) targets, in its recent report clearly underlines the fact that 14 countries, most of which are from sub-Saharan Africa but also include India, show a gender parity index (GPI; ratio of female–male enrolment) between 0.8 and 0.9. In India's case it is 0.84. Thus, there was no hope for any of these countries achieving gender parity in enrolment by 2005 (UNESCO 2003). In any case, GPI only has limited significance as it is does not take into account the massive drop out, especially among girls. Also, it is widely acknowledged that the enrolment figures are generally overestimated. Hence, SSA's target of providing elementary education to all children by the year 2010 also seems far-fetched considering the high drop-out and retention rates at the primary and upper primary levels.

Even the achievement levels that are linked with the quality of education do not give any cause to rejoice. According to Jha and Jhingran (2002: 50), based on extensive fieldwork in 10 backward districts from 10 states, 'Children in class III or IV could not read or write properly or carry out simple multiplication/division exercises.' Aggarwal's earlier report (2000) on achievement studies of the DPEP showed an equally dismal picture and the latest Pratham Survey (the *Indian Express*, 13 September 2004) also demonstrates that on an average, 25 per cent of all school children cannot write a dictated sentence even at age 14. Also, 95 per cent children between the ages 7 and 10 could not do basic mathematics in Uttar Pradesh (ibid.). The 2005 edition of the *EFA Global Monitoring Report*, published by UNESCO, underlines the fact that in many low-income countries more than one-third of children have limited reading skills after several years in school (*Education Dialogue* 2005). A comparative evaluation of the education guarantee scheme (EGS) centres, alternative schools (ASs), Prathmik Shiksha Karyakram (PRASHIKA) and Eklavya done by IIM, Ahmedabad, also illustrate that the achievement levels in the EGS schools in mathematics and languages drop drastically after class III (Kothari et al. 2000). 'Even the states that have attained universal access, enrolment and retention, the quality of education is very poor,' according to Mehta (2004a: 12).

Not that any of these are profound findings in themselves. Given the declining quality of educational inputs, both academic and administrative, even as new promises and programmes are announced, nothing better could be expected. In fact, low expenditure rates (absorption of funds) in the SSA districts and its impact on quality also need to be investigated. There are reports that the absorption of funds at the district level is inadequate. It cannot be explained solely on the basis of red tapism. Bad expenditure pattern may also be an indicator of lack of creative ideas at the level where funds are controlled. SSA district-level proposals and the earlier DPEP proposals gave ample indication of lack of ideas as most of these proposals followed a standard pattern, without many insights regarding regional diversities and pluralities.

POVERTY AND EDUCATION   The Tapas Majumdar Committee Report (1999) estimated the number of out-of-school children to be about 60 to 70 million. Jha and Jhingran (2002) emphasise that 'it is not only the size of out-of-school children that poses a challenge'; in fact, recent trends in enrolment make it clear that it is more difficult for children who remain outside of the school system now, at the beginning of the new century, to get into school, as compared to those who were already enrolled in schools. The report refers to Aggarwal's (2001) study which indicates stagnation or decline in overall enrolments in many districts seen during the second half of the 1990s. This is not only in the districts 'where the age specific population ratio is on the decline; it includes many districts from states yet far from that plateau' (Jha and Jhingran 2002: 2). The authors clarify that stagnation in enrolment does occur almost universally, but only after attaining a high rate of enrolment. 'However,' they underline, 'what is really disturbing is the fact that many states or districts in educationally backward districts appear to have reached, or are going through, a period of stagnation in school participation rates at a much lower stage' (ibid.).

Mehta (2004b) also points out that despite improvements in retention rates, the drop-out rates are still high at 40 and 57 per cent respectively at primary and elementary levels. There is unevenness across districts and states. Retention rates computed during 1998–99 showed that at the primary level, 'Bihar, Rajasthan, West Bengal, Uttar Pradesh, etc. had a dropout rate higher than 50 per cent' (ibid.: 10). The report points out that the trends in growth of primary schools reveal that the rates of growth were higher during decades following independence and declined continuously thereafter. 'Growth rates in the number of primary schools and upper primary levels are low in Bihar and negative in Uttar Pradesh, the two populous states' (ibid.: 2004).

Jha and Jhingran (2002: 3) also underline the fact that, 'the available evidence, based on analyses of large sample survey-based statistics, clearly reveals that the majority of in-school children come from economically better-off and majority of out-of-school children from the poorer sections of the society'. The report asserts that the positive and strong correlation between poverty and school participation rates for children makes it clear that the issue of non-participation needs to be understood in the specific context of low-income or expenditure of households. This becomes more pertinent as there is a high incidence of poverty in India, with nearly 300 to 350 million people living below the official poverty line (ibid.: 5).[3] The report exposes a glaring disparity wherein more than 50 million children who are out of school belong to lower castes, class and Scheduled Tribes. On the basis of their study in Jharkhand, Rana and Das (2004: 1176) conclude that, 'abject poverty forces parents to employ children in activities other than studying', and 'forces many children to go out and gather their own food'. Their study shows that the intricate relationship of poverty, ill health and indebtedness also has a grave effect on enrolment and attendance. They argue that in such situations, setting up more schools and thereby increasing their numbers cannot succeed in making primary education available to all. In her recent study, Vaid (2004) also found that class emerged as a strong determinant of the relative chances of a child continuing in school.[4] Various studies show that income or expenditure poverty 'is only one aspect of deprivation'. Apart from food insecurity, illness, lack of choices and opportunities, forced livelihood options, vulnerability to crisis, and social deprivation due to belonging to an ascribed caste, tribe or religion are other crucial forms of deprivation, especially in highly stratified rural areas. These have severe impacts on education.

These findings are not new discoveries. However, they need to be reiterated as the poverty–education relationship is increasingly marginalised in the discourse of universalisation of elementary education. Such studies bring out the starkness of poverty–education correlation systematically and emphasise the need to re-examine the structural constraints in achieving universal education. They may also help in making the discourse of education more nuanced, something that has been confined to either the mechanistic target-oriented access retention levels or to the demand–supply model, and lend it the complexity it demands/deserves. The mainstream space for such a discourse is highly restricted and is informed only by the high-profile propaganda on universalisation or on the issue of fundamental rights.

A new slogan that 'a child outside the school is a child labour' and the construct that drop-outs are primarily due to bad schools, is gaining currency and acceptability (for a comprehensive discussion on child labour and education, see Krishna [1996]; Kumar [1996]; Lieten [2004] and Saxena [2000]). It is true that schools with inadequate infrastructure and other resources, corporal punishment, and caste, class and gender discrimination do contribute to drop-out rates. However, the obfuscation of these structural constraints has not helped the cause of universalisation of education. At such a juncture it becomes important to explore the relationship between the aim of universalisation of education and the current character of the state policy in light of the neo-liberals providing it a decisive direction.

Despite the overwhelming constraints and slow overall progress, if not stagnation, of the universalisation of elementary education, the call for universalisation has enormous appeal. Two notions— one, that adult ignorance and indifference, if not irresponsibility, deprive children of formal education; and two, that bad schools keep children from schools—enjoy widespread acceptability. What explains the enormous appeal of this argument in the media and among the middle class, including professionals? Is it the propaganda that illiteracy and lack of education lies at the core of a range of social and economic problems that we face, or deep anxiety that uneducated masses are responsible for backwardness? Does it also stem from the atavistic anxiety of the ruling élite that the deprived may actually subvert the agenda of the élite if not 'schooled'? Or is it because of its evident simplicity in explaining a deeply fractured world?

In the absence of a comprehensive understanding of this and much more, including the phenomenon of indifference to schooling among the economically and socially deprived sections, the age-old wastage and stagnation debate may rear its head again. This not only crucifies the 'ignorant masses' for not sending their children to schools and thus contributing to the wastage of national resources, but also legitimises the privatisation of school education and thus marginalising the issues of poverty, inequity and injustice. Comprehending the interplay of economic and social deprivation in pushing children out of the school system is important. Equally important is having an objective assessment of the relevance of the given type of formal education in the lives of these sections of society.

Undermining the significance of education is not the objective. Here, the effort is to highlight that the wider social and economic realities of children also play an important role in determining their education. Therefore, there is a need for a deeper engagement with this issue in the light of grim education indicators. Stagnation in enrolment and high drop-out rates at one level indicate the structural constraints linked to social and economic deprivation. On another level, low achievements are also indicative of the kind of educational opportunities people have access to. Thus, the interplay of a variety of deprivations either does not allow them educational access, pushes them out of the system, or offers irrelevant and meaningless education. Therefore, despite odds, whoever manages to stay in the system learns little, if at all.

SECTION II

The Three-tier System of Education for Universalisation

The promise of universalisation of elementary education (UEE) has always been accompanied by the creation of parallel and cheaper alternatives of education for the marginalised people. Even the inclusion of basic education in the Kothari Commission had more to do with its promise of economic self-sustenance and less with its conceptual thrust. The idea of non-formal education was also rooted in this search for less expensive education alternatives for marginalised groups. However, the changes of the 1990s are different. During this phase, in addition to the creation of a variety of parallel systems, old institutions were transformed in a major way that may leave them beyond recognition 10 to 20 years hence.

In this section, some of these crucial changes that have been introduced in the formal education system in the past decade are discussed. For legitimacy, these ideas are couched in emotive articulation. For example, for justifying the creation of single, ill-paid contractual-teacher-dependent and infrastructure-less EGS centres instead of regular schools in the rural area of Madhya Pradesh, Gopalakrishnan and Sharma (1998) say, 'The unreached have been reached for the first time after independence.... Generations of children have been wasted away waiting for primary education.' The central concern is whether people should accept (or resist) the kind of schooling that the State provides in the name of universalisation, and the educationists who fit themselves in this role of promoters of this agenda when their role should be to provide a critical framework for analysing such changes in a wider perspective.

The paper argues that on the one hand, through its publicity machinery and promotional materials, the State is building up a favourable environment regarding its commitment towards UEE, but on the other hand, in reality, it is gradually dismantling the existing system. Though the pace of change is uneven, it is happening across states. African and Latin American countries witnessed such transformations in the 1970s and 1980s. It began in South Asia and China in the 1990s and the process is still unfolding. Such changes create insecurity, uncertainty and fragmentation amongst the teaching community to such an extent that collective action or organised resistance becomes extremely difficult, if not impossible. Such changes are first tested in one or two states, followed by their incorporation in national policies, as was the case with the EGS and para-teacher schemes. Focus on retention, access and quality that thwart any engagement with the political repercussions are helping a smooth transition.

Para-teachers

While conducting a study in one of the tribal blocks of a district in Madhya Pradesh in 2003, I encountered an interesting situation where an active *gram sabha* was trying to tackle the issue of teacher absenteeism in their village school. The members of the *gram sabha* were very keen on a *dharna* in front of the block development officer's office to demand action against the village schoolteacher. The teacher, I was told, was generally very irregular and did not come on that particular day despite it being the mid-term examination. While the members were busy deciding the punishment for the teacher, one of the panchayat members intervened and informed the gathering that this para-teacher had not been paid for the past four months. Incidentally, such delays in payment of emoluments, especially in case of contract teachers, are a rule rather than an exception. Despite this, the members reminded each other, the teacher was attending school, cycling almost 30 km through the forest to reach their village. The discussion changed track and the members started talking about the teacher's positive contributions despite being alone in a school of more than 120 students and three classes. They reminded each other that the school had been without a teacher for more than a year until his appointment. Since then the village middle school was being run by this single para-teacher regularly, people corrected themselves.

Here was an active *gram sabha*, willing to take a teacher to task, but ran out of ideas when it was realised that the responsibility rests with the education department. Could they discern the irony of the gradual degeneration of their middle school into a barely functional, single-para-teacher-dependent set-up on the one hand, and then still retaining village-with-middle-school status in the national data on the other hand? Incidentally, this was not an isolated incident. My investigations revealed that in that particular block itself many of the regular schools were being run primarily by para-teachers—with or without a single regular teacher. With a ban on regular appointments still in force in Madhya Pradesh and the government having found various 'less expensive' alternatives for regular teachers, duly endorsed by national policies, there seems to be no going back on this strategy. With a national consensus on blaming teachers for the decay of the system, even politically aware activists seem to lose sight of the larger policy/political issues detrimental to the fate of the school system as a whole.

One of the apparent reasons for banning the appointment of regular teachers in government schools is stagnant economic growth and the rising demand for teachers with the expansion of the school system in many of the states. Economic rationalisation, however, conceals the social and political compulsions that guided such policy decisions. Though the process has rendered powerful schoolteacher unions dysfunctional, a few states have witnessed sustained protests by such underpaid and under-trained teachers. Soon after the Parliament elections in 2004, Rajasthan witnessed massive protests by thousands of para-teachers who were appointed during the previous Congress regime and promised regular appointments by the BJP. They had worked hard for the BJP during the elections and were let down by them as the government did nothing to regularise their services after coming to power. Para-teachers in Madhya Pradesh went on a statewide strike that continued for more than two months. It was an unprecedented protest, almost ignored by the national media but widely reported locally, as after police action and arrests in Bhopal the strike continued at the district and block headquarters. Similar incidents were reported from Chhattisgarh. Decentralisation of recruitments and contractualisation of teaching has not only hit the profession economically and academically, it has reduced a once-prestigious profession to a profession dependent on political patronage of either a political party or the village education committee or the *gram sabha*.

Contractualisation of teaching services is common knowledge and is also acquiring middle-class sanction as the general perception about teachers, especially village teachers, is that they do not work. With teachers' unions being rendered almost defunct, apart from sporadic protests like the ones that happened in Rajasthan and Chhattisgarh, or like the sustained struggle of teachers in Madhya Pradesh, not much is happening in restoring the professional dignity of the teachers. Legal battles that have been fought in some states have really been within the larger frame that contractualisation is a better system of jobs and winning the battles have meant only marginal improvement in service conditions (Kumar et al. 2001b). Latest data on the appointment of teachers show that except Haryana, Gujarat and the southern states (except Andhra Pradesh), all other states are recruiting para-teachers against regular vacant posts. And except for Punjab, Gujarat, Sikkim and a few north-eastern states, all others are lagging behind in filling vacant posts. In the eastern and north-eastern regions only contractual appointments are being made (Ed.Cil. 2004). A recent report on Uttar Pradesh informs that the state is in the process of appointing 31,000 more para-teachers (also known as *shiksha mitras*) to bring down the pupil–teacher ratio, and this will take the total number of para-teachers in the state to 70,000 (Shukla 2004).

Job insecurity combined with limited training, bad service conditions, low emoluments, limited or no access to academic support and a decentralised recruitment policy has actually eroded the status and authority of teachers and has been a major source of discontent and lack of motivation. Madhya Pradesh is one state where regular appointments have been banned and for over a decade the burden of universalisation and quality education is more or less on the shoulders of a variety of para-teachers. The survival of such teachers in the system is often dependent not on their sincerity and quality of work, but on the patronage of the Village Education Committee (VEC) or the village panchayat.

The emergence of the concept of para-teachers could be traced to the much acclaimed *shiksha karmi* (SK) scheme in Rajasthan that was implemented to resolve teacher absenteeism in village schools. Interestingly, this scheme came into being as regular teachers were not willing to go and stay in villages, indicating thereby a need for special planning to make the jobs in badly-connected habitations and backward villages attractive and challenging. Instead, the government opted for less expensive alternatives. From the government's own account, *shiksha karmis* were supposed to work as social workers. They were to be voluntary workers and not to be considered government employees. They are often compared to the barefoot doctors of China, and are called change agents. It is an admission of the fact that working conditions were such that regular trained government teachers were not willing to go and stay in these areas and they were obviously not expected to do social work. So, instead of improving working conditions, the state took an easier recourse by taking refuge in the argument that appointing local people would help the situation. Though such a decision had no empirical basis, it was appealing enough to allow the state to compromise on qualification, remuneration, infrastructure and working conditions in the teaching profession. The exploitation of *shiksha karmi*s has thus been justified by calling them change agents and social workers. Though according to Rohit Dhankar (2004), a major difference between Rajasthan's *shiksha karmi*s and the para-teachers is that former received better and sustained academic support.

This arrangement is not as innocent as it is made out to be. If one looks at the experiences of societies that started implementing the neo-liberal agenda a decade before India, it is evident that contractualisation of teaching services flows from overall structural adjustment policies. Cutting public expenditure on welfare programmes including health and education, privatisation of such services and restraint on wages and public sector employment are the steps for 'stabilisation' of the economy. In any case, the change agent argument fails to impress as now in most of the states para-teachers are appointed in lieu of regular teachers, and these may or may not be interim arrangements. The following story cited by Susan George, a primary school teacher in Bolivia, on strike for a living wage, may help in seeing the changes from a global perspective:

Under pressure from the IMF, the government has frozen salaries. Depending on the category, a teacher earns between [US$ 10 and 40 monthly at the May 1986 rate].... The minimum food basket as calculated by the [Central Trade Union Organisation] costs [US$ 160]. We knew that we would never get that from the government so we asked for [US$ 60]. Well, the government won't even negotiate. They just said that any teacher who wasn't in the classroom on Monday was fired and his job would be considered vacant.

I don't think enough will go back to stop the movement. Teachers all have to [take] another job anyway to survive. Some drive taxis or deal on [the] black market.

The real long-term problem is the quality of teaching. Nobody is motivated to teach with salaries like that, or to prepare the lessons. A lot of children are dropping out in the early grades now in order to work trampling the coca leaves [the first stage of cocaine processing].... The ones that do come to school are malnourished—their parents don't have enough money to feed them—and they arrive with empty stomachs so they cannot concentrate or they fall asleep in class. (Graham-Brown 1991: 39).

China has been liberalising its economy at a feverish pace and the general impression of the outside world is that considering the growth rates it is probably doing very well. However, the social consequences of economic reforms, which affect the lower strata most, remain invisible. Regarding school education, the *Monthly Review* reports:

Chinese schools have become increasingly privatized, they charge the parents steeper fees ... [and] rising school fees and low incomes are keeping an increasing number of children out of the classrooms especially in rural areas. [With the central government having] largely stopped subsidizing primary education a decade ago ... education is increasingly a luxury item in China's poorest villages, purchased only when finances allow—and far more often for boys than for girls. In some villages only 20 per cent girls and 40 per cent boys attend school. There are entire provinces where less than half of the girls attend any schools at all—and many who drop out before completing the elementary level. (2004: 54–78)

Critics argue that undue service protection for school teachers on the lines of government employees, without suitable arrangement for performance assessment and accountability, finally lead to emergence of powerful teachers' unions with stateside membership (Govinda and Josephine 2005). However, many crucial issues on which this policy shift is based have not been documented or researched so far. Trends clearly indicate that by and large it is the rural government schools and its various alternatives that cater to the deprived sections of the population which are undergoing these changes. Also, apart from the economic logic, the policy is based on the assumption that privatisation and contractualisation of services would increase teachers' accountability. However, there is neither much evidence to support this assumption, nor many studies on the working conditions, their non-academic responsibilities, quality of academic support and inputs and, most importantly, the reasons of their absenteeism. The general perception is that teachers remain absent for personal reasons, and Kingdon and Muzammil (2001) observes that teachers' political activities keep them away from school too often, reducing teaching time. A World Bank study of Karnataka and Uttar Pradesh schools, however, raises questions on such perceptions:

> Perhaps the most surprising finding from these survey data are that while the incidence of teacher absence from school is quite high, the main reason for leave is authorised leave ... unauthorised absence does not appear to be greater than 3 to 4 percent of all teachers absence on any day in the sample districts in both states. (World Bank 2004: 25)

EGS and Other Alternatives

In the Indian situation we may draw solace from the fact that we have worked out alternative strategies for reaching the unreached through EGS centres, alternative schools and back-to-school camps, as listed in the SSA's action plan. These alternatives make the education system a three-tier one—private schools, government schools and alternative arrangements for people who cannot access the regular government schools. The emergence of such alternative arrangements at the state level, and their subsequent legitimisation and appearance in the national document shows the failure of the State in providing quality education to its masses. The idea of such alternatives draws its justification by claiming that the EGS 'supplied' education to the unreached for the first time since Independence and ensures community participation. Such poorer versions of existing ill-equipped government schools eliminate whatever commitment to equity in education existed prior to this.

Participation of the community here implies withdrawal of the State, as it does not take the responsibility of providing infrastructure for such schemes. The government only provides meagre funds for one or two contract teachers and learning material. The onus of providing space for conducting classes falls on the community, an arrangement that deprives children of their right to have a decent public place for their education. Surely this distinction of public and private (somebody's house or courtyard for conducting classes) space cannot be glorified in the name of community ownership as has been done in Madhya Pradesh from where the idea originated. Although in the face of criticism the Madhya Pradesh government was compelled to construct a few buildings under this scheme, these were exceptions rather than the norm. Taking a cue from this experience, the EGS found respectable space in the national policy and now the 'community-owned' scheme for the deprived sections is firmly in place. The only systematic study of the EGS and other primary schools in the state in the context of studying the impact of education policy reforms on the school system stated the following in its conclusions:

> To conclude definitely, field work done in Shahpur and Tonk Khurd block suggests that changes taking place in the primary school supply of rural Madhya Pradesh consist in extension via division of the school system rather than its universalisation. The impact on society (and the economy) of these changes risks being limited, as it is the state's conception of education which is being adapted to current social structures rather than social structures being challenged by the introduction of the 'revolutionary' concept of universal education .... The current trend is towards making the school supply the outcome of local *market* mechanisms under the control of the same influential social groups either through decentralisation or through privatisation. A 'schooling revolution' will be achieved only if local *politics* are made to promote a democratic but radical *policy* of education for all. (Leclercq 2002: 166–67)

It is a fairly common experience that decentralisation and community participation in the stratified rural society invariably implies continued domination of influential people who can provide resources, including space, for running a centre or school. Public funding neutralises this domination to a certain extent, at least in principle, as it is a matter of right for all citizens and the school is a public place. Such is obviously not the case with individual benevolence. The deprived sections generally have no resources to contribute except their labour. Hence, such arrangements by and large strengthen the existing power hierarchy. Commenting on the impact of decentralisation in the context of setting up village education committees (VECs), Sarangpani and Vasavi (2003: 3404) state: 'These have been effective only in some villages, where the landed and relatively well off and powerful families have been able to engage with teachers and the education bureaucracy.' And the situation 'where the communities that have not been able to mobilise funds or resources such as land, or wield significant political influence, continue to be either without schools or have very inadequate structures'.

Privatisation of schools, especially at the primary levels, has also emerged as one of the ways of making the system more accountable and efficient. It is based on the assumption that people are willing to pay for their children's education. People may be willing to pay, but a majority of them who are out of the education system are also the ones who have no resources to pay. There is not much need to go into the validity of this argument as the poverty data already cited clearly defies any such claims. Dilution of the conditions for recognising private schools in various states has given a boost to the emergence of this parallel system in a big way, although in the SSA document private schools do not find a place in the list of alternatives for universalisation of elementary education. On the basis of their intensive study on private schools and universalisation strategies, De et al. (2002) say that private schools have a right to exist under the Constitution and that a pluralistic framework of education and a variety of delivery mechanisms within this framework have been in place for a long while. 'However,' the authors emphasise, 'private education initiatives have gained new prominence in recent years, though in a somewhat different way from the old— as substitute for, not supplement to, government schools.' Further, they add, 'The question is not one of permitting private schooling but of its promotion or otherwise, and even, by extension, one of revival or retreat of the state-supported school system.' (Ibid.: 132)

Another Fundamental Right

Free and compulsory education for all children in the 6 to 14 age group has become a fundamental right through the 86th Constitutional Amendment Act, 2002. In compliance with this, the first draft legislation was prepared and posted on the Web site for inviting comments from the public. The draft Bill, prepared by the previous government, was in circulation in the public domain and has been critiqued by several people (Balagopalan 2004; Sadgopal 2004; Tilak 2004) until it was finally withdrawn by the then regime. Presumably, the Bill will be drafted again. Generally, it is believed that the fundamental right will at least provide space for negotiating resources for the education of the deprived sections. Keeping this focus, the Bill has been critiqued primarily on two counts: it legitimises the two- (three?) tier system of education and its clauses regarding penalising parents or guardians of the children, which effectively puts the onus of the universalisation of education on the poor parents. In other states where such Acts existed long before the central government woke up, there are instances of penalising the parents. Whether these two factors are taken care of in the new draft is a crucial issue. The relevance of this has to be seen in the context of the SSA policy, the framework and action plan for universalisation, as the two- (three?) tier system of education flows from there.

However, the issue of the right to education has to be discerned in the context of the right to livelihood, as this has to be distinguished from the rights that are called first-generation rights, traditional liberties and privileges of citizenship: religious toleration, freedom from arbitrary arrest, free speech, the right to vote and so on. Second-generation rights are, according to Waldron (1993: 578), 'socio-economic claims: the right to education, housing, health care, employment and adequate standard of living'. And further, that 'no one can fully enjoy or exercise any right that she is supposed to have if she lacks the essentials for a healthy and active life'. And that, 'death disease, malnutrition and exposure are as much matter of concern as any denials of political or civil liberty. Where such predicaments are unavoidable, a refusal to address them is an evident insult to human dignity and failure to take seriously the unconditional worth of each person'. In the context of the rights discourse and the sense of achievement that the constitutional amendment produced, one is tempted to ask a question: how is this right in isolation going to make any difference to at least those 300 to 350 million people who live below the official poverty line and thus whose right to life is tampered with?

Concluding Remarks

The agenda of universalisation of elementary education has diminished the goal of education on the following counts:

1. The issue of equality has finally been abandoned, not in principle, but certainly in practice, at the level of policy formulation and action plan that flow from the policy statement.
2. By the inclusion of alternatives for schooling without the commitment of proper funding even for such alternatives, holding the community responsible for providing the major infrastructure facilities, and encouraging privatising of schooling, the State has ensured no education for the majority of children from a disadvantaged background.
3. Why should every child go through the experience of 'schooling' only the way it is envisaged in the agenda of universalisation of elementary education? Such and many more fundamental issues are not even considered. The role of the majority of educationists has thus been reduced to the level of promoters of the State agenda instead of critical thinkers.

Notes

1. Graham-Brown (1991: 23) writes that 'structural adjustment' has actually meant further squeezing the poor: 'The numbers of people who are living in absolute poverty—that is, unable to meet basic needs for food, shelter and clothing—has

been increasing. In Central America, for example, up to 40 to 50 per cent of the population now considered to be living in absolute poverty'. Further, 'Declining wages evidently hit the urban population hardest. In some cases the declines are the sharpest for low earners: in Chile, for example, real wages fell 16 per cent between 1981 and 1984, but in 1981–82 alone, real income for the poorest 40 per cent of wage earners fell 10 per cent. In Brazil, in 1986–87 there was a 38 per cent drop in urban wages.... For the poorest families, this means longer hours of work to provide basic needs and more family members contributing to income'.

2. More so as the situation had not improved by 2005 either. According to the *Global Education Digest* released by UNESCO, the gross enrolment ratio, which measures the number of students at a given level as a percentage of the total population in the relevant age group, stands at 71 per cent at the lower secondary level, significantly lower than the world averages of 79 per cent, closer to the West Asian averages of 69 per cent. What is worse, of all the countries in the world with a gross enrolment ratio lesser than 80 per cent, there are only eight where the percentage intake into the last grade of primary education is expected to decline by more than 5 per cent over the next six years. India is one of them. What this reflects is the high drop-out rates in our primary schools and hence the lower probability of those enrolled actually finishing primary education (*Times News Network* 2005).

3. Jaya Mehta (2004a) questions the official poverty estimates. On the basis of the Planning Commission's own definition of fulfilling 2,400 Kcal and 2,100 Kcal norms, she shows that more than 80 per cent of the population is not able to afford food that can fulfil this calorie requirements. She says, 'Effectively, 80 per cent of the rural households do not have access to an adequate livelihood resource base'. Further, she adds, 'The recognition that rural poverty in India is nearly 75 per cent and urban poverty 55 per cent changes the policy perspective drastically' (p. 33).

4. Lieten (2004: 77) who investigates the complex relationship between child labour and poverty comments, 'Children, if not protected either by family adults or by *public institutions*, may end up in an abject dependency relationship with employers who may go to various extremes in exploiting the young child up to the hilt' (emphasis added). He indicates that poverty is responsible for child labour, but there are other factors as well, and institutional protection would make a difference.

References

Aggarwal, Yash. 2000. *Monitoring and Evaluation under DPEP: Measurement on Social Impact.* New Delhi: NIEPA.

———. 2001. Progress Towards Universal Access and Retention. New Delhi: NIEPA.

Balagopalan, Sarada. 2004. 'Free and Compulsory Education Bill, 2004', *Economic and Political Weekly*, 39(32): 3587–91.

De, Anuradha, Manabi Majumdar, Meera Samson and Claire Noronha. 2002. 'Private Schools and Universal Elementary Education'. In R. Govinda (ed.), *India Education Report: A Profile of Basic Education*. New Delhi: Oxford University Press.

Dhankar, Rohit. 2004. Unpublished Theme Paper on Rajasthan Education presented at a Seminar on 'Strategies and Dynamics of Change in Indian Education', CARE India and Institute of Applied Manpower Research, New Delhi, 25–27 November.

Ed.Cil. 2004. Technical Support Group For SSA (Unpublished Report).

Education Dialogue. 2005. 'Education For All: The Quality Imperative', 2(2): 264–67.

Gopalakrishna, R. and Amita Sharma 1998. 'EGS in Madhya Pradesh: Innovative Step to Universalise Education', *Economic and Political Weekly*, 32(39): 2546–54.

Government of India. (n.d.). *Sarva Siksha Abhiyan: Framework for Implementation*. Department of Elementary Education and Literacy, New Delhi: Ministry of Human Resource Development.

Government of India. 1999. *Tapas Majumdar Expert Committee Report*. New Delhi: Ministry of Human Resource Development, Government of India.

Govinda, R. and Y. Josephine. 2005. 'Para Teachers in India: a Review' Draft report, New Delhi, NIEPA.

Graham-Brown, Sarah. 1991. *Education in the Developing World: Conflict and Crisis*. London and New york: Longman.

Jha, Jyotsana and Dhir Jhingran. 2002. *Elementary Education for the Poorest and Other Deprived Groups: The Real Challenge of Universalisation*. New Delhi: Centre for Policy Research.

Karlekar, Malavika (ed.). 2004. *Paradigms of Learning: The Total Literacy Campaigns in India*. New Delhi: Sage Publications.

Kingdon, Geeta Gandhi and Muzammil, Mohd. (2001). 'A Political Economy of Education in India: The Case of UP', *Economic and Political Weekly*, August 11.

Kothari, Brij, P.G. Vijaya Sherry Chand and R. Sharma. 2000. *A Review of Primary Education Packages in Madhya Pradesh*. Ahmedabad: IIM.

Krishna, Sumi. 1996. *Restoring Childhood*. New Delhi: Konark.

Kumar, K. 1996. 'Agriculture Modernisation and Education: Contours of Points of Departure', *Economic and Political Weekly*, 31(35–37): 2367–73.

Kumar, K., M. Priyam and S. Saxena. 2001a. 'Looking Beyond the Smokescreen: DPEP and Primary Education in India', *Economic and Political Weekly*, 34(7): 560–68.

———. 2001b. 'The Trouble With Para Teachers', *Frontline*, 9 November: 93–94.

Leclerq, F. 2002. *The Impact of Education Policy Reform on the School System: A Field Study of EGS and Other Primary Schools in Madhya Pradesh*, (CSH Occasional Paper 5). New Delhi: Centre de Sciences Humaine.

Lieten, G.K. (ed.) 2004. *Working Children Around the World*. New Delhi: Institue for Human Development, and Amsterdam: IREWOC Foundation.

Mehta, Jaya. 2004a. 'Poverty'. In Alternative Survey Group, *Alternative Economic Survey, India: Magnifying Mal-Development*. New Delhi: Rainbow, and London: Zed Books.

Mehta, C. Arun. 2004b. 'Education for All in India with Focus on Elementary Education: Current Status, Recent and Future Prospects', http://www.educationforall inindia.com, accessed in December 2003.

Mukherjee, Aditi and Duggirala Vasanta. 2002. *Practice and Research in Literacy*. New Delhi: Sage Publication.

Rana, K. and Samantak Das. 2004. 'Primary Education in Jharkhand', *Economic and Political Weekly*, 39(11): 1173–78.

Sadgopal, Anil. 2004. 'Globalisation and Education: Defining the Indian Crisis', XVI Zakir Hussain Memorial Lecture, Zakir Hussain College, University of Delhi.

Sarva Shiksha Abhiyan (SSA). 2001. *A Programme for Universal Elementary Education.* New Delhi: Department of Education and Literacy, Ministry of Human Resource Development.

Sarangpani, P.M. and A.R. Vasavi. 2003. 'Aided Programmes or Guided Policies? DPEP Karnataka', *Economic and Political Weekly*, 38(32): 3401–7.

Saxena, S. 2000. *Shiksha aur Janandolan.* New Delhi: Granthshilpi.

Shukla, Suresh. 1979. 'Indian Education Thoughts and Experiments: A Review', *Teacher Today*, October–December: 1–19.

———. 1997. 'Nationalist Education Thought: Continuity and Change', *Economic and Political Weekly*, 31(29): 1825–31.

Shukla, Shravan. 2004. 'Rs. 430 Crores for Primary Education in UP'. *Times News Network*, 10 September.

The Indian Express. 13 September 2004.

Tilak, J.B.G. 2004. 'Free and Compulsory Education: Legislative Intervention', *Economic and Political Weekly*, available at http://www.epw.org.in, accessed in February 2005.

Times News Network. 2005. 'Dream For Girls: UNESCO', 5 May. Available at http://www.timesofindia.indiatimes.com/articleshow/1098920.cms, accessed in June 2005.

UNESCO 2003. *EFA Global Monitoring Report: Gender and Education for All—The Leap to Equality*, Paris: UNESCO.

Vaid, Divya. 2004. 'Gendered Inequality in Educational Transitions', *Economic and Political Weekly*, 39(35): 3927–37.

Waldron, Jeremy. 1993. 'Rights', in *A Companion to Contemporary Political Philosophy* by Robert E. Gooddin and Philip Pettit (eds.), Oxford: Blackwell.

World Bank. 2004. *Teacher Management Issues in Karnataka and Utter Pradesh: Critical Issues in Reforming State Education Systems.* New Delhi: South Asia Development Sector, South Asia Region.

6

EDUCATE GIRLS, PREPARE THEM FOR LIFE?

Karuna Chanana

INTRODUCTION

In as much as education is a critical indicator of status, provision of elementary education and raising the status of women must be a priority for India. The central premise of this paper is that the exclusion of girls from elementary education or all of education will continue so long as schools are sites for the maintenance of gender identity and inequality with the active support of educational policies and programmes. Further, the Indian educational policies designed to promote the education of girls and women are not expected to be change agents since they are conceptualised within a narrow framework. Moreover, in spite of the insights and understanding gained from the women's movement, an overall framework which will mainstream gender and will encompass all children, girls as well as boys, has not emerged. This narrow conceptualisation has not helped in bridging the gender gap and in providing the right to elementary education to Indian girls. Therefore, while looking at elementary education and issues of exclusion and discrimination, one has to look not only at access, which includes enrolment, drop-out and retention, but also at the conceptual framework underlying Indian educational policies and programmes, which are characterised by a discourse of inclusion and exclusion (Gale and Densmore 2000).

Education has been at the centre of early (liberal) feminism and feminist educational thinking is influenced by feminist theory. The use of feminist sociological perspectives in educational theory, research, teaching and pedagogy has become central, and the contribution of feminist discourse to women's educational experience has been considerable. Feminist educational research stands at the intersection of gender and education through a variety of perspectives. There are those who explain educational inequality between women and men by differential socialisation of girls and boys (Boudreau et al. 1986; Chapman 1986; Deem 1978). Others have argued that schools reflect and perpetuate patriarchal relations (Spender 1982). Other important areas of concern are: schools and universities being sites for enacting gender; the ways in which the formal educational system is shaped by gender; the resistance of all subordinated groups, including women, to hegemonic knowledge and power; and the educational policy analysis from a gender perspective. Scholars argue that the construction of educational policy is basically political and, therefore, it fails to overcome the gender bias.

The main purpose of this paper is to analyse educational policy so as to demonstrate how it 'genders social relations' (Lesley and Watson 1999: 1). It is an attempt to put together some of the key points that I have been making in my published papers, namely, that the emphasis on the instrumental value of education in the context of girls denies them agency (Chanana 1994); that even the most informed educational policy adopts a compartmentalised approach in which, at the most, women are assigned a chapter along with separate chapters to others from the disadvantaged sections of society; that the educational policy for girls is constructed around the social roles of women (Chanana 2001); even when it overcomes the social roles as was the case with the National Policy on Education (1986) as the basic frame, the final document does not circumvent this thinking; and, further, that there is hardly any policy analysis from a gendered perspective. Therefore, a great deal has to be done before the right of women to education in India becomes a reality, and the process of exclusion and discrimination can come to an end. Therefore, the questions that need to be asked are: Why are women given education? How is the need for their education conceptualised—historically and contemporaneously?

Four views emerged regarding the need and justification for girls' education during the pre- and post-Independence period. The first view, which was salient in the pre-Independence period, was that reform in the social position of women (and education was an important instrument) would reform society. Therefore, the demand for their education arose as a concomitant of the social reform movement (Chanana 1988). These considerations had an impact on the curriculum for girls, as discussed later in this paper.

The second view or conception is based on the premise that men and women are equal and, therefore, equality is to be provided to women. It is embedded in the political ideology of democracy and equality. It assumes that equality is fundamental to a democratic society. At the time of attaining independence in 1947, when Indian political leaders decided to establish a democratic political system, promotion of egalitarianism through education was on top of the agenda. Thus, discrimination on the basis of race, caste or sex was to be eliminated. This view was incorporated in the Constitution.

Although there are a number of institutions that reproduce inequality between women and men, what imbues education system or school with special significance is the contradictory role assigned to it. Since the Industrial Revolution, education has been regarded as the instrument for promoting social mobility and eliminating inequality. It has also been the central parameter in discourses on development, change and modernisation. However, many sociologists also regard it as central in reproducing inequality. Thus, the views about education range from optimism and positive expectations to negative perceptions related to perpetuation of inequality, domination and hegemony. Yet both groups of sociologists also recognise its instrumental value in promoting equality under certain conditions. Thus, education remains a contested site in sociological discourse.

Although initially feminist educational theory also agreed with this formulation, yet by the 1980s 'feminist critiques of social democracy bit deeper and deeper, challenged liberal philosophy at the heart of educational policy and the specific sets of relations constructed within the liberal democratic state and its institutional arrangements' (Arnot 1993: 46). Arnot maintains that research on women in the 1970s highlights an increasing disillusionment with the 'social democratic principles underlying educational and social policy. Thus, many of the central beliefs of social democratic principles, such as equal opportunity and universalism, have been challenged by feminist theory and research as they were in sociology and educational discourse'.

The third conception of women's education emphasises the need to develop all human resources (men as well as women) for the development of a society. Thus, the development of society is dependent on women and men, and any view of 'development' must not omit them. It is argued that the lacuna so far in development-oriented programmes has been their focus only on men to the exclusion of women, and that education is a necessary precondition for the development of all human resources and for equality.

Moreover, in recent times, gender as a principle underlying distribution of resources and entitlements within the household and the society—namely, education, economic rights, health care and political participation—has become crucial in educational discourse due to the linkages of education with indicators of social development. In this discourse, education is viewed as an important resource to which, historically, women have been denied access (Dreze and Sen 1995).

Recently, there have been critics of this approach because it denied women agency. They argue that this discourse on the education of girls assigns a utilitarian function to female literacy and education (Gale and Densmore 2000: 9). For example, female literacy and education is socially desirable because it leads to reduction in maternal and child mortality, increases female literacy and education, and is good for the general well-being of the family. The assumptions underlying this position are two-fold. First, women lack what education is expected to give them, that is, they lack the information and knowledge to reduce/plan childbirth, to increase child survival rate, etc. In other words, the role of female literacy in social development is emphasised. It also assumes that planning a family, ensuring good health and child survival is the responsibility solely of women as mothers. Men/males have been absent in this discourse.[1]

Development, thus, has had a dynamic definition, changing from GNP as its main indicator to human development, with gender development now constituting important dimensions of societal development. What emerges in the debate on development is the pre-eminence of the instrumental value of education and the need to bring women into the educational stream so that society benefits from their education.

The fourth, and most recent, conception underscores equality and empowerment of women as the aims of education which were articulated in the NPE (1986). It is now generally accepted that education, as a source of equality and empowerment—both at the individual and collective levels, is imperative for women, who constitute half of humankind, if societies have to develop in any meaningful way. For the first time there was a shift from the means to the ends perspective at the policy level. However, in spite of this shift, the policy has been criticised for reinforcing patriarchy, and this aspect is discussed later.

However, none of these conceptions questions the existing structure of social relations and social roles of men and women, or visualise the use of education as a tool to transcend the social division of labour within schools and society. Moreover, there are no debates around the education of boys. The exclusion of boys from the discourse on education for girls indicates an assumption that the goals of education for boys can be assumed and taken for granted. Is it because education is a means for girls and an end for boys?

Female Sexuality and the Exclusion of Girls from Education

Although declarations have been made by the Government of India time and again that elementary education is a right, yet there is a gap between promise and practice. This is because rights can be granted in theory and laws can be set in place to spearhead change, but social reality takes longer to change. Also, there is a simultaneous process of exclusion and inclusion of girls from schooling, which has to be seen and understood with reference to the societal concern with protection of female sexuality and the attendant notions of female purity/impurity. This is linked to caste status, and the honour of the agnatic kin group and familial consideration put severe constraints on the schooling of girls and women. This has to be seen along with the practice of female seclusion or *parda* and segregation, especially around puberty, to control female sexuality (Ahmad 1985: 16–19; Minault 1981: 87–88; Papanek and Minault 1982). These social practices led to the exclusion of girls from public spaces. Formal education or schooling involves moving into public spaces, interaction with males (in co-educational schools and with men teachers); or being socialised (through the curriculum) as boys; and supposedly moving away from the eventual goal of wifehood and motherhood (Chanana 1993: 87, 2001: 38).

Thus, familial and societal concern with protection of female sexuality accounts for whether girls have access to education. It also determines the quality, type and duration of education they receive, and what they do with it later, that is, whether they work or not, and what kind of jobs they take up, whether they work to earn before or after marriage. Furthermore, adaptations to changing situations are basically adjustments that do not call for social structural changes, or changes in sex role stereotypes, or question the basic premises of the value system surrounding female sexuality.

Therefore, it is critical to have an understanding of the nature and functioning of familial socialisation as the process of gender construction and its impact on the education of the girl child. Socialisation and formal schooling or education interact and react with each other. Both are processes of social control and train the individual to conform to the expectations of the social group. Although the family is the site of primary socialisation, schools are sites of secondary socialisation, and generally reproduce primary socialisation. Protection of female sexuality and 'purity' are central to the socialisation of the female child, and socialisation practices and their different significance for boys and girls are crucial to uncover the constraints imposed on girls' and women's education (Chanana 2001:38). If this is the social context, then do the latest official instruments transcend these constraints?

THE PRESENT CONTEXT

Several developments in the recent past have brought primary education to the centre stage. For instance, the introduction of economic liberalisation in 1991 pitted primary education against higher education. Since then it has become an accepted part of the public discourse on education. It is integral to the official discourse and is reflected in the policies, programmes and funding pattern of higher education. It is also being promoted by national non-governmental organisations and international development agencies. Although the entry of Indian NGOs has been salutary, the entry of international agencies has been criticised by scholars and activists in the field. In fact, international agencies are competing with one another for a share of the cake in the field of primary education. Three implications of the shift in the government's position deserve serious consideration.

The first is the use of external funds in primary education from the early 1990s. The District Primary Education Programme (DPEP) was started in 1994 with a soft loan from the World Bank. This was a departure from the post-Independence policy of the Government of India of self-reliance in education, and reflected a dilution of the state's responsibility to universalise elementary education.

The second relates to the reduction of the constitutional goal of providing free and compulsory education from eight years to five years of primary education (Chanana and Rao 1999: 445; Sadgopal: 2004: 60). The World Bank provided the soft loan to promote primary education under the highly publicised DPEP, and the Indian government willingly accepted this dilution and became an active partner of international funding agencies and their agenda. According to Sadgopal (2004: 60), it was not only a matter of primary education of five years instead of eight years of elementary education, but 'the state is rapidly abdicating its constitutional obligations towards the provision of elementary education of equitable quality for all children'.

Third, higher education is pitted against primary education as if they were two isolated parts of the system. The holistic view of education was given up for a fractured view, thereby defusing the focus from the larger philosophical and pedagogical goals of education. If primary education provides the roots of higher education, the latter provides support through the development of curriculum, pedagogy, training of teachers, etc.

In addition, three new instruments have been made available by the government, which raise hopes of those interested in education to rethink elementary schooling and its impact on girls. The first relates to the 73rd and 74th amendments of the Constitution, which decentralised schooling and brought it within the purview of the local self-government or *panchayati raj*. The second is the 86th Amendment Bill, 2002, which makes education a fundamental right for children between 6 and 14 years of age. The third is the Sarva Shiksha Abhiyan, launched at the end of the Ninth Five-Year Plan, a programme that promises to universalise elementary education for all children between 6 and 14 years of age throughout the country (Government of India undated). At this juncture, reflection and rethinking are critical and all the more necessary given the continued problem of non-enrolment, drop-out, poor quality of schooling, coupled with the marginalisation of girls, especially those from the Scheduled Castes and Tribes and rural areas.

It is by now a well-known fact that the gender gap at all levels of education has been persistent since Independence. Even though statistics show that this gender gap has decreased, it is also true that it is nowhere nearing closing. In other words, the enrolment of girls continues to be lower than that of boys. Further, the drop-out rate among girls is higher, which has an impact on the retention rate. Additionally, three-fourths of out-of-school children (33 million out of 44 million) are girls (Government of India: 2001: 42). A majority of them belong to the Scheduled Castes and Tribes, minorities, and from rural and inaccessible areas. Moreover, poverty

208 ◆ Karuna Chanana

affects girls more than boys (Filmer and Pritchett 1999). Nevertheless, the social, regional and economic diversity of India has also to be taken note of while one is looking at the gender dimension of elementary education. For example, specific states have been identified as being very backward in education generally and in the education of girls specifically.[2] There is enough data to show that a sizeable proportion of out-of-school drop-outs, working children, non-enrolled children, children of migrants and the poor, and the disabled are girls (Government of India 2001: 42). These trends are reflected whichever way one presents the statistics, that is, whether one is looking at gross enrolment rates, net enrolment rates or at completion rates. It is also true that while caste, tribe and economic factors keep girls from specific social groups out of the schools, socio-cultural factors, cutting across class, caste, tribe, rurality and so on, keep all girls out (Chanana 2001).

Is the conceptual framework underlying most policy instruments, apparently informed with this understanding, able to transcend the constraints imposed by social reality? If not, how then can education be an instrument of social change in the lives of girls and women? It is contended here that a set of considerations flowing from the concern with protection of female sexuality and the feminine role have had an effect on formulation of policies. For example, what subjects to teach or not to teach girls in schools—a concern that has been there ever since formal education was introduced for girls in colonial India.

ELEMENTARY EDUCATION: POLICY INITIATIVES

Curriculum content and its relevance for the social role of girls has been a salient issue since the late 19th century. For example, the Indian Education Commission (1882–83) dealt extensively with female education and made several recommendations. Even as early as that there was an awareness that girls may not attend full-day schools, that incentives such as scholarships and waiver of tuition fee had to be provided; that female teachers were needed to attract girl students, and that schools had to be situated in suitable localities. So far as the curriculum and teaching were concerned, 'the standard of instruction for primary girls' schools be… drawn up with special reference to the requirements of home life, and to the occupations open to women… that the greatest care be exercised in the selection of suitable textbooks for girls' schools…' (Garg 2001: 233). The Educational Policy of 1904 mentioned the social customs of the people that act as barriers to female education. In spite of this, the government supported it through scholarships and fees because 'far greater proportional impulse is imparted to the educational and moral tone of the people than by the education of men' (ibid.: 257). The Educational Policy of 1913 continued in the same vein. Although it noted that social customs differ in different parts of India, it recommended that 'the education of girls should be practical with reference to the position which they will fill in social life. It should not seek to imitate the education suitable for boys' (ibid.: 289).

This kind of argument continued throughout the colonial period with a few exceptions. It was argued by social reformers and 'enlightened' Indians that schools should offer relevant curriculum and subjects to girls. In the colonial period the majority view was that the school curriculum should be different for girls and boys. It should meet the special needs of girls (Chanana 1988). Arguments were given that even though men and women may be emotionally and intellectually similar, psychologically and physically they were different (Chiplunkar 1930: 232; Siqiera 1939: 129). However, there were some exceptions to the majority view. For example, Choksi (1929: 68, 72) and Menon (1944: 17) argued that the primary function of education should be to inculcate critical thinking, particularly at the university stage. According to Choksi:

> It is doubtful whether a university can so circumscribe cultural aims as to propose and equip women as housekeepers, wives or even mothers. Its great aim should finally be to produce accurate, far reaching and critical thought. (1929: 65)

Menon (1944), far more radical than Choksi, mentioned that the clamour for a change in curriculum came mainly from men. She also emphasised the need for intellectual training and suggested that mathematics, physics and social sciences should not be excluded from girls' curricula even though certain subjects meant only for them might also be included.

Hannah Sen (1938) and Hansa Mehta (1945) took a middle position. They agreed that the curriculum for girls had to be related to life and home and, therefore, domestic science should be part of the curricula. However, Sen also said that:

> It seems paradoxical that, while the progress of higher education has reduced the inevitability of marriage as the only career for women, greater stress is being laid on the study of domestic subjects. The present attitude is but a reaffirmation of the age-old principle that, whether women marry or follow other pursuits, on them will devolve the main task of managing the home, at least for decades to come. (1938: 100–101)

Mehta favoured a broad-based curriculum that would include what was offered in the general curriculum along with subjects meant for girls so that they could make a choice. In other words, even if a woman's social role is highlighted, school and home were not perceived as incompatible.

The post-Independence period is also not free of these concerns because political freedom did not bring with it an overnight change in sex roles and expectations from formal education. Nonetheless, the resolve to universalise elementary education was incorporated in the Constitution. There was also the awareness that the Indian society is far too complex and heterogeneous for a uniform programme. This framework was reflected in the Constitution in which

> minorities needed to be brought into the mainstream, Scheduled Castes and Scheduled Tribes required social justice and equality. Women, on the other hand, deserved equality. Thus, Constitutional provisions were made to achieve these aims, specially, those relating to the first two categories.... (Chanana 1993: 69)

The major concern about the minorities and the Scheduled Castes/Tribes relates to the fulfilment of Constitutional provisions. Women have neither enjoyed similar concern not legal backup. Subsequently, the policymakers looked at the three social categories in isolation of one another instead of treating equality as the overarching parameter and looking at girls within all the social categories. As a result of the fragmented approach, subsequent policies have lacked an overall conceptual framework.

However, there has been much better articulation of the aims of education for women as a result of the women's movement during the last 20 years (ibid.: 86). As a result of this, the NPE (1986) articulated the goals of education for girls and women as equality and empowerment as is evident in the following quote:

> Education will be used as an agent of basic change in the status of women. In order to neutralise the accumulated distortions of the past, there will be well-conceived edge in favour of women. The National Education System will play a positive, interventionist role in the empowerment of women. It will foster the development of new values through redesigned curricula, textbooks, the training and orientation of teachers, decision-makers and administrators, and the active involvement of educational institutions. This will be an act of faith and social engineering.... The removal of women's illiteracy and of obstacles inhibiting their access to, and retention in, elementary education will receive overriding priority. (NPE 1986: 6)

It was an improvement on the earlier policy documents and government instruments in that it brought together the insights and understanding gained from research and action by the women's movement. Therefore, equality and empowerment were well thought out and debated upon before they were incorporated in the NPE (1986). For once the focus was on women themselves and not on their instrumentality. This reflected a marked improvement in articulating the goals of education for girls. A notable example of how a proper perspective and understanding before the policy initiatives are put on the ground is the 10+2 system at the school level. According to this decision of the government, school education was to be of 12 years' duration all over India and science a compulsory subject for all students up to class X. This resulted in girls taking to science and in eliminating discrimination against them by the family and school. Till date this is a notable example of a gender-positive initiative.

Unfortunately, over time, the focus on education as an end, by itself and for itself, in the context of women[3] has been diluted. It is another matter that policy diluted this goal through some other provisions, for example, the introduction of an alternative to formal education (non-formal education) for girls, which will be discussed later.

Programme of Education (POA) (1992) continues the thrust of the National Policy on Education (1986). It states:

> Education for Women's Equality is a vital component of the overall strategy of securing equity and social justice in education.... [W]hat comes out clearly is the need for institutional mechanisms to ensure that greater sensitivity is reflected in the implementation of educational programmes across-the-board.... [I]t should be incumbent on all actors, agencies and institutions in the field of education at all levels to be gender sensitive and ensure that women have their rightful share in all educational programmes and activities. (Government of India 1992: 1)

It devotes the first chapter to education for women's equality followed by a chapter each on the education of the Scheduled Castes, Scheduled Tribes and Other Backward Sections, minorities, handicapped, etc. It focuses on the role of education in changing the status of women, but stops short of presenting a conceptual framework for this purpose. In continuation of the programmes and strategies of the NPE (1986), it limits itself to suggesting ad hoc and piecemeal strategies, such as, opening boarding schools and alternative schools, and Early Childhood Care and Education (ECCE) centres, setting up alternative schools, thereby accepting the sex role stereotypes about girls. According to Sadgopal (2004: 27), the Indian government has willingly surrendered to the international agenda:[4]

> Significantly, the Jomtien–Dakar Framework does not the even refer to patriarchy as an issue and essentially reduces girls' education to merely enrolling them on school registers and giving them literacy skills. This is exactly what happened when World Bank-sponsored DPEP adopted Mahila Samakhya.... [I]t became a mere girl child enrolment programme.... Unfortunately, the notion of gender parity (ratio of enrolment of girls and boys) in UNESCO's EFA Global Monitoring Report 2003/04 reinforces this confusion. Also, the World Bank diluted the goal of women's education to just raising their literacy

levels and productivity (rather than educating or empowering them).... The Dakar framework has now added ambiguous notion of Life Skills that seems to be yet another mechanism for social manipulation and market control of the adolescent mindset, particularly the girls. (2004: 27)

Research and action have provided enough feedback to understand that there is a need to identify girls in all groups among the minorities, the disabled, the urban deprived, those living in isolated areas, among certain castes and tribes, and among working children. (Government of India 2001: 6). However, educational policy documents continue to use a compartmentalised approach to education. For example, a separate chapter is generally written on the education of girls, and others on the education of the Scheduled Castes and Tribes, another on children with disability, one on child labour, the urban disadvantaged, etc. Each of these chapters may not refer to gender. In other words, gender may be excluded from the social groups based on caste, tribe, disability and working status of the children. These then become exclusive categories and not inclusive as they are expected to be. As new groups are identified, such as working children or children with disability, gender is not necessarily included. There is a considerable time lag between the identification of a new parameter (such as disability or working status) and its incorporation in policy documents. Even then the integration remains at best fragmentary or compartmentalised.

This approach has led to another anomaly. Even the most well-worked-out policy documents mention separate strategies for improving the enrolment and retention of girls and children from other social groups and categories. For example, the NPE (1986) devotes a section to the role of education in promoting equality. It underscores the twin dimensions of education, namely, the removal of disparities and equalisation of educational opportunities. Strategies are outlined separately for women, the Scheduled Castes, Scheduled Tribes and minorities. However, their specific needs and suggested strategies are neither integrated, nor an overall comprehensive framework provided for the education of all the disadvantaged groups (Chanana 1993: 86). This happens even when the problem is of a general nature, for example, out-of-school children (because they dropped out or never enrolled) who have to be given education. Again, non-formal education for children of the 9 to 14 age group was meant mainly for girls who were out of school. It was to be provided for two to three hours in the evening so that girls could assist with domestic chores (Chanana 1996: 374) and sibling care during the day. The implications are that the social roles of girls need not change, and their poor parents need not be given proper employment and wages. Instead, a parallel and alternative system of education with lesser financial, human and pedagogical inputs, such as the non-formal system, will provide equality in terms of access/enrolment and quality of education. In other words, education is viewed as an instrument of reinforcing the traditional sex role division. 'This implied the willingness of the policymakers to adjust with, rather than challenge, the gender stereotypes of the role of girls in domestic chores and sibling care. In this sense, NPE 1986 legitimised both child labour and patriarchy' (Sadgopal 2004: 11).

The 10th Plan document on elementary education (Government of India 2001: 7) is critical of earlier programmes, which were 'disjointed in nature' because their targets were either specific regions or merely covered specific aspects of elementary education or did not cover the whole country. It is proposed in the 10th Plan 'to have a holistic and convergent approach'. It mentions a two-pronged approach that will mainstream gender and also introduce specific schemes for the promotion of education of girls and women. For example, it is mentioned that all the programmes will continue even though educationists have criticised them, notably the DPEP, for reinforcing gender differences and patriarchy (Sadgopal 2004: 6). When specific schemes are mentioned, such as the National Programme for Education of Girls at the Elementary Level (NPEGEL), the fragmentary approach is very evident although there is also recognition that girls are the most disadvantaged in all the identified social groups.

The SSA aims to universalise elementary education for the 6 to 14 age group by the year 2010. The purpose is to bridge the social, regional and gender gaps. Community participation is central to the programme. One section is devoted to the coverage of special focus groups. The first one is on the education of girls. Like the

10th Plan paper, it also mentions that the emphasis will be on 'mainstreaming gender concerns in all the activities under the SSA programme.... Every activity under the programme will be adjudged in terms of its gender component'. (Government of India 2001: 40) It also mentions that girls from among out-of-school children, especially girls from disadvantaged groups, have to be taken back to school. There is also mention of local contexts. But then, almost in continuation, one reads 'relating education to their life'. Is it not going back to the old paradigm?

A notable refrain in the policy documents is that the education of girls should be relevant and should prepare them for life (ibid.). Nowhere is it mentioned that education should prepare all the children for life. What should one infer from this differentiation in policy perspective? Is it not obvious that while there is need for differentiation, through affirmative action, at the implementation level, there is need to have a common conceptual framework?

In addition, one has to look at the bifurcation of elementary education into primary and upper primary schools (Nayar 2002). This division in the structure of the schools and their physical location affects girls much more than the boys. The transition from primary to middle school corresponds with transition from girlhood to womanhood, that is, puberty, and the social concerns mentioned earlier affect the decision of the parents to withdraw them from school. Furthermore, this institutional arrangement assumed, after the independence of the country, that every child who is able to access primary schooling will not be able to or will not be interested in completing the upper primary grades. How else is one to explain the acceptance of different norms for the primary school and for the upper primary schools, and also the fact that classes I to VIII are not taught in one school? While the primary school had to be set up within a distance of 1 km of the village, the upper primary school was to be set up within a distance of 3 km. Thus, children who could not walk that distance were automatically excluded from upper primary schooling. This was in spite of the fact that the Constitution promised free and compulsory schooling for the first eight years. Were these norms not in violation of the constitutional promise of universal education? If children cannot physically access upper primary schools, how does one ensure universal elementary education? The 10th Plan also mentions that the primary schools are to be upgraded to upper primary schools if norms permit (Government of India 2001: 44). The question is: why not change the norms?

Moreover, there is the problem of social access, which is pertinent in the case of young girls who are not allowed to go to school that are not at a safe distance from their homes.[5] This has been known for a pretty long time to the policy makers, educational administrators and government, yet till date primary schools are not upgraded to upper primary schools. In fact, if education in rural areas has to be made accessible up to the elementary level, a new thinking has to go into it.

CONCLUSION

The persistent gender gap in education indicates that policies have not been implemented realistically. It is also not enough to formulate policies and programmes or to enact laws because even the best ones may not be implemented. Compulsory elementary education is a very good example. Again, even the official stance of positive discrimination in favour of the Scheduled Castes and Tribes does not benefit their women (Chanana 1993). Moreover, there is discrimination at the implementation stage when young girls receive fewer and lesser benefits from various schemes, and when the State and the households spend less on their education, or when the parents do not send them to schools because they provide domestic help (ibid. 1996).

In addition, large numbers of out-of-school girls are a symptom of systemic failure and of the State's inability to provide this basic human right to them. Socio-cultural biases and the emphasis on domestic role are almost universal, yet their combination with poverty has an extremely detrimental effect on the participation of girls in education.

The impact of privatisation of education, due to economic liber-alisation and globalisation, is expected to be adverse. There are more unaided expensive private secondary schools than government schools in Delhi. There is enough information to substantiate the point that parents spend less on their schoolgoing daughters than on the sons (ibid.), and they prefer to send sons to private schools and daughters to government schools. Although macro statistics are yet to be put together, it is a foregone conclusion that girls are more likely to be excluded from this kind of education. Further, the impact of market forces in determining the choice of subjects and future options will also discriminate against girls. Sadgopal (2004: 60) has this to say about globalisation and the international agenda on India's education:

> Women will be turned into a marketable commodity, thereby further strength-ening the patriarchal stranglehold. Girls' education will be aimed at turning them into mere transmitters of fertility control, health or nutritional messages and making them 'efficient' producers for the global economy; their right to education and development as a human will be further marginalised.

As stated earlier, socialisation of girls and the gender-based div-ision of labour determine whether girls will be sent to school, for how long and why. In other words, gender ideology underlies the societal perceptions of the goals of women's education. Therefore, the parameters of educational policy, which delimit women's role as well as the functions of formal education, need critical examin-ation because they continue to affect the approach and programmes relating to elementary education of girls.

> Gender operates in a manner so that women are at the bottom of all the groups. Thus, gender becomes an all-encompassing negative parameter con-ferring cumulative and competing disadvantages on women in their race for equality (as women), for social justice (as Scheduled Caste/Scheduled Tribe women) and for mainstreaming (as minority women).... While the constitu-tional safeguards reflect the hierarchical and fragmented social reality, the educational policy and programmes are unable to take this into account. They are also unable to perceive the disjunction among the sectoral aims of education. It is also problematic to 'mainstream' one section, provide social justice to another and equality to those who are members of all sections of society. (Chanana 1993: 90)

To reiterate:

> Educational policies and programmes are rooted in social values and premises. Even when they are made gender inclusive, they are constantly subverted by the gendered vision of parents, administrators, policy makers, and teachers who are the custodians of formal education. Thus, the process of subversion continues unhindered.[6] This subversion may be conscious and explicit or indirect and implicit but it is fine-tuned to familial and societal expectations, socialisation and sex role stereotypes. It is possible to move along with every stage of the life cycle of a girl through school and college to highlight the concerns around female sexuality and female body that colour and determine the options available to her and the options she makes. Thus, schooling of girls is essentially embedded in the societal context even though it provides an expanded space for growth to women. It ensures that women remain passive actors in the process of schooling, do not question the patrifocal ideology and do not transgress the social boundaries and work within the accepted system of values. In fact, schools and schooling become active instruments of cultural reproduction and social control. (Chanana 2001: 57)

The educational discourse emerging from the development and modernisation paradigm imbues education with the powers of engineering societal change at the collective level. Within this paradigm, the individual who experiences mobility and attitudinal change through education assumes the role of the change agent. This model assumes a positive relationship between formal education, occupational mobility and change. Formal education bestows necessary skills for the market and also 'modern' attitudes suited for a changing society, while the school is a site of transformation of individuals. It is ironical that this is not expected from girls' education. They are denied agency because the goals of familial socialisation and schooling as processes have to converge. Thus, they continue to remain objects, not subjects, of social policy.

Policy makers do not want to learn from experience because programmes that excluded men, such as the family planning programme, and those that excluded women, such as the community development programme, failed to achieve their goals and have been critically evaluated for this lacuna. While differences between women and men are to be recognised, one has to be conscious 'that a reductive notion of femininity has underpinned many of the exclusions women face, and in arguing that some attributes are inherently feminine we find ourselves on weak ground when arguing that others are not. Gender is either a social construct or is not a social construct' (Lesley and Watson 1999: 2).

Moreover, preparation for life, making education relevant, and imparting of life skills are indeed very desirable goals of education; yet they should be meant for all children who enter the school system. It will also depend on how 'relevance', 'life skills' and 'preparation for life' are defined. Lesley and Watson (ibid.: 6) refer to the embeddedness of women's exclusion in some of the critical concepts in social policy discourse. Therefore, the discourse of inclusion and exclusion has to be replaced with an inclusive discourse of difference (Gale and Densmore 2000: 123).

We need policies to neutralise or circumvent the ideological, structural and familial impediments so that the educational facilities are fully utilised by girls. However, even though there is an apparent shift in emphasis in educational policy from equal educational opportunity for men and women to education for women's equality and empowerment, the instrumental value of education for women remains paramount. Sadgopal (2004: 59) argues that exclusion and discrimination are inherent in the present operating education policy, and instead of focusing on implementation, 'attention must remain focused on analysis of the character of the policy itself' (1999). Rees (1999) contends that it is possible to integrate equality into all policies and programmes, from the stage of formulation to implementation. What is needed is a paradigm shift. According to Lesley and Watson (1999: 1), 'There are many ways in which the... state both constructed and was underpinned by, delineated roles for women, mainstream social policy analysis remains sadly uninformed by questions of gender'.

Is it not time that the debate on girls' education and the role of the state begins to focus on girls themselves and also integrates it with that of boys or for all children at the conceptual level before formulating a policy? In other words, common goals be identified for all children and gender concerns be integrated in the overall policy? What is pertinent is that education should be a means as well as an end, for both boys and girls. In other words, education should be not only a means (instrumental value) for societal improvement, but also for the sake of women as persons, for knowledge and for self. Without this shift in perspective, universalisation of elementary education is unlikely to be achieved in view of the paradoxical situation of India's commitment to promoting universal elementary education, and the large gender gap in the educational field.

The history of women's education reveals a dialectic between the demand for women's education and the opposition encountered in the process: how to live up to the promise of education and also perform the feminine role. The state policy can neutralise the adverse impact of socio-cultural practices. Further, emphasis on social access (Acker 1984) should not be an excuse to encourage conservatism; educational policies have to be informed by social sensibilities, but be forward looking in mainstreaming gender.

Notes

1. Scholars and social activists have criticised the lack of focus on men in family planning programmes. Socially and politically this makes sense. Socially because the well-being of the family in a patriarchal society may, at least, provide educational access to girls. Politically, too, in the same vein and in a society where gender overlaps the other parameters of poverty, caste, tribe and rurality, those in charge of education may at least push it forward to support family and society.
2. The seven states in the north-eastern region are socio-culturally different from the rest of the country (Chanana 1993). Some of the states have a majority population of tribals. Here poverty does not impact gender differences adversely nor is the gender gap in literacy and education as wide as in the rest of India (Srivastav and Dubey 2002).
3. Although the 10th Plan mentions self-esteem and self-confidence of girls through education, it does not articulate it within any framework.
4. The latest example is the *India Education Report* (Govinda 2002), which has chapters on all these groups. Except for the chapters on Dalit children and tribal children, gender is not identified as a parameter.
5. Economists have started using economic jargon in explaining the problems in elementary education. For example, instead of identifying barriers to the universalisation of primary education, the World Bank report talks of supply-side factors that influence enrolment and attendance.

6. For instance, when feminists raised the issue of 'home science' being labelled a feminine discipline, they were arguing for a broader framework and for making it gender neutral. But several élite private co-educational schools in Delhi discontinued this subject, thereby closing the option of a career (as home science schoolteachers) to women. Perhaps considerations of cost went into this myopic decision because home science entails setting up laboratories. It also meant saving on teacher salary.

References

Ahmad, Karuna. 1985. 'The Social Context of Women's Education in India, 1921–81'. *New Frontiers of Education*, 15 (3): 1–36.

Acker, Sandra. 1984. 'Women in Higher Education: What is the Problem?' In S. Acker and P.D. Piper (eds), *Is Higher Education Fair to Women?* Surrey: Society for Research into Higher Education and NIER.

Arnot, M. 1993. 'Introduction'. In M. Arnot and K. Weiler (eds), *Feminism and Social Justice in Education*. London: Falmer Press.

Boudreau, F.A. and Wilson, M. (eds). 1986. *Sex Roles and Social Patterns*. New York: Praeger.

Chanana, Karuna (ed.). 1988. 'The Social Context of Women's Education in India, 1921–81'. In K. Chanana (ed.), *Socialisation, Education and Women: Explorations in Gender Identity*. New Delhi: Orient Longman.

Chanana, Karuna. 1993. 'Accessing Higher Education: The Dilemma of Schooling Women, Minorities and Scheduled Castes and Tribes in Contemporary India'. In P.G. Altbach and Suma Chitnis (eds), *Reform and Change in Higher Education in India*. New Delhi: Sage Publications.

————. 1994. 'Social Change or Social Reform: Women, Education, and Family in Pre-Independence India'. In Carol C. Mukhopadhyay and Susan Seymour (eds), *Women, Education and Family Structure in India*. Boulder: Westview Press.

————. 1996. 'Gender Equality in Primary Schooling of Girls in India: The Human Rights Perspective', *Journal of Educational Planning and Administration*, 10 (4): 361–81. New Delhi: NIEPA; also in J.B.G. Tilak (ed.), 2003, *Education Society and Development: National and International Perspectives*. New Delhi: APH Publishing Corporation.

————. 2001. 'Hinduism and Female Sexuality: Social Control and Education of Girls in India', *Sociological Bulletin*. 50 (1): 37–63. Also in S. Rege (ed.), 2003, *Sociology of Gender: The Challenge of Feminist Sociological Knowledge*. New Delhi: Sage Publications, pp. 287–317.

Chanana, Karuna and S.S. Rao. 1999. 'Primary Education in India: Some Policy Perspectives'. In *Basic Rural Infrastructure and Services for Improved Quality of Life* (Vol. II, Proceedings of the NIRD Foundation day Workshop). Hyderabad: National Institute of Rural Development.

Chiplunkar, G.M. 1930. *Scientific Basis of Women's Education.* Poona: S.B. Hudlikar.

Choksi, Mithan. 1929. 'Some Impressions of Indian Women's Colleges'. In Evelyn C. Gedge and M. Choksi (eds), *Women in Modern India.* Bombay: D.B. Taraporewal Sons.

Deem, Rosemary. 1978. *Women and Schooling.* London: Routledge and Kegan Paul.

Dreze, Jean and Amartya Sen. 1995. *India: Economic Development and Social Opportunity.* New Delhi: Oxford University Press.

Filmer, Deon and Lant Pritchett. 1999. 'Educational Enrolment and Attainment in India: Household Wealth, Gender, Village and State Effects'. *Journal of Educational Planning and Administration,* 13 (2): 135–64.

Gale, Trevor and Kathleen Densmore. 2000. *Just Schooling: Explorations in the Cultural Politics of Teaching.* Buckingham: Open University Press.

Garg, B.R. 2001. *Policy Documents on Indian Education.* Ambala Cantonment, Punjab: The Associated Press.

Govinda, R. (ed.). 2002. *India Education Report: A Profile of Basic Education,* National Institute of Educational Planning and Administration, New Delhi and UNESCO: Oxford University Press.

Government of India, (undated). *Sarva Shiksha Abhiyan: A Programme for Universal Elementary Education: Framework for Implementation,* Dept. of Elementary Education and Literacy, New Delhi: Ministry of Human Resource and Development.

Government of India. 1992. *Programme of Action,* 1992. New Delhi: Ministry of Human Resource Development.

———. 2001. *Working Group Report on Elementary and Adult Education: Tenth Five Year Plan 2002–2007.* New Delhi: Department of Elementary Education and Literacy, Ministry of Human Resource Development.

Lesley, Doyal and Sophie Watson (eds). 1999. *Engendering Social Policy.* Buckingham: Open University Press.

Mehta, Hansa M. 1945. *Post-War Educational Reconstruction: With Special Reference to Women's Education in India.* Bombay: Pratibha Publications.

Menon, Lakshmi N. 1944. *Position of Women* (Oxford pamphlets on India Affairs, No. 2). Madras: Oxford University Press.

Minault, Gail. 1981. 'Sisterhood or Separation? The All-India Muslim Ladies Conference and the Nationalist Movement'. In Gail Minault (ed.), *The Extended Family: Women and Political Participation in India and Pakistan.* New Delhi: Chanakya Publications.

National Policy on Education (NPE). 1986. New Delhi: Ministry of Human Resource Development, Government of India.

Nayar, Usha. 2002. 'Education of Girls in India: An Assessment'. In R.Govinda (ed.), *India Education Report.* New Delhi and UNESCO: Oxford University Press.

Papanek, Hanna and Gail Minault (eds). 1982. *Separate Worlds: Studies of Purdah in South Asia.* New Delhi: Chanakya Publications.

Rees, Teresa. 1999. 'Mainstreaming Equality'. In Lesley Doyal and Sophie Watson (eds), *Engendering Social Policy.* Buckingham: Open University Press.

Sadgopal, Anil. 2004, *Globalisation and Education: Defining the Indian Crisis* (XVI Zakir Hussain Memorial Lecture). New Delhi: Zakir Hussain College, University of Delhi.

Sen, Hannah. 1938. 'Education of Women and Girls'. In Shyam Kumari Nehru (ed.), *Our Cause: A Symposium by Indian Women*. Allahabad: Kitabistan.

Siquiera, T.N. 1939. *The Education of India: History and Problems*. Madras: Oxford University Press.

Spender, Dale. 1982. *Invisible Women: The Schooling Scandal*. London: Writers and Readers.

Srivastav, Nirankar and Amaresh Dubey. 2002. 'Elementary Education, Poverty and Gender Differentials in North-East India: Some Issues'. *Journal of Educational Planning and Administration*, 16 (3): 375–98.

7

TERMS OF INCLUSION

DALITS AND THE RIGHT TO EDUCATION

Geetha B. Nambissan

INTRODUCTION

The decade of the 1990s witnessed considerable efforts by the State and civil society in India to universalise elementary education. While free and compulsory education for all children up to the age of 14 years was written into the Directive Principles of State Policy of the Indian Constitution in 1950, it had been reduced to the level of rhetoric by the constant setting and resetting of official deadlines over the years, completely oblivious of ground realities in education. What has happened in a little over a decade was a change in both the international and national scenario in relation to the priority given to education and the efforts to ensure that education is the right of every child. Internationally, conventions such as the Rights of the Child and declarations at Jomtien and Dakar, the availability of aid for education, donor pressure to achieve stated goals, and successive human development reports that highlighted India's dismal record in education, created an environment in which the Indian State was obliged to set in motion new policy initiatives and programmes to bring all children to school. There has also been a significant focus by the judiciary as well as NGOs and citizens groups in India on the right to education. More recently, the corporate sector has also come forward with independent initiates in primary education as well as in support of government programmes of universal elementary education (UEE).

A significant emphasis in policy and programmes has thus been on hitherto educationally deprived groups such as Dalits, Adivasis and minorities (and girls) who comprise the majority of children who are out of school. These are children who belong to socially vulnerable groups, denied education not only because of poverty but also because of low status derived from their position in the traditional social structure in relation to caste and culture. In addition, the fact of generations of educational deprivation has also meant that these children come from non-literate or poorly schooled backgrounds that are unable to provide the necessary cognitive, language and social skills that make for relatively greater school readiness among the more privileged classes. Thus, these communities are not easily able to access schooling, and when they are in a situation to do so, often do not have the economic, social and academic wherewithal to complete at least eight years of basic education. Given such a scenario, what does the right to education for hitherto educationally excluded groups really mean in substantive terms? What is the magnitude of the task, and what are the critical issues that need to be addressed?

In this paper the focus is on the education of Dalits (Scheduled Castes) in the light of the fundamental right to education. I have written on the education of Dalit communities, emphasising that their caste status as former 'untouchables' is still a barrier to school entry and influences their experience of education (Nambissan 1996). I have also highlighted the growing inter-regional and intra-caste variations in school participation among Dalits, and pointed to the need to address educational disparities that are quite visible within these communities (Nambissan and Sedwal 2002). In the discussion that follows, I reiterate these as issues that need to be addressed if Dalit children are to realise their right to education. However, greater emphasis is placed on the 'institutional framework' that has come into place in the wake of policy initiatives for UEE, more specifically on the increasing stratification of schools on the one hand, and the setting in place of decentralised and participative structures for public participation in and academic support for education on the other. I argue that this framework has important implications for the terms of inclusion of Dalit children in education. I view inclusion not merely in relation to quantitative indices of school entry, attendance and completion rates that are being presently used to assess social parity, or equality of educational opportunity as understood in policy documents. But following Kabeer (2000), I view inclusion in education as a far more complex process that positions social groups differently in relation valued resources: knowledge, skills and cultural attributes, future opportunities and life chances, sense of dignity, self-worth and social respect. Kabeer's notion of 'adverse incorporation' or 'problematic inclusion', as against 'privileged inclusion', draws attention to the importance of interrogating the process of institutional inclusion of hitherto excluded groups from the per-spective of equity—that is, against the criteria of social justice and fairness.

Situating the education of Dalits in the context of poverty, hierarchical caste relations and an increasingly stratified school system, I argue that while the large majority of Dalit children are now being included in schools at the point of entry, the terms of their inclusion in relation to institutional structures and processes are discriminatory. However, I suggest that the institutional interventions in primary/elementary education also provide opportunities for enabling education among disadvantaged groups, and must be explored and strengthened. I have based the discussion that follows mainly on research studies and surveys (of the late 1990s) so that the context in which the right to education must be realised is in focus.

Education Policy Frame and the Right to Education

The right to education must be seen in conjunction with policy framework laid down by the State for the universalisation of elementary education. The thrust in the National Policy on Education (Government of India 1986) was on universal access, enrolment and retention up to 14 years of age, and improvement in the quality of education to enable all children to achieve 'essential levels of learning' (Government of India 1992: 18). More recently the objectives laid down for the Sarva Shiksha Abhiyan (SSA) emphasise that all children will complete five years of schooling by 2007, eight years of schooling by 2010, and provision of education of quality (SSA document undated). The perspective in relation to educationally deprived groups has been to 'equalise educational opportunity by attending to the specific needs of those who have been denied equality so far' (Government of India 1992: 9), and to 'bridge all gender and social category gaps at the elementary level' (SSA document undated). Thus, the policy objective has largely been to bring excluded groups such as the Scheduled Castes and Scheduled Tribes on par with the general population in terms of enrolment, retention and learning levels (attaining minimum levels of learning). However, the process of schooling, which is integral to the quality of the learning experience and hence equity in education, has received little attention.

Institutionally, the 1986 policy brought in the non-formal system of education (NFE) ostensibly to meet the needs of children who could not access formal education and remained outside the school system. The NFE was closed in 1997 in response to criticism that it served as a parallel, inferior stream of education. The alternative school system that claims parity with regular primary schools has been put in its place. In 1994 the District Primary Education Programme (DPEP) provided a major thrust to primary education, targeting children hitherto out of school and emphasising quality of schooling, and creating district, cluster- and village-level structures that would facilitate decentralised planning, community participation, academic support and monitoring of education. The SSA has also laid emphasis on 'community ownership' of the school system.

The 86th Amendment to the Constitution is an important step in the process of UEE as it makes education for children a fundamental right and not merely a directive principle of state policy.

It has been critiqued for a number of reasons such as its narrow coverage of only the 6 to 14-year age group and the glossing over of concerns of quality, both of which are likely to be detrimental to the schooling of marginal groups whose access to early childhood care and preschooling, as well as quality education is far poorer than that of the middle classes/higher castes. The draft legislation makes a distinction between schools, alternative schools and transitional arrangements for education (that are especially targeted at hitherto out-of-school children among whom Dalits predominate) and fails to provide pedagogically meaningful minimum norms for infrastructure, basic facilities and teacher qualifications in alternative/proposed 'transitional' schools. It also appears to make the management and administration of schooling more bureaucratic and duplicates authority structures at the local level. In what follows, I discuss the substantive implications of the right to education for Dalit children given their social and economic context, the institutional structures they engage with, and their learning experiences within schools.

DALITS: SOCIAL AND ECONOMIC REALITIES

What is the status of Dalit communities in India today? While the situation from all accounts has improved and the majority no longer lives in the inhuman conditions that was their lot even 50 years ago, they still occupy the lowest echelons in Indian society both economically and socially. Dalits predominate the more marginal groups in rural areas as land-poor agricultural labour, and can be found largely engaged in wage labour and menial services in urban areas. Data on poverty ratios indicate that the proportion of Dalits below the poverty line (36.2 per cent in rural and 38.6 per cent in urban areas) was significantly higher than that of the non SC/ST population in both rural (21.6 per cent) and urban India (23.7 per cent) in 1999.[1] Their low social and ritual status in rural society is compounded by their economic dependence on higher (and dominant) caste groups, rendering them vulnerable in the context of inter-caste relations.[2] Scholars have observed that incidents of blatant untouchability are less visible and are now restricted mainly to the private sphere, especially in urban areas. However Dalits continue to live in clusters physically segregated from other households in villages in India, and are often relegated to the most inhospitable terrain of the village with poorest access to basic facilities and amenities:

> The SC clusters often happen to the more difficult localities in terms of access and facilities. If it is a low-lying area without transportation in one village, it is located on a hilltop in another. This has severe implications for the daily lives of adults as well as children. They have to walk longer for fetching water, fuel wood and work, and in some cases have to remain cut-off for months together during the rains.... Further these are the last clusters to receive facilities and services which usually are brought to high caste localities. Thus SC communities are discriminated against in location of facilities and services and other benefits provided under different schemes. (Jha and Jhingran 2002: 92–93).[3]

Dalit communities are not homogeneous and they live in a wide range of social situations. The traditional social oppression of Dalits is linked to their position as 'untouchables' in the caste system whereby they were prohibited from owning land and other assets, and denied access to education. The nature of caste relations and how it has historically and in more recent times influenced access to resources, opportunities and livelihood strategies of Dalits has been critical. Where Dalits have been able to access alternative sources of income, they are less bound to the oppressive caste framework of economic and social relations. Jha and Jhingran's study indicates that non-traditional opportunities for Dalits as a result of economic changes has meant a decline in their dependence on high-caste families, 'reduction in the practice of attached labour', 'greater negotiation power with local landlords', and 'greater ability to survive and cope' (2002: 99). Education has been an important channel for social mobility, and Dalits who had a relatively early exposure to education because of historical and social circumstances were able to benefit from the policy of reservations in the public sector in post-independence India. Adult franchise and democratic politics have facilitated social mobilisation and political assertion by Dalit communities in which educated youth are seen to play an important role in these movements (Pai 2000). However, only a small section have reaped the benefits of formal education and the occupational opportunities that it provides access to, and the majority of Dalit families 'happen to be over-represented among the poorest, the landless, the low-paying, low-skilled wage earners and illiterates, categories that signify deprivation and vulnerability' (Jha and Jhingran 2002: 83).

PARTICIPATION IN SCHOOLS IN THE 1990S: ENROLMENT, ATTENDANCE AND RETENTION

School participation data from the NFHS (1998–99) (IIPS and ORC Macro 2000) for the 6 to 14 age group indicates that the task of ensuring that all children are receiving education is an enormous one. As seen in Table 7.1, by the end of the 1990s, there was still 16 per cent of the 6 to 10 age group and 23 per cent in the 11 to 14 age group not attending school. The percentage of non-attendance was higher in rural (19.3 per cent) as compared to urban areas (9.7 per cent), and girls as compared to boys (23.4 per cent and 15.4 per cent respectively in rural areas). The proportion of schoolgoing children from Dalit communities had significantly increased in the 1990s. However, non-attendance among Dalits was higher than in the general population (around 20 per cent in the 6 to 10 and 29 per cent in the 11 to 14 age group in 1998). Inter-caste disparities of the magnitude of over 10 percentage points can be seen if attendance rates of Dalits and 'other-caste' children (a category that excludes Other Backward Castes) are compared (for instance, 76.1 per cent and 87.3 per cent of children in the 6 to 14 age group respectively were attending schools). Inequalities on the basis of gender are pronounced and are far sharper when attendance rates among Dalit girls are compared with 'other-caste' girls even in the primary schoolgoing age group (for instance 72.3 per cent and 84.2 per cent respectively in rural areas) as well as 'other-caste' boys (90.5 per cent in rural areas).

TABLE 7.1
HOUSEHOLD POPULATION AGED 6 TO 17
ATTENDING SCHOOL BY GENDER, RESIDENCE AND SOCIAL GROUP IN INDIA,
1998–99 (%)

Age (Years)	Total			Rural			Urban		
	Total	Male	Female	Total	Male	Female	Total	Male	Female
Dalit									
6–10	79.5	83.6	75.1	77.3	82.0	72.3	86.6	88.6	84.3
11–14	71.0	78.4	62.9	67.4	76.6	57.4	78.1	83.3	72.1
6–14	76.1	81.5	70.2	73.4	79.9	66.5	82.8	86.2	79.0
15–17	45.8	55.2	35.8	41.3	52.1	29.9	57.4	63.2	51.2
Other Castes									
6–10	89.6	91.8	87.2	87.5	90.5	84.2	93.3	94.0	92.5
11–14	84.3	88.3	80.0	80.8	86.8	74.4	89.8	90.5	89.1
6–14	87.3	90.3	84.1	84.7	89.0	80.1	91.8	92.4	91.0
15–17	63.0	69.6	56.3	56.1	67.2	45.2	73.6	73.0	74.2
All									
6–10	83.6	86.7	80.3	80.7	84.6	76.6	91.3	92.4	90.1
11–14	77.1	82.7	71.2	73.2	80.7	65.4	86.2	87.3	84.9
6–14	80.9	85.0	76.5	77.7	83.0	72.1	89.0	90.1	87.8
15–17	54.3	61.8	46.6	48.6	58.8	38.3	66.7	68.2	65.0

Source: NFHS-2 (IIPS and ORC Macro 2000).

Intra-regional variations in school attendance rates can be seen among Dalit groups across the country. Primary school attendance rates range from a high of over 94 per cent among Dalit children in Kerala, Tamil Nadu and Maharashtra to a low of 76.2 per cent and 73.7 per cent in Uttar Pradesh and Rajasthan respectively.[4] In the former states attendance rates of Dalits compare well with that of other children. Comparison across age groups suggests that there have been significant improvement in attendance rates among young Dalit children in the 1990s. Attendance rates in the 6 to 10 age group in all these states increased by more than 10 percentage points over that in the 11 to 14 age group (the largest gains being among girl children in rural areas; in Rajasthan, for instance, the increase was to the tune of more than 20 percentage points) in all these states, pointing to the growing demand for schooling among Dalits.

While the proportion of Dalit children who enter school has increased significantly in the last decade and more, successful completion of eight years of elementary education is important if education up to 14 years is to be ensured in substantive terms.[5] The decline in school attendance rates in the older age groups is indication enough that large numbers of children leave school well before the age of 14 years. While this may be so for the child population in general, the rate of discontinuation appears far higher for Dalits as compared to higher-caste groups. NFHS data show that only around 50 per cent of children aged 10 to 14 years (the broad age group factors in for late entry and stagnation) completed primary school, and 42 per cent have completed middle school in 1998–99 (IIPS and ORC Macro 2000). Dalits perform even more poorly where school completion rates are concerned, particularly in comparison with children from other castes. The proportion of Dalit children who have completed primary schooling was only 43 per cent (as compared to 58 per cent for other castes), and middle school around 42 per cent (as compared to 63 per cent for other castes) in the respective age groups. The World Bank (2003) has computed primary school completion rates of children aged 12 years and 16 years from the NFHS-2. Primary school completion rates for Dalits are relatively high in Kerala (96 per cent as compared to 100 per cent for the other castes). However, the proportion of children who completed primary school is relatively low in states such as Maharashtra (79.21 per cent) and particularly Tamil Nadu (41.96 per cent). Rajasthan (35.15 per cent) and Uttar Pradesh (30.52 per cent) figure at the lower end as far as completion rates for Dalits are concerned, the lowest surprisingly being West Bengal with a shockingly low rate of only 19.28 per cent of Dalit children aged 12 years having completed primary school. Middle school completion rates for Dalit children at age 16 range from a low of around 21 per cent in Bihar and 31 per cent in Rajasthan to 74 per cent in Maharashtra, 63.89 per cent in Tamil Nadu and 90.8 per cent in Kerala (ibid.). The 'caste gap' in school completion rates can be seen in all states.

There are two points of concern that emerge from the earlier discussion. First, a significant proportion of children continue to remain out of school, particularly in the younger age group, which suggests that school entry for a section of children is still a problem, particularly in the educationally backward states. Second, the relatively low school completion rates in 1999 highlights the fact that despite efforts towards Education for All (EFA) and UEE gathering full steam from the early 1990s, schools were unable to retain the majority of children even till the end of the primary stage of education. That caste status is an important barrier to school completion is seen in the fact that school attendance and completion rates for Dalit children are well below that of the other-caste groups in most states, the magnitude of disparity varying across states. Even states that have been able to bring the majority of Dalit children to school, such as Tamil Nadu and Maharashtra, appear to have failed to ensure school completion for a significant proportion of children, pointing towards the need to integrate concerns of completion of elementary schooling and quality of education with that of universal school enrolment.

CASTE, POVERTY AND SCHOOL ACCESS

One of the continuing casualties of 'ex-untouchable' caste status is easy access to schooling. Though the official position is that primary schools are available to as many as around 95 per cent of the population within a kilometre of their habitation, a closer look at the available data as well as recent research suggests that lack of easy access to schools for Dalit children is likely to continue to be an obstacle to their education. In many instances this follows from the segregated pattern of living in rural India, where Dalit house-holds are usually in clusters that are on the outskirts of the villages and at a distance from higher-caste habitations. Schools serve not only as learning spaces, but also as election offices, polling booths and marriage houses. The politics of school location ensures that they are usually located in upper-caste habitations, making them not only physically distant from Dalit habitations, but often socially inaccessible as well. Navigating their way into upper-caste habitations may prove daunting for Dalit children, and instances have been reported of their encountering hostility and even being barred from entering these areas (Nambissan and Sedwal 2002).[6] Further, Dalit clusters are located in the more inhospitable terrain in villages and are often vulnerable to rains/floods, thus cutting them off from the main village where the school is usually located (Jha and Jhingran 2002: 93–94).

Until the late 1980s, policy efforts to increase access of Dalits to schools were largely limited to relaxing of norms for the estab-lishment of schools in predominantly Dalit habitations. Thus, though the official norm was that habitations with a population of 300 and more were entitled to a primary school within 1 km, for Dalits (and tribals) this norm was relaxed to a population of 200 and more. However, since Dalit habitations formed part of larger villages, official distance norms were met even if schools were lo-cated within upper-caste habitations, often resulting in physical but not necessarily social access for children from these commu-nities. Data from the All India Education Survey (AIES) in 1993 showed that Dalit habitations did not differ significantly from general rural habitations where access to schooling within a kilo-metre was concerned. Around 82 to 83 per cent of these habitations had access to primary schools within this distance (NCERT 1999). However, the proportion of Dalit habitations with a school (37 per cent) was smaller than that was available within rural habitations in general (50 per cent). Again, access is more favourable for Dalits where they are in higher numerical strength. For instance, more than 90 per cent of Dalit habitations in the population slab of 2,000 and more have schools. But the majority of Dalit habitations are relatively small. As many as 50 per cent have a population of less than 300 persons and only around 21 per cent of these have primary schools within the habitation (Nambissan and Sedwal 2002: 78).

The DPEP placed special emphasis on universal access through formal or non-formal schools[7] equivalent to formal schools. The latter emerged as the Alternative School (AS) programme in which the problem of inadequate access to schooling received prominence. By 2001 there were more than 58,000 AS in DPEP (phases 1 and 2) states, accounting for as much as 10.3 per cent of the total enrolment in schools in these states.[8] The Education Guarantee Scheme (EGS) that was initiated by the Madhya Pradesh Government and specifically targeted towards 'school-less' habitations received prominence. That physical and social access was a major barrier to the schooling of Dalits (and other educationally deprived groups) was clear as these communities overwhelmingly came forward to enrol their children in AS. In Madhya Pradesh, as many as 24 per cent of primary school enrolments were in EGS centres that attracted a large number of Dalit girls because it was also possible for them to combine schooling with their other responsibilities. Though there is every effort to project the AS programme as comparable with formal schools, it has introduced another tier within the publicly funded school system. Thus, as a consequence of the initial glossing over of the vulnerability of the education of Dalits within local-level caste dynamics and the politics of school location, their habitations by default became the sites of alternative schools that expanded access to schooling, but one that was informed by watered-down norms as compared to regular government schools.[9] This will be discussed in greater detail in a later section.

Poverty and insecure livelihoods are also important factors that impinge on school enrolment and continuation in schools. Table 7.2 gives the distribution of school attendance by economic status or standard of living index (SLI). As can be seen, attendance rates are almost universal in households in the highest SLI (SLI-3) category. The proportion of children attending school falls in household in lower SLI. When attendance rates are compared between Dalits and other castes, it can be seen that in each SLI category Dalit children's school attendance rates are poorer than that of 'other-caste' children. Disparities in attendance rates in the 6 to 14 age group are most pronounced between Dalit (64.8 per cent) and other-caste children (70.2 per cent) in the lowest SLI category (SLI-1), suggesting that Dalit status compounds the disadvantages that the poor face in the education of their children. The interlocking of poverty, caste and gender makes Dalit girls among the most vulnerable in relation to schooling. Only 44.1 per cent of Dalit girls in the 11 to 14 age group were attending schools in rural areas as compared to 55.4 per cent of other-caste girls and 68.2 per cent of Dalit boys in the same age group (see Table 7.2).

A number of studies have suggested that poverty as a barrier in the education of the poor has been exaggerated and that there is growing demand among marginal groups for educating their children.[10] Parental aspirations for education for their children cited in research as well as the increasing enrolment/attendance rates recorded in national surveys have been highlighted to draw attention away from the earlier emphasised lack of demand for education to the poor quality of its supply. The latter has been highlighted as one of the primary reasons for children remaining out of school rather than the poverty of the household as reflected in the drawing upon of children's labour and the costs of schooling. However, more recent research suggests that poverty is likely to continue to be critical barrier to school entry and retention. In 1994 a national survey conducted by the National Council of Applied Economic Research (NCAER) quite clearly points to the burden of costs of schooling for the poorest segment of rural households among whom the annual expenditure on education was around Rs. 510 per annum (Shariff 1999: 280). The Pratichi Trust reports that in the West Bengal villages covered by their study, yearly expenses on education even among poor agricultural labour households were a minimum of around Rs. 200 per year per child, with the relatively better-off families paying much more. The cost of private tuitions alone (out of reach for many among the poor) is estimated at a minimum of around Rs. 200 per child per year. Dalit, Adivasi and Muslim children reportedly complained, 'How can we bear the expenses when we cannot even provide the children their daily meals' (Pratichi 2002: 33).

TABLE 7.2
HOUSEHOLD POPULATION AGED 6 TO 17
ATTENDING SCHOOL BY GENDER, STANDARD OF LIVING INDEX (SLI)
AND SOCIAL GROUP IN INDIA, 1998–99 (%)

	Total			Rural			Urban		
	Total	Male	Female	Total	Male	Female	Total	Male	Female
Dalit									
SLI-1									
6–10	69.3	75.3	63.0	68.9	74.9	62.5	72.5	78.1	66.7
11–14	57.4	68.3	45.2	56.7	68.2	44.1	62.2	68.9	53.2
6–14	64.8	72.6	56.3	64.3	72.4	55.6	68.4	74.2	61.8
15–17	29.7	39.4	18.3	29.6	39.8	17.7	30.2	36.7	22.7
SLI-2									
6–10	87.5	90.2	84.5	86.6	90.0	82.9	89.7	90.8	88.6
11–14	78.4	84.0	72.2	76.9	83.7	69.3	81.8	84.7	78.7
6–14	83.7	87.6	79.4	82.6	87.4	77.4	86.2	88.1	84.2
15–17	51.2	61.7	40.5	49.1	61.0	37.0	55.8	63.3	48.0
SLI-3									
6–10	87.5	90.2	84.5	86.6	90.0	82.9	89.7	90.8	88.6
11–14	78.4	84.0	72.2	76.9	83.7	69.3	81.8	84.7	78.7
6–14	83.7	87.6	79.4	82.6	87.4	77.4	86.2	88.1	84.2
15–17	51.2	61.7	40.5	49.1	61.0	37.0	55.8	63.3	48.0
Other Castes									
SLI-1									
6–10	75.1	79.4	70.3	75.2	80.0	70.0	74.4	76.1	72.2
11–14	62.4	68.9	55.7	62.9	70.4	55.4	59.2	60.2	57.8
6–14	70.2	75.5	64.6	70.5	76.4	64.2	68.7	70.2	66.8
15–17	31.8	38.7	25.0	31.7	40.3	23.4	32.5	29.9	35.4
SLI-2									
6–10	89.8	92.2	87.3	89.6	92.7	86.3	90.4	91.2	89.6
11–14	82.7	88.3	76.7	82.0	89.6	74.1	84.1	85.6	82.5
6–14	86.8	90.6	82.8	86.4	91.4	81.1	87.7	88.8	86.6
15–17	56.0	65.3	46.3	55.1	68.8	41.4	58.0	58.0	58.0
SLI-3									
6–10	97.6	98.2	96.9	96.9	97.6	96.2	98.0	98.6	97.4
11–14	95.6	96.3	94.9	94.2	95.7	92.8	96.6	96.8	96.3
6–14	96.7	97.3	96.0	95.7	96.7	94.6	97.3	97.7	96.9
15–17	83.2	85.8	80.5	76.9	83.8	70.2	87.5	87.2	87.8

Source: NFHS-2 (IIPS and ORC Macro 2000).
Notes: SLI-1: Lowest SLI; SLI-3: Highest SLI.

Given the incidence of poverty and high costs of schooling (the major cost being on uniforms, books and stationery), incentives such as free uniforms and books as well as midday meals lighten the burden of expenditure for poor households. Dalit and Adivasi pupils, particularly girls, are meant to receive a number of such incentives. However, incentives have to be meaningful. This is not the case where their coverage is narrow, when they are received irregularly, or when, instead of cooked meals provided daily in school, dry rations are distributed to children at infrequent intervals. Many teachers in the village studied by Pratichi felt that 'a properly administered midday meal scheme can have a positive impact on attendance...' (Pratichi : 58). Sen goes on to argue for 'actual midday meals' which, he emphasizes, will 'contribute greatly to the nutrition of children', 'enhance school attendence' and also 'reduce the abuse and corruption typically associated with the distribution of dry rations, which are more easily fungible' (ibid.: 10).

Though the formally recorded number of children who are in regular work has declined over the years, in 1993–94 they comprised a relatively larger proportion among Dalit children (8.1 per cent) as compared to the general child population (7.2 per cent). Further, as many as around 31 per cent of Dalit children (35 per cent of Dalit girls) in rural areas are engaged in domestic chores (NSSO 1997). Jha and Jhingran's (2002) research in villages, where there was a significant proportion of Dalits, shows that children's work comprises an important survival strategy of poor Dalit households. In addition to household tasks, children were often engaged as contract domestic servants and cattle herds with local landlords. They make the important point that where there are rigid caste hierarchies and feudal relations, and inadequate work opportunities for adults, children are drawn quite early on into the world of work (ibid. 2002: 99–101). The Pratichi study found more non-schoolgoing male children from poor families engaged in income-earning activities such as tending cattle, and hiring out labour as *bagal*. Teachers reported that, 'If they hire out labour as *bagal* they can earn at least their own food and sometimes they can help out the family by contributing some money' (Pratichi 2002: 49). The report also cites the case of a girl who had completed class IV and was good in her studies, but had to be pulled out of school since her father can neither provide private tuition (which, he believed, was essential for studying), nor could he arrange money for books and other stationery needed. 'It is difficult enough to provide a square meal,' he says. Thus, Munni has joined her mother in agricultural wage work during the cultivation seasons (ibid.: 51).

Migration forms an important component of livelihood strategies of poor households and brings with it possibilities of income, reduces dependence on higher castes for work in villages of origin, and so on. However, it has important consequences for children's right to education. Often parents migrate with their children, who at an early age are entrusted with family responsibilities and in time also work alongside adult family members. Some of the case studies indicate that parents are quite helpless when it comes to the education of their children. The Pratichi study cites the case of a Bauri (Dalit) family that was forced to migrate in search of agricultural wage work. The eldest daughter was never enrolled in school, but was entrusted with the task of caring for the younger children till she was in a position to hire out her own labour. When asked if she wanted to go to school, the 15-year-old said, 'Give me money and I will go to study…. First we need to fill our bellies' (ibid.: 48). Though parents often acknowledge the value of education, they tend to rationalise the non enrolment of their children by suggesting that while education is important, it was not relevant for their children, and, further, that they were not in a position to see that their children were enrolled and attended school (Jha and Jhingran 2002).

For Dalits, migration to urban areas, historically, has provided a relief from the oppressive regime of caste relations, and also better opportunities for education and alternative occupations for their children. Relatively early migration to urban areas was one of the factors that gave some Dalit communities (for instance, the Mahars of Maharashtra) a head start in accessing educational and occupational opportunities in the colonial period, and subsequently from independent India's policy of affirmative action for Dalits. However, with rapid and unplanned urbanisation and migration of the rural poor to the cities in search of employment, an increasingly large proportion of the urban population today resides in slums and shanty towns characterised by nonavailability of basic amenities, insecure lives and livelihoods, and inadequate facilities for education and health care. The NIAS (2002) cites evidence from a recent survey of 279 slums of Jaipur city indicating that as many as 71 per cent families were SC who were engaged in menial jobs. The study also reveals that though these slums are home to as many as 30 per cent of the population of the city, they are poorly provided with facilities for education: as many as 73.48 per cent of slums do not have any government schools and 37.28 per cent do not have any provision for schooling. Further, 'more than 50 per cent of children in about 86 per cent of the *basti*s do not attend any school' (ibid.: 16).

Research on poverty and education, thus, suggests the need to make a distinction between the value (in terms of aspirations and preferences) of education among poor parents, their decision to invest in children's education, enrolment of children in school, and actually ensuring regularity of their attendance. Livelihood strategies, the weighing of costs and benefits of educating each child, as well as the support received for their schooling significantly affect the nature of school participation of children. While enrolment rates (including what the NSSO calls 'attendance rates') may be high, they are meaningful only when children regularly attend school. Among marginal groups, enrolment drives are often common and teachers are expected to go to the homes of children and enter their names in the school register. However, little attention is paid to see whether children go to school on a regular basis. Jha and Jhingran's study is significant in that it is one of the few attempts to make a distinction between enrolment in school and regularity of school attendance. This is especially important where children are first-generation learners and their families are unable to provide the academic support that schools expect from them. In the villages that the authors studied, there was invariably a gap between the proportion of children enrolled and those who attended schools regularly. Wide variations in the regularity of school attendance of Dalit children were also seen across states. For instance, in Maharashtra and Karnataka 'more than 90 per cent of enrolled Dalit children regularly attend school. At the other end in villages in UP and Bihar, barely 20 to 25 per cent of dalit children attend school regularly' (Jha and Jhingran 2002: 83).

A number of factors appear to influence the regularity of school attendance. For instance, physical location and climatic conditions. Because the habitations in which Dalit children live are more likely to be unfavourably located, they are particularly affected by such factors. Jha and Jhingran observe that where Dalit settlements are in low-lying areas, heavy rains can prevent children from attending school. In one case mentioned by them, an entire hamlet was cut off for almost three months in the rainy season.[11] Physical quality of the school also influences children's attendance. In my own study of a few schools catering to poor households in Kolkata, teachers mentioned that children were keen on attending schools even during the monsoons as their homes became damp and uncomfortable, and they could not play out side during the rains (Nambissan 2003: 31). On the other hand the *sishu siksha kendra*s (SSKs [AS in rural West Bengal]), which were easily accessible to children, constrained attendance because of their poor physical quality. One *sahayika* (AS teacher) complained: 'Parents don't send little children as they have to sit in the mud' (Pratichi 2002: 87).

The nature of livelihoods of poor households also constrains regular attendance. For instance, where both parents are engaged in wage labour, adult responsibilities devolve on young children who are expected to stay at home to look after younger siblings, care for domestic animals, and shoulder other household responsibilities. Children are also expected to help out with farm work. One of the primary teachers in the Pratichi study said:

You are seeing some children in the school now. If you come during the cultivation season you may see almost zero attendance from the SC and ST children. They all take some household responsibilities while the parents are out to work. And the girl children of these communities seldom attend school as they do various kinds of work both domestic and income generating. A 10 year old girl picks dry cow dung to sell, for example. (Pratichi 2002: 60)

Migration of families also results in absence from school and leads to a situation where children may not be re-enrolled when they return, and even if they are, they are unlikely to be able to adequately cope with their studies. Other reasons that have been given for irregular attendance of children include the ill health of family members and 'lack of interest' of parents in education of their children. Ill health of family members in fact comprised 19 per cent of reasons for children's absence, the largest single reason cited by parents interviewed in the Pratichi study (ibid.: 61). Parental perception of lack of relevance of schooling in situations of poverty and migration has been referred to. This is likely to be compounded where parents and elders are non-literate or have low levels of education. The NFHS-2 (IIPS and ORC Macro 2000), for instance, shows sharp inter-group disparities in educational attainment of the adult population. Only around 23 per cent of Dalits as compared with 47 per cent from other castes in the 20 to 29 age group (that comprises a large number of young parents) had completed high school. This starkly reflects the effects of exclusion from education of generations of Dalits, and makes for unequal learning environments offered to children by the home and community. Thus, the mention of children's 'own agency', where by they 'vote with their feet' where school attendance is concerned: playing truant from school, refusing to go to school, wanting to stay home to help parents, and so on, must be seen in the context of their family and community contexts, where the value and wherewithal for education may be not adequate for sustained schooling. In this context, the role of the school in providing an inclusive learning space that is sustainable for groups hitherto excluded from education must not be glossed over. What then is the experience of the Dalit child who is enrolled in school, often under extremely difficult conditions?

THE QUALITY OF SCHOOLING: DALIT IDENTITY AND THE EXPERIENCE OF EDUCATION

Poor infrastructure, lack of basic amenities and facilities, as well as inadequate number of teachers is a feature of schools that Dalit children encounter as they enter government (local body managed) schools. In addition, curriculum transaction in schools is dominated by conventional pedagogy based on the textbook, 'chalk and talk' and absence of relevant teaching aids, and dominated by rote learning. Ongoing academic support, monitoring and feedback is also not a feature of primary schools, less so in more and backward rural areas and poverty zones in cities. This provides an unattractive learning environment for Dalit children (the majority of whom enter government schools) and contrasts with the quality of schooling (in 'public'–private institutions) enjoyed by the more privileged strata.[12]

Many of the studies that referred to the experiences of Dalit students as well as adult reminiscences prior to the 1980s spoke of the discrimination they faced in schools at the hands of teachers. More recent research suggests that Dalit identity continues to influence the treatment of children in schools. Studies have shown that teachers (who are predominantly higher/upper caste) bring their own commonsense understanding of the legitimacy of caste relations into the classroom, and that these pervade their interaction with Dalit and lower-caste children, and is reflected in discriminatory attitudes and practices within school. Researchers report the often demeaning and harsh treatment of Dalit pupils. Thus, for instance, a recent study of schools, many in predominant Dalit localities says, 'The most uniform finding of this research project has been the widespread nature of verbal abuse that Dalit and Adivasi children suffer at the hands of their upper-caste teachers in primary schools, which has a critical impact on the ways in which these first generation school attendees view themselves as learners'

(Balagopal and Subrahmanian 2003: 43). Jha and Jhingran's (2002: 95) research also points out that Dalit children are 'unnecessarily beaten, abused and harassed by upper caste teachers'.

Teachers expect Dalit and lower caste children to 'do a number of personal tasks such as fetching firewood and if the children did not oblige, physical punishment is meted out to them' (ibid.). There are also instances reported of lower-caste children being assigned menial tasks such as sweeping and cleaning of the classroom (Ramachandran 2002). Teachers are also reported to have low expectations of Dalit children and fail to give them adequate attention. Exclusion of children from classroom activities and making them sit in the last row is also reported (Jha and Jhingran 2002: 95). Equally serious is the observation that teachers tend to absent themselves more frequently if pupils are mainly from disadvantaged communities. For instance, it has been observed that in cases 'where all children belong to Dalit or other disadvantaged communities, it is common for teachers to absent themselves or come for fewer hours' (ibid.). The Pratichi study of schools in villages in West Bengal makes a mention of 'disturbing evidence that primary school teachers often show much less regard for the interests of children from poorer and lower caste backgrounds'. It was observed that there was 'much greater teacher absenteeism in schools with a majority of children from scheduled castes and scheduled tribes (75 per cent), compared with other schools (33 per cent)'. Also, in some schools with children from 'lowly families, the teachers, on a regular basis, do not take classes on certain days of the week;' in one case, 'no classes on Saturdays and Mondays, and sometimes the hours are arbitrarily reduced' (Sen 2002: 6).

Teachers also view parents of first-generation learners within middle-class frames, expecting them to provide the academic support and orientation to school that the latter give their children. When children arrive in school without their clothes and books in order and their homework incomplete, they receive punishment (often corporal) rather than concern from teachers for the difficult conditions under which they avail of education. Sreedhar (1999) underscores the inability of non-literate parents to help with their children's studies or even provide them with the space to concentrate on their schoolwork. He says, 'The importance of homework in the traditional primary schools is a major reason that Dalit children lag behind other children in class' (Sreedhar 1999: 14). The NIAS (2002) observes that most teachers do not empathise with parents' working and living conditions, and do not understand the limitations faced by children who are first-generation learners. In fact, the Pratichi study says that one of the reasons why even poor parents seek private tutoring for their children is to see that the child is able to complete her homework, something that non-literate and poorly educated parents are unable to help with. Studies rarely mention efforts by teachers to provide any additional inputs to first-generation learners. Balagopal and Subrahmanian (2003) observe that their research recorded little effort, if any, on the part of these teachers to make classroom learning for these first-generation learners more interesting. They continued to teach through traditional methods, and their inordinate reliance on homework contributed to these children (particularly in the Adivasi villages, where the children's home language is different from the medium of instruction) being unable to keep up with classroom learning and therefore remaining quiet and unresponsive in class. Many teachers appeared to be disapproving of incentives being given to children from these communities and often passed disparaging remarks about Dalit parents 'being more interested in the monthly grain installments that they received and the scholarships that their children brought home rather than in their children's academic performance' (ibid.: 52).

Though poor financial condition of the household is cited by parents as a major reason for absenteeism and the dropping-out of children from school, teachers' absence, hostile environment and lack of children's interest in what is taught are also mentioned as reasons for children not attending school (Pratichi 2002: 30). Parents from Dalit (and Adivasi) communities in the villages studied by Pratichi complained of the 'stepmotherly' treatment that their children received in primary schools. They felt that discontinuation

was 'precipitated by the poor quality of teaching, excessive punishment and children's failure in qualifying for higher classes' (Pratichi
2002: 32).

Where peer relations are concerned, research reports mixed
findings. In the mid 1970s, Chitnis (1981) observes that for majority
of high school Dalit children surveyed, friendships were confined
to members of their own sub-caste or those that were closer to them
in terms of ritual status. More recent studies suggest that there
may be greater interaction across castes within schools, but this
may not extend outside the boundaries of the institution, particularly to the private space of the home. This is likely to be more
common in towns and cities than in the villages. Balagopal and
Subrahmanian refer to friendships formed among children across
castes in the primary school/section they studied in Ganganagar
and Ujjain towns. However, it must be remembered that these
schools were dominated by low-ranked castes. Their comment that
'within the classroom, these peer friendships were important resources that enabled students to cope with abuse or victimisation
by teachers', is significant and needs to be explored. Drawing attention to a different context, Jha and Jhingran (2002: 9) report that
in the more economically backward villages where rigid social
hierarchies persist, Dalits do indeed face hostile peer behaviour in
schools and that 'children belonging to the upper castes generally
bully them and do not allow them to mix as equals'. They go on to
conclude that 'the general experience of Dalit children in school,
therefore, is that of neglect and indifference, when not outright
discrimination and rejection'.

STRATIFICATION, SEGREGATION AND EQUITY

The reference to unequal treatment of Dalits within school in a
few studies may be seen as mere instances and as aberrations rather
than integral to the experience of formal education of children
from these communities in school. However, when placed within

the larger context of the institutional stratification and social segregation that is increasingly visible in elementary education in India, it appears that despite being 'included' in schools in significant numbers in recent years (which project a semblance of equality of opportunity), the terms of inclusion of Dalit children are inequitable when judged against criteria of fairness or justice.

The entry of large numbers of Dalit and other socially and economically marginal groups into the school system, often the first generation to receive formal education, has also witnessed second- and third-generation learners of other social groups moving out of publicly funded schools and into private institutions (Ramachandran 2002). Government (local body managed) primary schools increasingly cater mainly to low-ranked castes (and lower classes). For instance, the NIAS (2002: 13) shows that in Thanjavur, children mainly from the Scheduled Castes (Thoti, Parayal, Pallar and Chakliyas) and a sprinkling from the Most Backward Castes (such as Ottan) attend the local municipal primary school. Some scholars have argued that movement of the middle (and lower middle) classes away from government schools to privately managed institutions is likely to result in greater equity as public resources can then be used for the most needy. However, the flight of the middle class, the vocal and opinion-making section of society, results in a social fragmentation of the community of parents who access schooling. Those who remain in government schools lack the voice to ensure that they receive quality service, setting in a process of further decline in the quality of education on offer. Further, the neglect of elementary education over the post-independent decades and the urgency to realise targets for UEE in the 1990s amidst economic restructuring has resulted in spreading thin the inadequate resources allocated to this sector. This is reflected in the poor physical quality of schools and availability of teachers as mentioned earlier. The situation is likely to change for the worse rather than the better to the detriment of children from hitherto educationally deprived groups who are increasingly attending these schools. The NIAS describes the decline of the municipal school in Tanjavur town, considered a model school in the early 20th century when it was catering to Brahmins and upper-caste families. The 'deterioration

of the school' over the decades is reflected in its 'sporadic functioning' with 'high teacher absenteeism' and decline in strength of
students. The NIAS report observes, 'Far from being a model
school, it is now in a state of decay with few of the neighbourhood
children attending it and with only the very poor enrolling their
children in it'. In 2002 only Dalit and lower-caste children remained
in the school, and that too primarily because they could not afford
to send their children to privately managed schools that had sprung
up in the city over the years and which were catering to the demand
for quality education from the higher castes. The report makes the
following important point:

> As middle-class and better-educated and professional parents withdraw their
> children from government schools, the accountability of teachers and the
> pressure on them to teach or perform their other duties in school decreases.
> As working-class parents, especially the labouring poor, cannot wield authority
> and exert pressure like the educated and professional parents, they and their
> children are seen as liabilities and dependent recipients who are unworthy of
> being educated. Further, such differentiation has other implications for the
> children's experience of schooling, the authority and rights of teachers, and
> the larger purpose of education. (NIAS 2002: 24)

The poor physical quality of local body managed (government)
schools, lack of relevant aids and inadequate resources is likely to
provide a work environment that in itself is unlikely to elicit and
sustain teacher motivation. However, it is also important to remember that school teachers at the elementary stage are overwhelmingly
from non-Dalit backgrounds, largely higher caste and middle class,
while their pupils, as mentioned, are from low-ranked castes that
are also poor.[13] The growing chasm between teachers and children
in terms of social class or economic and educational backgrounds
is often seen to underlie negative teacher attitudes to poor students
and their disparaging comments on the absence of parental support
for education (Sen 2002). What is also significant is that higher-
caste teachers may also resent the crowding of Dalit children into
'institutional space' that was hitherto taboo for 'polluted' castes,
and see this as a transgression of traditional social hierarchies.
Balagopal and Subrahmanian (2003: 43) view 'the abuse [of Dalits]

as a manifestation of a more systemic disjuncture associated with the entry of traditionally excluded groups into spaces that were hitherto the preserve of caste and class élites.

In keeping with the changing times, teachers, as reported in many instances, may not directly speak disparagingly of 'caste status' and 'pollution', but use the more acceptable 'secular' discourse of 'ability' and 'merit' to relegate lower-caste and Dalit children as 'uneducable'. Velaskar (1998: 227), for instance, observes that, 'The stigmatized identity [of Dalits] is carried forward but is now attributed with new criteria, new labels and new disabilities and is now justified not on traditional, religious criteria, but "modern", "objective", "secular" ones of merit, excellence and fairplay'. It is also commonplace for teachers to point to 'non-conducive family environments' as responsible for failure and drop-out of children from poor and marginal groups (Nambissan 2003: 33–34). Balagopal and Subrahmanian (2003: 49) observe that teachers in their study 'seldom said that the child was intrinsically unable to study but described the difficulties involved in teaching them in language that blamed parents for their lack of interest, their "drunkenness", their failure to create a more conducive "home" environment and their continued reliance on traditional occupations'.

The social segregation in government schools presents a diversity that has to be handled in pedagogic terms for which teachers are neither trained for nor oriented to. Children are often first-generation learners, of different age groups (they often come to school as a result of mobilisation and enrolment drives), drop-outs from different grades, child workers, former child workers, children with special needs and so on. In terms of language and ways of living, the cultural backgrounds children come from are likely to vary not only vis-à-vis the teacher, but also among themselves. The educational needs of these children are unlikely to be met at home and there is little evidence that they are being addressed in school. Conventional teacher training is yet to acknowledge the need for pedagogy that is informed by social and economic realities that these children have experienced. Curricular transaction is hence largely informed by teachers' beliefs about children's abilities that usually stem from common sense notions and stereotypical attitudes about these social groups. The NIAS (2002) observes that the belief in the lack of ability of Dalit and marginal groups provides government school teachers an excuse to justify the lax and indifferent manner in which they discharge their duties:

> By associating capability and orientation of students to their background many teachers shirk their responsibility of ensuring that children gain from being in the class. In their assessment of students, many teachers mark some students as being educable and many as not educable. Such an orientation largely accounts for why many teachers do not seek to expend much time or energy on teaching. (Ibid.: 29)

Alternatively, it may encourage corporal punishment, often seen as the only way to make some children learn. The NIAS study quotes the headmaster of a municipal school justifying corporal punishment by saying, 'these children do not respond to kindness. They have to be beaten to discipline them'; a teacher says, 'Just as bullocks need to be whipped to make them pull the cart, so must these students be whipped to get them to start studying' (ibid.: 15).

The perception of Dalits as 'polluted' and 'backward' is likely to have deleterious implications for their sense of dignity, identity and self-worth. Children's own experiences within the classroom have hardly received any attention. However, there are reflections of Dalit adults about being made to feel 'inferior' and 'different' from their classmates in school and excluded from classroom activities (Nambissan 1996). Krishna Kumar (1989) also draws attention to the fact that identity as 'Dalit' or 'Adivasi' influences engagement with school knowledge and the transaction of the curriculum to the detriment of children from these communities. Illaiah (1996) points to the alienation of Dalit and lower-caste children from the knowledge, cultural experiences, as well as the medium of communication considered legitimate for schooling.

Mention has already been made of the institutionalisation of alternative schools as introducing another, albeit inferior, tier within publicly provided primary schooling. The AS, by targeting Dalit and tribal habitations in rural areas and poverty zones in some cities, has further increased social segregation within government schools.[14] AS teachers are locally recruited, and are accountable to the community to which their pupils belong. Thus, absenteeism is seen to be lower and social relations within the classroom less hier-archical as compared to regular primary schools. Researchers who see functioning AS (where teachers come to school) amidst the dysfunctional regular primary schools tend to be ecstatic about the former without looking at how equitable such schooling really is. What is usually ignored is that the norms that underlie this tier of schooling in relation to physical infrastructure (no minimal norms exist), teacher recruitment (on contract and at lower salaries than regular teachers), and qualifications and training (a minimum of high school with barely three to 20 days of training) may ensure teacher 'presence', but set limits to the quality of education that children receive. Thus, though schools are said to be 'functioning', this is mainly in terms of regularity of teacher attendance and tak-ing of lessons, while the quality of classroom instruction is likely to be poor. An earlier study did draw attention to the poor quality of education being imparted in 'para-teacher' schools (DPEP 1999). Pratichi emphasises that one of the major constraints within which SSKs function is that of poor facilities as compared to regular schools: 'The situation in the SSKs is much worse, only 24 per cent of them have got small, single-room buildings. The rest con-duct classes in cowsheds, verandahs and in community rooms.' Further, AS children who are from deprived socially and econo-mically disadvantaged groups are not entitled to incentives such as free textbooks, midday meals and so on (Pratichi 2002: 32).

Available research suggests that the performance of Dalit chil-dren has been relatively poor. DPEP baseline studies carried out in 1993 showed that Dalit (and Adivasi) children 'performed less well than other students in tests of language and Mathematics' (World Bank 1997: 133). However, it is reported that differences in the average achievement in maths and language declined when family background of Dalit, tribal and 'other' students were statistically controlled for in the eight states that were studied (ibid.). The con-clusion that 'difference in average achievement between Sched-uled Caste and Scheduled Tribe students and other students are attributable largely to differences in socio-economic status' gives the schools that children attend, hardly anything to cheer about.

The review of the performance in schools in DPEP states in 2002 suggests that while progress has been made by Dalit children in relation to learning outcomes, a large proportion have failed to achieve the minimum targeted 40 per cent in language and math. This is more pronounced in the senior grades in primary school (World Bank 2003).[15]

DYSFUNCTIONAL SCHOOLS AND PRIVATE OPTIONS

Given the poorly functioning government school sector, it is not surprising that parents of Dalit children are looking to the private sector for quality education for their children. The NCAER data shows that in 1994 around 30 per cent of Dalit children (aged 6 to 14 years) were enrolled in privately managed schools (aided and unaided) in rural areas. In urban areas the shift to private schools is more significant though less than in the general population. Between 1986 and 1993, as much 31 per cent of the increase in primary school enrolment of Dalit boys in urban areas was in privately managed unaided schools (NCERT 1999). Dalit parents tend to see private schools as having quality education on offer as compared to what their children receive in government schools. As mentioned earlier in the NIAS study (2002) on Tanjavur, Dalit parents were keeping their children in the municipal school only because they could not afford to put them in private schools in the city. In the Balagopal and Subrahmanian study in Ujjain city, only a few Valmikis (low-ranked Dalit sub-castes) were sending their children to private schools. However, there was a belief that 'academic mobility' came with private schooling, and the 'entire community had not only imbibed the culturally hegemonic language around the failure of government schools, but also used this to criticise the lack of academic rigour in the local Lower Primary School' (Balagopal and Subrahmanian 2003: 46). Speaking of the local school, they make the significant observation that the Valmikis 'construct this school only as a temporary space for their children, until they could put them into private school' (ibid.: 48).

Within private schooling as well, a number of tiers have emerged in relation to management and quality of education on offer. In addition to the officially 'recognised' privately managed aided and unaided schools are the 'unrecognised' schools that do not come under the purview of government norms and regulations. Such schools are mushrooming in cities and small towns as well as in the more developed villages where there is a demand for quality education, viewed as that which is privately provided and in the medium of English. These schools also flourish because the state usually turns a blind eye to private schools at the primary stage, while regulations come into force at the secondary level. It is to these primary schools that sections of the poor and lower middle class turn to in order to improve the life chances of their children. In Jaipur a study notes that as many as 4,000 small primary schools were catering to the demand for private schooling among the lower middle classes. Many of them were located within or near the poverty zones in the city (cited in NIAS 2002). Many Dalits enrol their children in such unregulated schools. Though there has been no research regarding the quality of private schooling that Dalits avail of, scattered references in some studies suggest that they are likely to be short-changed in relation to quality education within the private sector as well. There are implications for gender equity, as parents attempt to secure what they see as 'private', good-quality education for their sons while sending their daughters to government/municipal schools. This trend is now reflected among the relatively better-off Dalits who are also accessing private education for their children. According to the NIAS study, 'When parents can afford it they send their son to the private and daughter to the corporation school' (NIAS 2002: 15). The increasing public–private divide in schools according to gender has been reported in a number of studies. Manjrekar (2003) points to the hitherto unexplored detrimental consequences for self-esteem as girls continue to be sent to government while their male siblings access privately provided schools.

Dysfunctional schools also force parents to seek private tutoring for their children. The poor quality of education offered by the public school system is one of the main reasons for the flourishing tuition industry that today caters even to the poor. West Bengal is probably the state where private 'coaching' is most rampant. Families in the Pratichi study saw private tuition as an important input in school education. A fifth of children whose parents were agricultural labourers (mostly Dalits and Adivasis) were sending their children for private tuition. The accessing of private tuition by the poor not only increases the burden of cost of primary education, but also differentiates them on the basis of those who can provide this extra academic support for their children and those who cannot (Pratichi 2002: 32–33). As mentioned, private tuition is seen as important not only in relation to what is taught in class, but for the completion of homework as well, which, if not done, brings the wrath of the teachers upon the children.

INSTITUTIONS AND OPPORTUNITIES

A significant feature of the education system at the primary stage today is the institutional space for participation of local communities in the affairs of the schools and academic support for teachers. An important thrust of the DPEP was on setting up of village- and school-level committees to enable participation in school education, and to create block and cluster resource centres (BRCs and CRCs) to provide ongoing academic support to teachers in local schools and organising training for the professional development of teachers. I would like to argue that though studies do indicate that structural constraints impede the effective functioning of these institutional interventions to a great extent, there is also evidence to believe that they offer possibilities for providing enabling conditions for the education of marginal groups, in this case, Dalits.

Village education committees (VEC) are formal structures envisaged to mobilise local communities to send their children to school as well participate in its functioning. Around 230,000 VECs, 170,000 parent–teacher associations (PTA)/mother–teacher associations and 61,000 school management development committees have been put in place (World Bank 2003). These committees provide for representation of Dalits, Adivasis and women. Have Dalits been able to participate in VECs and thereby strengthened their voice in relation to the functioning of schools? The World Bank review of research (ibid.), suggests that in general the functioning of VECs has been irregular. The Pratichi (2002) report observes that while VECs may have been formed in a number of villages, many are still to become functional. Subrahmanian (2003: 234) notes that VEC activities have mainly centred around construction, maintenance and expansion of school buildings, and that there was less focus on 'mobilizing participation and assessing what factors outside the physical availability of schooling hamper or facilitate greater school enrolment'. The 'limited empowerment of its members, especially from SC/ST communities and women', and their 'silent' and 'passive' attendance at meetings has also been commented upon (World Bank 2003). Given the marginal status of these communities in the village, reports of the exclusion of their educational needs from VEC concerns are not surprising. For instance, a study in 22 villages in Karnataka mentions that 'even micro-planning, identifying the status of non-enrolled students in the village is often not inclusive of the SC/ST communities' (ibid.). Another reports that the finding from a micro planning strategy that a section of the village wanted non-formal schools in the evening for children was summarily dismissed without addressing the larger concern of why children were not able to attend regular schools and initiating efforts to see that it was possible for them to do so (Subrahmanian 2003: 231). In addition to caste and gender hierarchies, an impediment to the regular participation of Dalit members in VECs was their dependence on wage labour wherein they had to often migrate out of the village. Teachers and higher-caste members were found to play an important role in decision making, and often sought the involvement of the more marginal groups mainly where there was need for mobilisation of labour and resources (ibid.).

The importance of local-level organisations for enabling schooling of children, especially girls, is drawn attention to by the NIAS (2002). It was found that membership of such organisations (Ambedkar Sangh, Mahila Sangh, church organisations) had provided poor parents 'support and encouragement for sending children to school' (NIAS 2002: 14). Women's groups at the local level have also played a significant role in enhancing school participation and functioning in some states. There are reports of school-level committees that have been able to intervene in the functioning of schools. Jha and Jhingran (2002) emphasise the importance of social mobilisation and political assertion in claiming the right to education. In villages where there have been histories of Dalit movements, parents were seen to be relatively more critical of school functioning and likely to be more active in the VEC. 'In course of time, the schooling of children becomes a norm at such places and every child is sent to school' (ibid.: 28).[16] However, poor parents have no control over the quality of classroom transactions and social relations within the classroom, and are likely to continue to witness drop-out, failure and poor school completion rates unless some attention is directed to academic support to teachers and their professional development.

BRCs and CRCs are an important institutional innovation to provide ongoing academic support to teachers within primary schools, monitor the quality of classroom instruction, and address constraints in subject knowledge and appropriate pedagogy that teachers face in the daily routine of curriculum transaction. There were at least around 800 BRCs and over 5,000 CRCs in the 272 DPEP districts by 2000.[17] A couple of evaluations do mention visits by CRC coordinators to schools, and developing of teacher skills. However, in the light of the discussion so far, it would be important to look at the role of BRCs and CRCs from the perspective of the specific needs and constraints of Dalit and marginal groups. As mentioned, Dalit children who mainly look outside the home for academic support are likely to draw a blank when face to face with teachers whose professional capacities are poorly developed and who are neither oriented nor sensitised to the realities of poverty and social discrimination in the lives of these children. Nor are they adequately trained to address the learning needs of their pupils within the classroom. Thus, while there are reports of the occasional teacher/principal who disapproves of discriminatory practices towards pupils from low-ranked castes and reaches out to them, there is need for a systemic response to these issues. Academic support structures that have been put in place across the country and are meant to cater specifically to local body-managed primary schools where children from hitherto educationally deprived groups predominate, provide an opportunity to seriously address issues of quality of schooling for these children.

The professional development of teachers was one of the objectives of the DPEP, and a fairly large number of teachers had received in-service training as part of the programme by 2000 (World Bank 2003). However, the actual training programmes were too brief (barely three to 20 days) to either address subject content or to build capacities to provide the academic support that first-generation learners urgently require. Nor were these crucial aspects of training seriously thought through in relation to diverse teaching and learning contexts. Further, training appears to have completely ignored the issue of caste-based social discrimination within schools and how to question mindsets on these issues. Other than reference to Karnataka state that had developed 'video material on teachers' sensitivity to students from SC and ST communities', training modules appeared to be silent on this issue (ibid.: 34). Batra makes an important point:

> Teacher perceptions of dalit children, as backward with poor learning capacities, continue to be viewed within the narrow domain of building positive attitudes and motivating teachers through in-service training. Teacher education needs to engage teachers with the subject of their belief systems and assumptions about children and how these bear upon classroom processes to reinforce marginalisation even where structural opportunities of access to schooling exist.[18]

It is important to also bear in mind that it was during this period (as part of the larger neo-liberal ideology that was influencing policy) that there was a policy shift towards dilution of norms of teacher recruitment (in terms of basic qualifications and pre-service training) and hiring of teachers on contract. Teachers on contract are being hired not only in AS, but against teacher vacancies in regular schools in many states. The neglect of pre-service teacher education, a cavalier attitude to in-service training, and lack of attention to subject competencies, pedagogy and the social context of schooling as well as the hiring of teachers on contract has led to the trivialising of the much-needed thrust to professional development of teachers. This is a sphere that needs reflection—informed by a perspective of providing education of equitable quality.

The framework of educational governance that today calls for greater decentralised planning and management of schools requires qualitatively different roles that educational administrators, lower-level officials and academic resource personnel are expected to play. In addition to specific capacities that local-level planning, monitoring, school mapping, resource support and so on require, educational functionaries have to be oriented to reaching out to marginal communities that may differ greatly from them in terms of social background, power and authority. As has been said, the administration has hitherto mainly been a carryover from the colonial period, largely oriented to the maintenance of law and order rather than facilitating development. Unless administrators are adequately oriented and obliged to do so, they are unlikely to bridge the social gap that they confront while carrying out their duties. Further, unless educational functionaries and teachers (who are often asked to play the role of petty administrators)[19] are informed by a rights perspective, and view themselves as 'educational professionals' rather than seeing themselves as moral change agents and dispensers of patronage, they are unlikely bring to their work the seriousness, commitment and sensitivity that is essential.

Vasavi (2004) emphasises the absence of 'education institution building' by the State resulting in the publicly funded school becoming 'marginal institutions'. On the one hand she points to the failure to set in place organisational structures (VECs, PTAs, etc.) and build their capacities to make them effective, and on the other to bureaucratisation and centralisation of decision making 'replicated at every level with the concomitant loss of meaning and orientation', 'the absence of a culture of democracy and professionalism', and the subsequent indifference of educational administrators down the line to their work (ibid.: 31). This is extremely important because not only does it highlight the neglect of educational institutions by the State, but also draws attention to nature of institutions themselves as social arrangements governed by norms, values and rules that define membership, access to resources, and modes of participation and 'work cultures'.

In the context of institutional building, it may be appropriate to revisit the Kothari Commission for the insights it offers for the develpment of equitable education in this country. It may be worthwhile to explore the idea of the 'school complex' proposed by it, but extend its scope and possibilities. It will be important to envision institutional linkages that would revitalise government elementary schools, improving school quality with specific focus on the educational needs of marginal groups. Thus, the building of linkages between schools, academic support structures, institutions of teacher education, as well as colleges and universities within a geographical area as well as with VECs/PRI and community-level organisations will help 'break the terrible isolation under which the school functions', mobilise the necessary expertise to build capacity of academic support structures, encourage research to provide feedback in relation to specific contexts of teaching and learning, and as the Commission says, 'make cooperative efforts to improve standards' (quotes are from Kothari [NCERT] 1971).

CONCLUSION

In the foregoing discussion, I have placed the education of Dalits within the larger educational and policy context in India. Dalits are increasingly enrolling their children in schools, reflecting the growing value that they place on education for the future of their children. However, irregular attendance in schools, relatively low middle school completion rates, and poor performance of children from these social groups presents a disturbing picture in relation to the fundamental right to education. I have attempted to show that caste status and poverty continue to constrain access to and participation in schools for a large section of the Dalit population. There are social disparities in education across castes, particularly when Dalits are compared to higher castes. Within Dalit communities also, indicators of school participation vary across region, class, sub-caste and gender. Dalit girls in rural areas in the more educationally backward states are most at risk where UEE is concerned.

A major emphasis of the paper has been on the increasingly differentiated and stratified structure of educational institutions even within the elementary stage where education is deemed a fundamental right. I have shown that elite class, overlapping with entrenched higher-caste interests, rather than the value of universal and equitable entitlement to a public good, continues to govern the school system. Exclusionary rules and practices come into play within educational institutions, leading to inequitable inclusion of Dalit and marginal groups in schools. A section of Dalits, the middle class, which has availed of the benefits of affirmative action, enjoys relatively more 'privileged inclusion' in schools. However, for the vast majority of Dalit children, low-ranked caste status (compounded by poverty) continues to pervade school processes often through more 'secular' ways and influences the quality of schooling they receive, raising the larger issue of whether equity is really a commitment of state and society.

The experience of Dalits in states where school attendance rates are high such as Kerala, Himachal Pradesh and Tamil Nadu points to diverse factors that have encouraged the spread of education. These include effective policy interventions, expanding economic opportunities, functioning schools, public participation and community organisation for educational advancement. There is today a network of resource centres and village/school-level committees across the country that aim to provide academic support to schools and encourage public participation in their functioning. I suggest that this institutional network provides the space to create enabling learning environments for the education of marginal groups. However, there is need to seriously reflect on how these institutions can be 'built' in order to embody principles and norms that facilitate the education of the most deprived, and engage their trust and confidence. In the absence of enabling and effective institutional supports, even ensuring universal school entry is unlikely leave alone universal completion of primary or middle schooling. There is hence need to critically review structures in education, analyse and address constraints and bottlenecks, evolve linkages between institutions, and set in place mechanisms that can energise institutional functioning and ensure accountability.

For Dalits, education is a crucial resource to better their life chances as well as for social and political mobilisation. Given the larger landscape of increasing market relations in education, and the shrinking of the public sector, which hitherto provided the main avenue for educational and social mobility for Dalits, it is essential that equitable elementary education, under Article 21A of the Constitution, is seen as providing a critical base that will enable them to expand their choices and opportunities for further education and occupation mobility, public participation and mobilisation for change.

Notes

1. The situation of Scheduled Tribes (ST) or Adivasi communities is relatively worse than Dalits in relation to economic conditions and education, especially in rural areas. For instance, around 46 per cent of the Adivasi population in rural areas was below the poverty line in 1999. Though Dalits and Adivasis are often clubbed together by in policy discourse, the specific reasons for the economic and educational backwardness in these two communities differ and they must be understood separately. I am focusing only on Dalit children in this paper.
2. Harsh Mander observes that where Dalits are concerned there is an 'overlap between the poverty and pollution line' (quoted in a recent seminar at the India International Centre, New Delhi).
3. The introduction of State Component Plan (SCP) specifically targeted at Dalits made possible the provision of publicly provided facilities targeted to the SCs in villages. If a road was built with state funds, it would stop at the upper-caste habitations under normal circumstances. Similar was the case with facilities for water. With SCP funds it was possible to extend these facilities to the Dalit *bastis* as well. (Sukhdeo K. Thorat, personal communication).
4. However, educationally advanced states do have districts and blocks with a significant Dalit population that have low literacy and enrolment rates. For instance, in Tamil Nadu, which had an overall average female literacy rate of 64.55 per cent in 2001, Dharmapuri district, with a relatively large Dalit population, had a literacy rate of around 49 per cent (Akhila 2004: 2618).
5. The Programme of Action's (of NPE 1986) ingenious interpretation of the constitutional provision of education for all up to the age of 14 years was that all children would complete five years of schooling by the age of 14 years, rather than that they would complete eight years of elementary education.

6. The politics of school location has only been hinted at in a few studies and is often mentioned in discussions by educational functionaries and social activists.

7. The non-formal education programme initiated post-NPE (1986) was meant to target children who were seen as unable to avail of formal schools because they were engaged in work within and outside the home. The emphasis was on 'flexibility' and 'relevance' of schools. Around 279,000 centres were sanctioned by 1995–96. There is no data on whether these centres catered to Dalit children and to what effect. The only information that the AIES gives is that in 1993, NFE centres were set up in only *5.9 per cent habitations that did not have primary schools/sections within a distance of a kilometre*, indicating that these were unlikely to have significantly expanded learning opportunities for children who lacked easy access to formal schools. As mentioned, the NFE programme was wound up in 1997 in the face of sustained criticism that it was an inferior poor-quality stream of education, encouraged child labour, and so on.

8. Figures are from a World Bank review of research on DPEP phase 1 and 2 states (World Bank 2003: 31). The review cites data from Aggarwal (2001).

9. The 'transitional schools' mentioned by the Bill introduce yet another tier into the school system.

10. Bhatty (1998) highlights some of these studies.

11. The attitudes of teachers, their treatment of children, and so on were also factors that impinged on the attendance of children in schools. These will be discussed in relation to the quality of schooling that these children receive.

12. There is a small Dalit middle class comprising mainly those who have availed of public sector employment that accesses 'quality' schooling for its children.

13. In 1993 Dalits comprised around 11 per cent of primary school teachers, 9 per cent of upper primary and 5 to 6 per cent of teachers in secondary/high schools (NCERT 1999).

14. There may also be a movement of Dalits from regular schools to AS located in their own habitations. For instance, regular higher-caste school teachers may deliberately direct Dalits to attend their *own* schools (as reported by a researcher, Subrahmanian; personal communication). There are also reports that a functioning AS is likely to draw Dalit and lower-caste children from regular schools.

15. There are programmes today that seek to 'guarantee' learning, bring in 'accelerated learning' and so on. The Learning Guarantee Programme of the Premji Foundation attempts to provide incentives (monetary benefits as well recognition) to schools in the educationally backward district of Karnataka in order that schools attain expected levels of achievement. This programme has received the support of the government of Karnataka. While a large number of schools appear to have supported this programme, external incentive-driven programmes are likely to make them focus largely on 'results' rather than process or quality of learning. Such an emphasis on 'outcomes' may have important implications for the education of first-generation learners as they may be seen as 'liabilities' in such programmes, that is, they are likely to bring down the performance levels of individual schools. On the other hand these children need enabling learning conditions for them to attend school regularly and perform well. Whether programmes that exhort schools to show measurable outcomes within a short

period of time actually provide the space required to focus on processes of schooling, the culture of the classroom, and the response of teachers, particularly towards educational and social deprivation, needs attention.

16. Subrahmanian (2003) suggests that while VECs attempt to officially sponsor
community mobilisation, their effectiveness depends upon a number of social
and political factors in addition to histories of popular mobilisations in different
contexts. In one of the villages in Karnataka that she studied, Subrahmanian
found that, though a committed headmaster was able to use his influence and
see that school facilities were brought close to Dalit habitations, the mobilisation
of parents and providing support to send their children to school did not follow.
This was reflected in relatively low school enrolment rates. Lack of occupational
opportunities within the village constrained the participation of Dalit members
in the VEC.

17. These are figures of the number of resource centres that were constructed by
2000 (World Bank 2003).

18. Poonam Batra, personal communication.

19. Teachers are called to play an 'extra-academic roles' such as carrying out census
and other surveys, conducting elections and so on. They are often given petty
administrative tasks at the block office. They also distribute textbooks and other
incentives, and organise midday meals.

References

Aggarwal, Y. 2001. *Progress Towards Universal Access and Retention*. New Delhi: NIEPA.

Akhila, R. 2004. 'Reaching Global Goals in Primary Education: Some Gender
Concerns for Tamil Nadu', *Economic and Political Weekly*, 39 (25): 2617–22.

Balagopal, S. and Subrahmanian. 2003. 'Dalit and Adivasi Children in Schools:
Some Preliminary Research Themes and Findings'. In R. Subrahmanian et al.
(ed.), *Education, Inclusion and Exclusion: Indian and South African Perspectives, IDS Bulletin*,
34 (1): 43–54.

Bhatty, Kiran. 1998. 'Educational Deprivation in India. A Survey of Field Investigations', *Economic and Political Weekly*, 33 (27): 1731–40.

Chitnis, Suma. 1981. *A Long Way to Go*. New Delhi: Allied Publishers.

District Primary Education Programme (DPEP). 1999. *Reaching Out Further: Para-
teachers in Primary Education. An In-depth Study of Selected Schemes*, Ministry of
Education. New Delhi: Government of India.

Government of India. 1986. *National Policy on Education (1986)*, Ministry of Human
Resource Development. New Delhi: Government of India.

———. 1992. *National Policy on Education 1992: Programme of Action 1992*. Ministry of
Human Resource Development. New Delhi: Government of India.

Illaiah, Kancha. 1996. *Why I am Not a Hindu: A Sudra Critique of Hindutva Philosophy,
Culture and Political Economy*. Calcutta: Samya Publications.

International Institute for Population Sciences (IIPS) and ORC Macro. 2000. *National
Family Health Survey (NFHS-2), 1998–99*. Mumbai: IIPS.

Jha, Jyotsna and Dhir Jhingran. 2002. *Elementary Education for the Poorest and other Deprived Groups: The Real Challenge of Universalisation.* New Delhi: Centre for Policy Research.

Kabeer, Naila. 2000. 'Social Exclusion, Poverty and Discrimination: Towards an Analytical Framework', *IDS Bulletin,* 31 (4): 83–97.

Kumar, Krishna. 1989. *Social Character of Learning.* New Delhi: Sage Publications.

Manjrekar, Nandini. 2003. 'Contemporary Challenges to Women's Education: Towards an Elusive Goal', *Economic and Political Weekly,* 38 (4): 4577–82.

Nambissan, Geetha B. 1996. 'Equity in Education? Schooling of Dalit Children in India', *Economic and Political Weekly,* 31 (16 and 17): 1011–24.

———. 2003. *Educational Deprivation and Primary School Provision: A Study of Providers in the City of Calcutta,* IDS Working Paper No. 187.

Nambissan, Geetha B. and Mona Sedwal. 2002. 'Education for All: The Situation of Dalit Children in India'. In R. Govinda (ed.), *India Education Report: A Profile of Basic Education.* New Delhi: Oxford University Press.

National Council of Educational Research and Training (NCERT). 1971. *Education and National Development: Report of the Education Commission 1964–66.* (First edition published by the Ministry of Education, Government of India, in 1966, rpt 1971). New Delhi: NCERT.

———. 1999. *Sixth All India Educational Survey: Main Report.* New Delhi: NCERT.

National Sample Survey Organisation (NSSO). 1997. *Economic Activities and School Attendance by Children of India* (Report No. 412. Fifth Quinquennial Survey). New Delhi: National Sample Survey of Statistics, Department of Statistics, Government of India.

National Institute of Advanced Studies (NIAS). 2002. *Caste, Class and School Tanjavur, Tamilnadu: Local Education Report.* Bangalore: NIAS.

Pai, Sudha. 2000. 'Changing Socio-economic and Political Profile of Scheduled Castes in Uttar Pradesh', *Journal of School of Political Economy,* 12 (3 and 4): 405–22.

Pratichi. 2002. *The Pratichi Education Report.* Delhi: Pratichi Trust.

Ramachandran, Vimla. 2002. *Gender and Social Equity in Primary Education: Hierarchies of Access.* New Delhi: European Commission.

Sarva Shiksha Abhiyan (SSA). (n.d.). *Sarva Shiksha Abhiyan: A Programme for Universal Elementary Education.* Department of Elementary Education and Literacy, Ministry of Human Resource Development. New Delhi: Government of India.

Sen, Amartya. 2002. 'Introduction'. In *The Pratichi Education Report.* Delhi: Pratichi Trust.

Shariff, Abusaleh. 1999. *India Human Development Report: A Profile of Indian States in the 1990s.* New Delhi: National Council of Applied Economic Research and Oxford University Press.

Sreedhar, M.V. 1999. 'Reaching the Unreached. Enabling Dalit Girls to Get Schooling', *Manushi,* 3 (III): 10–19.

Subrahmanian, Ramya. 2003. '"Community" at the Centre of Universal Primary Education Strategies: An Empirical Investigation'. In Kabeer et al. (eds), *Child Labour and the Right to Education in South Asia: Needs Versus Rights?* New Delhi: Sage Publications.

Velaskar, Padma. 1998. 'Ideology, Education and the Political Struggle for Liberation: Change and Challenge among the Dalits of Maharashtra'. In Shukla Sureshchandra and Rekha Kaul (eds), *Education, Development and Underdevelopment*. New Delhi: Sage Publications.

World Bank. 1997. *Primary Education in India*. New Delhi: Allied Publishers Limited and World Bank.

———. 2003. *A Review of Educational Progress and Reform in the District Primary Education Program (Phases I and II)* (Discussion Paper Series). New Delhi: Human Development Sector South Asian Region.

8

INCLUSIVE EDUCATION IN THE CONTEXT OF COMMON SCHOOLS

A QUESTION OF EQUITY, SOCIAL JUSTICE AND SCHOOL REFORMS

Madan Mohan Jha

INTRODUCTION

Inclusive education has become an important part of the education discourse in recent times. It is not only being incorporated by different civil society groups active in India, but is also seen in the policy discourse being put forth by the Indian state. The term finds a mention in the 10th Plan document, and now one of the Central Advisory Board of Education (CABE) committees in 2004 examined how to make 'the common school system a reality'. The same committee also looked into the promotion of 'inclusive education' and reducing gender disparity in girls' education in the country.

The term 'inclusive education' owes its origin to the education of children with disabilities and special needs, as a preference to educating them in a segregated special education environment, as in Western countries. It has become an international buzzword in school education, unlike its predecessor 'integration' used generally in Europe, Asia and Australia, and 'mainstreaming' in the USA and Canada (Thomas and Vaughan 2004). The popularity of the term has enhanced since the *Salamanca Statement* (UNESCO 1994) on 'special needs education' declared in June 1994 that 'regular schools with inclusive orientation are the most effective means of combating discriminatory attitudes, creating welcoming communities, building an inclusive society and achieving education for all'. A plethora of literature around educational theories and practices has been emerging across the world since 1990s on inclusive education. In India, special educationalists, some private schools in the metropolis and non-governmental organisations working in the 'area' of special education have been using the term liberally. However, the concept is yet to receive attention of general educationists and teachers in the mainstream school system.

A 'common school' is a school next door, a 'neighbourhood school' to be 'attended by *all* children in the neighbourhood' intended to eliminate 'the segregation that now takes place between the schools for the poor and the under privileged classes and those for the rich and the privileged ones' (Education Commission 1966: 449, 458; emphasis original). Contrasting against the '*selective* view' of special education intended to box children into different categories, the idea behind an inclusive or common school is to make it a part of the 'comprehensive community education' so as to increase the 'inclusion and participation of students in the cultures, curricula and communities of mainstream neighbourhood schools' (Booth 1998: 83; emphasis original).

The purpose of this paper is to present an analytical review of international literature guiding perspectives and discourses on educating children with special needs, from charity to rights and diversity, leading to the different forms of education—special, integration and inclusive. It further attempts to find relevance and linkages of these discourses within the Indian school system with multiple forms of schooling anchored to the socio-economic background of children. Besides, a large proportion of children are out of schools and those in schools are likely to be 'pushed out' before they could have received a minimum of eight years of 'free and compulsory education'. The question the paper finally seeks to find out is whether an appropriate policy instrument could make common schools inclusive of 'all children regardless of their physical, intellectual, social, emotional, linguistic or other conditions' (UNESCO 1994: 6).

Terms like 'disabilities' and 'special needs' have been used in the paper interchangeably as commonly understood for physical, sensory and learning disabilities or difficulties.

CHARITY AND DOING GOOD DISCOURSE

Children with disabilities have traditionally been considered as 'tragic figures', needing charity, sympathy and humanitarian responses (Allan 1999; Fulcher 1999). The theory of defect and deficit within children has influenced the charity discourse expecting society to be good to them, and solutions are attempted in the medical and psychological domain even to achieve educational objectives. It is assumed that special educational needs arising due to defects and deficits could be identified and accurately assessed, and prescriptive solutions could be found with the help of professionals in the field (Bailey 1998; Clough and Corbett 2000; Skidmore 1996). While it could be possible to understand and agree on some 'normative' conditions—physical and sensory—the origin and measurement of 'non-normative' conditions of special needs such as 'learning disability' and 'learning difficulty' are highly contested (Tomlinson 1982). It creates a dependence syndrome within the individual, 'medical need' predominating over the 'educational need', and children are made to accept disabilities 'as a tragedy personal to them' (Oliver 1990: 92).

Education of the handicapped has been traditionally considered as 'individual and charitable enterprise', records the Warnock Report (DES 1978) in England. In India the Education Commission (1966: 123) wanted the education of the handicapped to be 'organised not merely on the humanitarian grounds but also on grounds of utility'. It seems the Indian policy makers are still in the 'charity' mode for arranging education for children with disabilities. The 1986 National Education Policy (modified in 1992) calls for the encouragement of 'voluntary efforts in every possible manners' (MHRD 1998) and the Persons with Disabilities Act (1995) commits to set up special schools in 'government and private sector' (Government of India 1996). Presumably, the intention is to engage nongovernmental organisations, and not the profit-making private sector. However, in reality, a huge market in the special education, particularly for the identification and assessment of 'learning disability', 'slow learners' and IQ testing is emerging in the country. The development of special education as a separate system in the West is based upon the defect and deficit theory of disabilities and special needs, and on assumptions that these 'pathological conditions' can be 'objectively diagnosed' and be given 'a rationally conceived and coordinated system of [educational] services' (Skrtic 1991).

Sociological Factors

A discourse built upon charity, sympathy and 'doing good' obfuscates other issues grounded in the society, culture and environment. Tomlinson (1982) has questioned the theory of 'benevolent humanitarianism' behind the growth of special education, and refers to the 'economic and commercial interests of a developing industrial society' as the guiding factor behind such 'benevolence' (ibid.: 29). A separate special education served the 'needs of ordinary schools' and 'the specific interests of professionals' (ibid.: 57). The law on compulsory education requiring all children to join organised classrooms led to branding and removal of problematic children from schools so that the majority could study without any hindrances. Bennison (1987) traced this reason for the removal of the 'feeble minded' in the USA, and Tomlinson (1982) calls the growth of special education in England a 'safety valve' for a smooth functioning of regular schools. A number of educationists and commentators have been referring to the sociological interpretation of special education by Tomlinson (ibid.), and later by Barton and Tomlinson (1984) (see Clough and Corbett 2000; Skidmore 1996; Slee 1997).

The Indian Reality

Sociological factors help us in developing a better understanding for analysing the Indian situation with mass schooling yet to be institutionalised and the special education system in a nascent stage of development.

There is a perception largely influenced by the non-governmental organisations and unquestioned by the authorities in the government that only 1 to 5 per cent of children with disabilities in India are enrolled in schools (see Singal and Rouse 2003; Watkins 2000). The perception does not match reality. The literacy rate of 54.5 per cent among disabled (male 64 per cent and female 41.6 per cent) has been recently reported by the Census 2001. Comparing with the literacy rate of 64.5 per cent (male 75.3 per cent and female 53.7 per cent) of the total population, and keeping in view that there are only 2,500 special schools (RCI 2000), mostly run by voluntary agencies, against over 115,000 secondary schools and 900,000 primary and upper primary schools in the country, it could be concluded that a large number of ordinary schools are educating children with disabilities. These figures confirm that 'the number of children with disabilities *casually integrated in ordinary schools*' exceed those reported in official documents (Miles 1997: 101; emphasis added) and also 'the informal efforts of Indian families and neighborhoods ... to respond to special needs and disabilities' (ibid. 1994: 4).

Earlier, the 47th Round of National Sample Survey in 1991 reported 42 per cent (NSSO 1994) literacy rate among persons identified as disabled. Often these figures are disputed due to under-counting and differences in the definition of disability as used by the survey and the census, and those given in laws or applied by NGOs. The percentage of the disabled reported by the survey and the census is close to 2 per cent. NGOs and international agencies believe that disabled should be between 5 to 10 per cent. Even assuming a higher percentage of disabled, the literacy rate should not be as lower as is generally projected. As per the recent national survey data, only about 11 per cent disabled were enrolled in special schools in urban areas, while less than 1 per cent were enrolled in rural special schools. Under the integrated education scheme, over 120,000 children were getting benefits in over 24,000 mainstream schools (Jha 2002a: 98). It seems that those reporting lower literacy rates among the disabled could be referring only to children covered under the integrated education scheme of the education ministry and special schools under the social justice ministry.

These figures are being presented to suggest that in India, children with disabilities *are going to ordinary schools*, without the services of special teachers. There is no charity or 'doing good' factor behind such a natural entry of children into ordinary schools. We do not have a structure of special schools as in the West, where a special school system was created for the disabled parallel to the regular school system when law for compulsory mass education was passed. We are in a similar situation as Western countries were over 150 years ago since we are in the process of making mass schooling compulsory. A central Bill for 'free and compulsory education' for children of age 6 to 14 years is in the offing. Now the question is, should we adopt polices and practices of the Western countries that created a special school system, and which they are now trying to dismantle, or do we strengthen our common schools to make them inclusive of all children in the neighbourhood? In other words, should we totally follow the Western 'models' of special education, special needs and learning disabilities, or develop our own understanding, appreciation and values for all children learning together in common inclusive schools? Do we define learning disability and special needs while they want to un-define these exclusionary labels? Analysing the disability situation in South Asia, Miles (2002: 114) observes, 'Inclusion requires a fundamental rethinking of the aims and social context of education, from top to bottom'.

The social reality in India goes beyond the integration or inclusion of children with disabilities. There are a large number of children with adverse social and economic background and situations.

The policy design and instrumentalities have been creating hierarchies of schools for different categories of children (PROBE 1999). There may be a need to extend sociological theory to understand this phenomenon in the Indian school education, and engage a discourse around the rights, equity and social justice that led to a demand for a 'more integrated system' in the West to desegregate special education for the disabled (Skidmore 1996).

Rights, Equity and the Social Justice Discourse

Moving away from charity and benevolence, disabled people themselves are voicing for rights and entitlement, leading to equity and social justice discourse (Armstrong et al. 2000). Discourses help us in understanding the 'particular interests' they serve (Allan 1999). For instance, a corporate or market discourse has recently emerged for 'managing disabilities' (Fulcher 1999). In India, professionals often talk of working in the 'disability sector'. Under the rights and social justice discourse, disability and special needs, instead of being regarded as pathology of individual, is considered as a societal construct resulting from the social order and social arrangements (Allan 1999; Jha 2002a).

However, a rights argument could also be used for sustaining special schools, as education is a means to an end; special schools for some children could 'provide the most effective means towards achieving these ends' (Farrell 2000: 155). Hornby et al. (1997: 84) see rights as 'right to an appropriate education' and 'right to be fully integrated into the society', and so they argue, children's education in ordinary schools or special schools does not matter so long as they 'facilitate those two rights'.

The demand for rights and equality, nonetheless, has followed on a number of United Nations conventions. The Programme of Action Concerning Disabled Persons (1983) called for 'equal educational opportunity ... in the general education system' (Article 120). The Rights of the Child (1989) asks countries to 'ensure that the disabled child has effective access to and receives education...in a manner conducive to the child's fullest social integration' (Article 23.1/3). The Standard Rules (1993) recognised 'the principle of equal primary, secondary and tertiary education…in integrated settings' (Rule 6). A natural corollary of these declarations and conventions has been that states have been making policies and laws for 'integration' or 'mainstreaming' of children with special needs in regular schools to secure them equal opportunity and social justice.

Integration

The rights argument brought children with special needs to mainstream schools to 'integrate' them, but it did not follow any ideological shift in the process of schooling; as a result, 'special schools' began, being created within regular schools. The children came 'in' but could not become 'of' the class (Ferguson 1996). The Warnock Committee in England took a mechanical view of integration and grouped it into three categories: 'locational', when children come to the same school site but remain separate; 'social', when they could mix in out-of-class activities; and 'functional', when they share the same classroom (DES 1978). Most Indian private schools have begun 'locational' integration by setting up learning centres or resource centres in the same premises. Integration followed a 'fit-in' approach, whereby children with special needs were expected to assimilate into cultures, norms and curriculum of regular schools. Integration thus became an additional burden for these children.

Barton and Tomlinson (1984: 65) argue that the ideological justification for integration is no way different from those given for special education. It relates to the 'needs' of the wider society, the whole education system, rather than simply to the 'needs' of the individual children.

Normality and Sameness

The issue of rights calls for equality and equal opportunity to meet the objectives of social justice, the result being a demand for access to the 'normal'. In case of education, it would mean an admission into mainstream schools. There is a conflict between equal opportunity to the 'normal' and education as 'appropriate' to the needs of a particular child. There is a tendency not to question what is normal and not to challenge the 'conditions under which discriminatory and exclusionary social practices operate' (Armstrong et al. 2000: 11). Normality and sameness are defined and constructed by the powerful groups in a society where there are differences and diversities. Archer (1979: 3) says, 'Forms that education takes are the political products of power struggles'.

The unquestioned sameness and normality creates a dilemma between commonality and difference (Clark et al. 1999; Norwich 2002). The Supreme Court of India in one of its judgements has said, 'In order to treat some people equally, we must treat them differently...equality of opportunity admits discrimination with reason and prohibits discrimination without reason.'[1] The question is who decides the reason? 'In a society based on hierarchy, power and interest groups, "reason" is mostly decided by professionals and bureaucrats' (Jha 2002a: 46), who have nearly full control on education, special education in particular. Equality, therefore, is to be achieved not by forcing 'normality' and 'sameness' in a mainstream school, but by appreciating and positively valuing differences and diversities (Daniels and Garner 1999; Oliver 1988) calling for school reforms. Adverse experiences of integration seem to have led to a discourse on diversity and inclusive education.

Equal Opportunity in Indian Schools

Gandhi's basic education was the first official policy in India 'to change the established structure of opportunities for education' (Kumar 1994). What comes to mind when we talk of basic education? It was 'contemporary not modern, ideal not practical, and it might have achieved limited success but ultimately failed' (Jha 2002b). Fagg (2002) has contested these perceptions in his study based on primary sources on basic education, and he says that the education system unveiled by Gandhi in 1937 influenced government policy for the next thirty years until the Education Commission (1966–68) replaced it by 'work education' as a subject for study in Indian schools. The Indian Constitution offers an essential framework for equality in opportunity, and policy makers have consistently used this term in policy documents as a rhetoric but without bringing in any structural changes that would reduce 'cultural domination and ideological control' of the middle class (Scarse 1993) and monopoly of the higher castes and class in the 'use of the best available educational opportunities' by them for their children (Haq 1989: 50).

The polices relating to the Common School System, growth of non-formal education, and special needs education for the disabled are being examined from the perspectives of equal opportunity and social justice. It is argued that overall policy and practices in regard to equality in education is important to give legitimacy and strength to a discourse on education for children considered as having special needs, and on inclusive education. In the absence of an inherently inbuilt equality in the system, a discourse on inclusion cannot advance beyond a point.

The Common School System

The Education Commission (1964–66), popularly known as the Kothari Commission, coined the term for the first time without defining or explaining what was meant by a 'common school'. It was intended to improve 'administration and supervision of school education' (the subject has been dealt under the chapter 'School Education: Administration and Supervision') by evolving 'a Common School System of public education' 'in place of the existing system which divides the management of schools between a large number of agencies whose functioning is inadequately coordinated' (Education Commission 1966: 229), unlike in England where the 'comprehensive struggles' had been launched with the aim of ending 'two nations in education' divided by grammar and secondary modern schooling (Tomlinson 2001: 14). The country was moving towards a comprehensive system of school education, and 'a common school underpinned by egalitarian ideologies, and attended by middle- and working-class children, was envisaged and supported by all classes' (Ford 1969, cited in Tomlinson 1982: 175).

The 'common school' envisaged under the Kothari report seems to be largely concerned with the administration and supervision of school education. A major portion of the report has been devoted to ending discrimination between teachers of different schools—government, local authority and private organisations; establishment of district school boards; school committees for government and local authority schools; and grants-in-aid to and management of aided private schools joining the Common School System (CSS). It also suggests that 90 per cent scholarships at the universities should be given to students passing out from the common school system of public education.

In the absence of data and researches, it is difficult to evaluate the impact of the Kothari Commission's recommendations on the school system in the country. However, anomalies between teachers' salaries in government, local authority and aided schools seem to have been removed. But recommendations regarding establishment of the district school boards, 'school committees' with half of elected members, so that 'each [government school] is regarded as an individuality and given adequate freedom' (Education Commission 1966: 449) at par with private schools, have been completely ignored. Bureaucratic control over government schools has rather increased, though private schools enjoy much more freedom (in the matter of selection of children, teachers, textbooks, holidays, school timings, etc, and charging of tuition fees and many other types of fees). Despite such glaring contrasts between the two unequals, comparisons are often made between government and private schools. As a result, parents are losing faith in government schools and the market for private schools is increasing.

The recommendations of the Kothari Commission on the CSS need critical examination after 40 years. First, the establishment of district school boards may not be relevant now in the light of the 73rd and 74th Constitutional Amendments, which require primary and secondary education to be transferred to the *panchayati raj* institutions. Second, an empowered school committee for the government and local authority schools is yet to emerge and the inspector *raj* continues in its full form. So the functioning and performance of government schools cannot be compared with private schools. Third, the commission had given the option to fee-charging private schools to join the CSS and abolish tuition fees (grants-in-aid to be given by the government), or remain fee-charging 'independent' (unaided) schools. In the present environment of growth in the private school market, it is doubtful if any private school would exercise this option. Finally, the Commission had proposed 90 per cent scholarships to students passing out from CSS schools for university education. Even this has become irrelevant for an insignificant number of such scholarships, very low university fees, and private schools not being limited only to rich persons as assumed by the Commission.

THE NEIGHBOURHOOD SCHOOL CONCEPT   The most crucial part of the CSS addressing the issue of equal opportunity and social justice is the neighbourhood school concept, which was given inadequate space and importance in the report. The concept implies that 'each school should be attended by *all* children in the neighbourhood irrespective of caste, creed, community, religion, economic condition or social status, so that there would be no segregation in schools' (Education Commission 1966: 458; emphasis original). If the report were to be written today, one would have expected that terms like 'ability' and 'disability or special needs' are also included in the *all*.

There has not been any discourse on the neighbourhood school concept in India unlike in most developed countries and democracies where this is being practised. Any reference of the concept to the bureaucracy, the upwardly mobile middle class and elite provokes two reactions. First, how to send children to substandard government schools in the neighbourhood. Second, the idea would destroy 'good' private schools if they were asked to take children indiscriminately. The argument centres on 'talent' and 'merit' for making a 'good' (private) school and education. Policy makers and even educationists omit the 'two other arguments' advanced by the Commission in support of neighbourhood schooling apart from social and national integration, namely, '[First], a neighbourhood school will provide "good" education to children because sharing life with common people is…an essential ingredient of good education. Second, the establishment of such schools will compel rich, privileged and powerful classes to take an interest in the system of public education and thereby bring about its early improvement' (Education Commission 1966: 458).

The Commission seems to have an educational theory behind a neighbourhood school system for 'good' education. However, Archer (1979: 4) explains that 'there is no such thing as an educational theory…there are only sociological theories of educational development'. The developments in school education post-Kothari Commission demonstrate that the rich, privileged and powerful classes did *not* take an interest in the system of public education to bring about any improvement in it. The growth of private schools at the cost of public education (government schools) in recent years confirms another theory given by Archer (ibid.: 2) that 'education has the characteristics it does because of the goals pursued by those who control it'.

In the context of education of children regarded as having special needs, even in England, the comprehensive education movement in 1960s and early 1970s did not include them. It is only after the Warnock Committee's report in 1978 that the equal opportunity theory was extended. Warnock herself wrote later to make education for children with special needs 'a natural part of the comprehensive ideal' (Warnock 1980). Tomlinson (2001: 31) comments: 'This expressed an egalitarian belief that a common school should be inclusive of children of all abilities and disabilities and clashed [both] with beliefs that "natural" abilities and disabilities needed separate schools'.

NATIONAL POLICIES ON THE CSS   The government accepted the Education Commission's recommendations on the Common School System in the 1968 national policy for 'equalisation of educational opportunity'. The policy committed to make efforts to 'improve standard of education in general school', wanted 'all special schools like public schools to admit students on the basis of merit and also to provide a prescribed proportion of free-studentship to prevent segregation of social classes' (MHRD 1998: 41), but without adversely affecting the minorities' right to manage their institutions under Article 30 of the Constitution.

The 1986 national education policy on the CSS was borrowed from the 1968 policy but it (1986 policy) shifted its (CSS) emphasis from 'education for equality' to make it a part of the 'national system of education', implying that 'up to a given level, all students, irrespective of *caste, creed, location or sex*, have access to education of comparable quality' (ibid.: 5; emphasis added). The Education Commission (1966), however, had recommended the neighbour-hood school concept for all children irrespective of caste, creed, community, religion, *economic conditions and social status* (ibid.: 458). The 1986 policy had also assured to take 'effective measures' to implement the CSS. But no measure has been taken so far. The Programme of Action (1992) makes *no mention* of the Common School System. Another part of the national system of education that re-quired a uniform educational pattern of 10+2+3 in the country has been monitored and finds references in official documents.

The Ramamurti Committee (1990), while reviewing the 1986 policy, outlined the reasons for the CSS not gaining ground—low investment in government schools because the elite and privileged classes do not send their children, lack of political will, craze for English-medium (private) schools, and growth of institutions like Kendriya Vidyalayas meant for separate categories of children. The Committee expanded and extended the scope of the CSS as a 'first step in securing equity and social justice'. It looked at the CSS beyond 'administration and supervision' of the school system. Accordingly, it recommended that the CSS be extended to unaided private schools by giving incentives, bring in essential minimum legislation to dispense with early selection process, and introduce the mother tongue as the medium of education at primary levels, including in unaided private schools.

These recommendations had the potential to change the face of school education system in the country and remove increasing disparities in school access irrespective of *economic conditions and social status*. But none of the recommendations was incorporated in the modified policy of 1992. The CABE Committee on Policy (1992), while reviewing the Ramamurti Committee report, expected the 'privileged schools' to accept 'social responsibility by sharing their facilities and resources with other institutions, and facilitating access to children of disadvantaged groups' (MHRD 1992: 16). And we have a fallout of this policy: private schools running 'centres for the underprivileged' in the afternoon or in their outhouses, thereby doing 'excellence' for the privileged in the forenoon and equity in the afternoon. Skrtic (1991: 233) argues: 'The successful schools in the postindustrial era will be ones that achieve excellence and equity simultaneously—indeed one that recognizes equity as the way to excellence'.

THE MAKING OF COMMON SCHOOLS   There are misconceptions and misgivings about the common school system. First, it is felt that children will be *forced* to go to substandard government schools, and, second, it is an attempt to encroach upon the parental choice of sending children to private schools of 'excellence'. The fundamental principle of the CSS is to create a (public) school system so that parents ordinarily will not feel the need to send children outside the neighbourhoods. Second, a 'good' school—government or private—should be part of the neighbourhood, not isolated from it. While certain features of the Common School System proposed by the Kothari Commission may have become out of context, the essence for establishing common schools is far more relevant today than it was 40 years ago.

There has to be a well-defined commonality in all schools in a (common) school system; it has to have '*equitable* (not uniform) quality of education for all types of schools, be they private-unaided, private-aided, Government or local authority'.[2] He identifies 'six essential and non-negotiable attributes' (of commonality) in common schools—minimum physical infrastructure; professional quality of teachers and optimum teacher–student ratio; diversified and flexible curriculum; holistic and child-friendly pedagogy; sensitivity and pedagogic empathy for gender; Dalits, tribal, cultural and ethnic minorities and children viewed as disabled and learning disabled; and decentralised community control of schools.

On the face of it there should not be much disagreement on the prescription of Sadgopal for a CSS. However, questions may be raised and doubts may be expressed when one calls for mixing children from the rich and socially advanced families with the poor and the disadvantaged, particular those viewed as having ability compared to those considered 'disabled'. People might sense a compromise with the 'excellence' in the name of equity and social justice. The traditional notion of 'excellence' from out-of-children sorted out at a young age is being questioned in most democracies. England abolished such sorting out of children at the age of 11 by introducing comprehensive schools in 1960s and 1970s, and Americans are basing their schools on 'the triple play of basics, technology and *diversity*' (Elliott 2002; emphasis added). Literature is emerging at the international level, arguing to make collaboration in heterogamous classrooms the 'prime mode of learning' in 21st-century schools (Lipsky and Gartner 1999), and give equity precedence over the 'excellence' (Skrtic 1991).

The most essential features of common schools in England (called comprehensives) were mixing and educating children of different social classes together. When such mixing amongst children takes place, there are evidences that it 'enhances the school standards for all' (Kahelnberg 2001). Tomlinson gives some figures on 'comprehensive success' in England:

In 1962, when some 20 per cent were selected for grammar schools, 16 per cent of pupils obtained five O-level pass. In 2000–2001, 51 per cent achieved the equivalent five GCSE passes. The A-level exam, originally designed for less than 10 per cent of pupils, was achieved in two or more subjects by 37 per cent of pupils in 2001. In 1970, 47 per cent left school without any qualifications, by 2000 this had fallen to 10 per cent'.[3]

A common school system with *all* children getting together with equal opportunity for access and success in the neighbourhood school would pose a major challenge to the brahminical high-caste/class social order, and that is the call of social justice to be achieved through education as a potent instrumentality in a democracy.

Non-formal Education

The formal school system is designed for a very small minority to prepare them for higher education, and the vast majority is given 'some education' through a parallel system of non-formal education (NFE) (Ahmed 1975; Beare and Slaughter 1993; Watkins 2000). There is a perception that the NFE was invented for a small minority and is caste neutral. Both perceptions are wrong as may be seen from Table 8.1.

TABLE 8.1
DROP-OUT RATES IN INDIA IN 2001–02 (%)

Class and Gender	Non-SC/ST	SC	ST
Class V boys	34	45	51
Class V girls	46	48	53
Class VIII boys	49	59	67
Class VIII girls	53	64	73

Source: Compiled from Selected Educational Statistics, 2001–02, Ministry of Human Resource Development, Government of India.

NFE is meant for the majority and is biased against the Scheduled Castes and Tribes, and girls. Even at the time of policy formulation, the population of out-of-school children was half of those in the schoolgoing age (MHRD 1990: 123). Policy makers, instead of taking drop-outs as a systemic issue and rectifying the formal school system, chose to design the 'non-formal programme, meant for drop-outs, for children from habitations without schools, working children and girls who cannot attend whole day schools' (ibid. 1998: 14). On its face, it seemed the NFE policy was incidental or temporary. However, with the growth of the different types of NFEs under the Sarva Siksha Abhiyan (SSA), it is now clear that the intention was to create a *parallel system* of education, romanticising it as 'relevant and contextual', and it was advanced as a justification.

Inadequacy of resources was the hidden reason but never publicised beyond a point. While NFE was to run as learning centres to be provided by the community, with 'instructors' who would be untrained school-pass local youth and would offer 'education' only for a few hours to accommodate the working time of children, it was eulogised by characterising its features such as offering 'locally relevant' and 'flexible curriculum', 'joyful learning' and 'community participation' in its running. Sadgopal (2003) ridicules these vocabularies, and asks why children from the elite and middle classes are being delivered 'irrelevant', and 'joyless' curriculum in the formal system. Whether it is the question of 'content' or 'relevance', they are important not only for non-formal learning centres but for the school system as a whole.

The Ramamurti Committee recommended that the formal system itself be 'non-formalised' to include all children in its fold. But the CABE Committee on Policy, constituted to look into the recommendations in 1992 thought that the 'challenges [of retaining children who cannot afford to attend schools regularly]... are daunting enough and it does not seem desirable to overload the school system with yet another formidable challenge of meeting the educational needs of children with severe para educational constraints' (MHRD 1992: 31).

The data clearly indicate that the clientele for NFE would largely be Scheduled Castes, Scheduled Tribes and girls, who traditionally have been treated as groups of distinct (lower) social status and the educational system is used as 'a crucial agent in differential socialization [of school children] by status groups of origin' (Karabel and Halsey 1977: 32). NFE has been formalised as a parallel system of education with a variety of names under the broad umbrella programme of the SSA of the central government despite the Planning Commission evaluation report, which said, 'The NFE system has not made any significant contribution to the realisation of the goal of the UEE [and]... elementary education needs to be delivered primarily through the formal education system' (Planning Commission 1998: xi).

The rhetoric of 'education for all' following the Jomtien Conference (1990) and entry of the international agencies into primary education has taken shine off our commitment of 'Education for Equality', at least in theory/policy (Sadgopal 2003, 2004), and it has been replaced by education for few (largely through private schools) and literacy for all through learning centres and para-teachers under the national flagship programme of the SSA. NFE schemes with different attractive names are no longer just a parallel system of education; they are replacing schools by centres, teachers by para-teachers, and education by literacy, and all are meant for poor and underprivileged children. In many states regular teachers are not being appointed and para-teachers are replacing them as a matter of policy. England ushered in the comprehensive ideal of schooling by abolishing 'two nations in education' (Tomlinson 2001), but we are creating 'many nations in education' by contemptuously dumping a common school system.

The draft education Bill of the elementary education department, intended to give effect to Article 21A of the recently amended provision of the Constitution to guarantee a fundamental right to children of the 6 to 14 age group, proposes to legalise the parallel non-formal education system, in utter contempt for the principles of equality and social justice. The Bill having been referred to the CABE committees, it was hoped they will take an egalitarian view of school education in India and abolish all forms of low-quality parallel education for the poor and under privileged.

Educating Children with Special Needs

The policy issue regarding education of children with disabilities and special needs does not seem to have been considered as part of the discourse of rights, equal opportunity and social justice in India. As pointed out elsewhere in this paper, it has been designed largely keeping in view charity and volunteerism. Further, it has been considered in isolation, treating these children as a separate group.

CABE 1944   'The first official attempt to analyse the problem [of educating the handicapped]' was made in the CABE report of

1944 (Sargent 1968: 100). The report, also known as the John Sargent Report (after the British chief educational adviser at that time), asked for making education of these children 'an essential part of a national system of education and [to] be administered by the Education Department' (CABE 1944). It further said, '*Wherever possible*, [the] handicapped should not be segregated from normal children' (ibid.; emphasis added), and 10 per cent of the total budget for basic and high schools should be spent on provisions and services for the education of the 'handicapped'. The special education is yet to be a part of mainstream education, though a number of UN conventions and declarations, including the *Salamanca Statement*, have called for making special education a part of mainstream education, and as per a survey of the UNESCO, 95 per cent countries in the world have already removed systemic segregation of special education (UNESCO 1995). Many civil society groups recently petitioned the President and the Government of India for removing bureaucratic barriers from making the education system inclusive.

SPECIAL NEEDS EDUCATION IN NPEs   The 1966 Education Commission noted that the Indian constitutional directive on compulsory education under Article 45 included handicapped children as well, but its subsequent observations had questionable foundations and were pessimistic (Jha 2002a). While observing that not much had been done in this regard, it recorded, 'any great improvement in the situation does not seem to be practicable in the near future'; and wanted the country to 'learn from educationally advanced countries' (Education Commission 1966: 123), though special education in those countries was under criticism. Further, it felt that the assumption that many (handicapped) children might 'find it psychologically disturbing to be placed in an ordinary school' (ibid.) against the spirit of integration. It made a target of covering only 10 per cent of children with disabilities by 1986. Drawing upon the report, the government, under the section 'Equalisation of Educational Opportunity' of the 1968 policy, committed to make attempts 'to *develop integrated programmes* enabling the handicapped children to study in regular schools' (MHRD 1998; emphasis added).

After eight years of the policy, a programme named Integrated Education of Disabled Children (IEDC) was launched by the government in 1974, which was revised in 1992. In the 1986 and 1992 policies, though 'Education for the Handicapped' was listed as a part of 'Education for Equality' in addition to the education for Scheduled Castes, Scheduled Tribes and minorities, the encouragement for 'voluntary effort' and the policy of opening special schools (at the district headquarters for 'severe disabilities') continued. It called for 'the education of children with motor handicaps and other mild handicaps' to be common with the others *'wherever it is feasible'* (ibid.: 11; emphasis added).

The Ramamurti Committee (1990) made a critical review of the 1986 policy, and observed that education for the handicapped is being regarded as a social welfare activity; 'special schools have been treated in isolation from other educational institutions', and the IEDC scheme is run as 'mini special schools' (MHRD 1990: 85). The modified policy in 1992 continued without making any changes. Jangira (1997: 496) finds the policy 'hesitant in full commitment to universalisation of elementary education' for them, and it remained 'silent on the department of education assuming full responsibility for education of children with disabilities'.

Education in Disabilty-Related Acts   In 1995 Parliament passed the Persons with Disabilities (PWD) Act, giving a full chapter on education for children with disabilities. There does not seem to be any major policy deviation after the *Salamanca Statement* (1994). It provided for setting up of special schools in the 'government and private sector', which seems inconsistent with the Supreme Court judgement and education policies that do not allow privatisation and commercialisation of education. It, however, assures that the government shall, *'endeavour to promote the integration* of students with disabilities in the normal schools' (Gazette of India 1996: 12; emphasis added). As a variant of NFE, the labour ministry of the government is running 'special schools' for the child labour as one of its projects (Government of India 2004a).

The PWD Act defines a 'person with disability' as one 'suffering from not less than forty percent of any disability certified by a medical authority' (Government of India 2004a). Such a criterion for measuring disability in terms of percentages creates utter confusion and problems in education, and deprives children of support and services, which they are otherwise entitled to, even if the disability is certified as less than 40 per cent, since education after all is 'free and compulsory' for all children.

The Act does not define 'learning disability', 'special needs' or 'learning difficulty', but 'mental retardation' has been defined as 'a condition of arrested or incomplete development of [the] mind of a person which is specially characterised by sub-normality of intelligence'; and 'mental illness' has been defined as 'any mental disorder other than mental retardation' (ibid.: 3). The phrases in the definition of mental retardation are similar to the ones used in the British Mental Deficiency Act of 1913 (amended in 1927), which defined mental defectiveness as 'a condition of arrested or incomplete development of mind'. While these definitions may be useful for giving some incentives and administering welfare programmes for the disabled, they do not have much relevance for providing education to all. At times it becomes limiting and stigmatising for children in schools.

Subsequent Acts have either copied the definitions of the PWD Act, or have added more categories of disabilities. For instance, the Act made in 1999 for creating a trust for the 'welfare' of persons with autism, cerebral palsy, mental retardation and multiple disabilities has kept the same definition of mental retardation and disability as given in the PWD Act, but has defined 'severe disability' as 80 per cent of disability, rather than 40 per cent. Notably, the National Trust Act does not refer to education of persons for whose 'welfare' it has been created. About autism, it says, 'Autism means a condition of uneven skill development primarily affecting the communication and social abilities of a person, marked by repetitive and ritualistic behaviour' (Gazette of India 1999). The same definition of mental retardation has been used in the Rehabilitation Council of India (RCI) Act (1992) (amended in 2000). The RCI decides the curriculum on special education, and accredits institutions and course for special education, thus keeping it outside the domain of mainstream educational institutions and maintaining a clear divide between the two.

THE DRAFT EDUCATION BILL   A Bill has been drafted following Article 21A of the Indian Constitution to secure a fundamental right to education for children of age 6 to 14 years. Though the Bill was placed before one of the CABE committees, it may not be inappropriate to look at the elements of equality and inclusion in the Bill.

The Bill defined a child with special needs as one 'with a disability or a learning disability or both'. Learning disability is defined as 'dyslexia, attention deficit disorder, autism, Down's syndrome and such other conditions as NCERT may notify' (Government of India 2004a). Local authorities shall '*promote integration* of children with special needs in normal schools' (ibid.; emphasis added). In the absence of a government school, recognised schools, including private unaided schools, would be directed to admit these children without specifying who should pay for them. In the subsequent section, the draft Bill says the child will be sent to a special school existing within a prescribed distance from his/her residence. It is silent on what happens if a special school is not within the 'prescribed distance' and the child is not able to 'integrate' in a normal school.

The Bill intends to create a non-existent category of 'learning disability' that would drive a large number of children from the mainstream school system into the hands of professionals and specialists who have begun growing in the private sector. To say the least, if the Bill becomes law in this shape, it would be out of tune with international perspectives and inclusion movements across the world that is questioning the theory of special needs and learning disability *within* children. In addition, it would open a big market for special and private schools and 'professionals' in this 'sector', excluding a large number of the poor and the disadvantaged from mainstream education. There are many study evidences at the international level which indicate that the proportion of the working class and ethnic classes have always been significantly high among those labelled as having 'learning disabilities' and 'special needs' (Dunn 1968; Tomlinson 1982). In case of India, it would largely mean Scheduled Castes, Scheduled Tribes and other children with poor social and economic background.

IS POLICY MOVING? It seems polices since 1944, while continuing to promote segregated special education, have been using variants of phraseologies on bringing children with disabilities in regular schools (see Table 8.2). In substance, however, there has been no progress, like someone running on a treadmill.

TABLE 8.2
A TYPOLOGY OF INDIAN POLICIES ON SPECIAL EDUCATION

Policy	Major Features	On Integration/Inclusion
CABE (1944)	Special education to be a part of the national system of education under the education department.	*Wherever possible* not be segregated from normal children.
NPE (1968)	Reference to 'special schools' for public schools; concept of the CSS introduced.	*Attempts to develop integrated* programmes in regular schools.
NPE (1986 and 1992)	Special schools at district headquarters; CSS as a part of national system of education.	*Wherever feasible*, education of disabled... common with others.
PWD (1995)	Special schools in 'private sector'; free education up to 18 in an 'appropriate environment'.	*Endeavour to promote integration* in normal schools.
Draft education bill (2004)	Defines special needs and learning disabilities (vague and confusing), and promotes special schools.	*Promote integration* (if not prevented).

DISABILITY: A DIVERSITY DISCOURSE

A man (or a woman) has a short leg making him (or her) unable to reach up to the shelf in a library. One could try to rectify this 'defect' and attempt a medical correction; or the person could be compensated for the 'deficit' within him (or her) either by putting up a ladder or by placing the services of another person to assist him/her. Another alternative could be to enter into a dialogue and find out the books generally of his (or her) interest, and arrange those on lower shelves.[4]

This simple example is given to explain a paradigm shift from the defect and deficit theory of disability to the diversity discourse. It does not suggest that the person should be denied of any resources or facility to overcome or minimise the impact of a 'disability' on him/her. It only demonstrates a shift from the pathological and dependence syndrome of disability to one of understanding and valuing. The diversity discourse can be used in planning programmes for the 'poor', in creating an understanding with groups belonging to different cultures and ideologies, and very effectively in education for creating inclusive settings for children with disabilities and special needs.

A diversity discourse on special needs education existing otherwise in the society, in its culture, language, ethnicity, religion and socio-economic situation, calls for treating disability not as something 'inherent' and 'categorical', but as 'transactional' and 'historical' (Lipsky and Gartner 1999). Valuing 'special need' as diversity and as a resource would mean that children will not be seen as 'other' or 'them' (Booth and Ainscow 1998), and it would become a foundation for creating inclusive and responsive schools (Booth 1987, 1996; Clark et al. 1997, Emanuelsson 1998; Wedell 1995).

From a study of the history of education and school, it is clear that school, as an institution for learning, is a creation of the industrial age in the 19th century (Beare and Salughter 1993; Simmons 1983). We are already in the 21st century and the 'industrial age' has been replaced by the 'information age'. Educational philosophers have questioned the meaning and practice of education in schools in the 20th century—Dewy and Whitehead in the West, and Gandhi and Krishnamurti in India. It is an important question to ask, particularly keeping in mind those termed as having disabilities and special needs, as there is now an agreement in theory, if not in practice, that whatever is decided upon as 'education' in any society, all children should enjoy it equally (Tomlinson).[5] However, who decides what is education and how one should get it. The questions remain unresolved in a hierarchical and power-centric society.

The nature of society and workplace in the meantime has changed in the 21st century; therefore, there is a need to redesign the school system wherein the emphasis would shift from 'knowledge transmission' to 'knowledge building', from individual excellence to teamwork and group achievements, and from addressing a homogeneous to a heterogeneous group of learners and workforce (Lipsky and Gartner 1999; Lloyd 2000). Giving a general plan for restructuring schools in the post-industrial era, Skrtic (1991: 233) argues for 'developing students' capacity for experiential learning through collaborative problem solving within a community of interests', for which he recommends the presence of children with diverse 'interests, abilities, skills and cultural perspectives' in a classroom. It would require a reconstruction of the mainstream curriculum so that children with special needs are not accepted and tolerated, but their diversity and difference is 'positively valued and celebrated' (Oliver 1995), with 21st century schools being organised around 'the idea of difference': '[It] implies nothing less than a total reconstruction of the whole enterprise of education...for societies in the twenty first century, which will be organized around the idea of difference; a radical departure from twentieth century societies, which have been organized around the idea of normality (ibid., cited in Thomas and Vaughan 2004: 114).

Inclusive Education

As integration emerged without much ideological discourse in response to a demand for human rights and equity on behalf of disabled and children with special educational needs in the 1980s, 'inclusion' seems informed by *diverse* educational needs of children in the 1990s. However, inclusion as a concept is yet to develop into school cultures and practices, and children are still expected to 'fit in' with the rigidity of the school structure. There seems to be no ideological shift towards viewing children with special needs as a part of the comprehensive school community, a factor missed out when policy makers and educationalists were opting for the integration (Barton and Tomlinson 1984).

A common school as a natural receiver of all children is to be imbibed as an educational philosophy, making it simpler to transform the school system. Schools, in the meantime, are using the term 'inclusion' rhetorically and converting themselves overnight from 'special' or 'integrating' to 'inclusive'. While it is difficult to say how the word was coined, it has become very popular in educational vocabulary in a very short period of time, particularly among brand-driven schools, NGOs and professionals. In a random survey conducted in Delhi schools in 2004 by the author, nearly all schools heads—private and government—confirmed that they had heard about special schools; 59 per cent government school heads and 64 per cent private school heads had heard about 'integration'; and 41 per cent government and 51 per cent private heads had heard of inclusive education.

A plethora of literature has emerged on inclusive education and inclusive schools since the World Conference on Special Needs Education in 1994 at Salamanca (Spain). The *Salamanca Statement*, issued following the World Conference represented by 92 governments and 25 international organisations, believed that 'every child has unique characteristics, interests, abilities and learning needs' and 'education systems should...take into account the wide *diversity* (emphasis added) of these characteristics and needs' (UNESCO 1994).

Despite references to diversity and to all children, which the statement further elaborates as 'disabled and gifted children, street and working children, children from remote and nomadic populations, children from linguistic, ethnic and cultural minorities and children from other disadvantaged and marginalized areas or groups' (ibid.: 6), the definition of the term 'special educational needs' does not seem going beyond the one introduced by the Warnock Committee (DES 1978) in the UK. The Committee's concept of special educational needs (SEN) was largely rooted in the *within-child-deficit* theory; it assumed the *accommodating capacity* of the existing school system, and remained confined to a 'discourse emphasizing professionalism, difference and deficit (Ballard 1995: 3), and creating more professionals 'claiming a legitimate involvement in special education process' (Galloway et al. 1994: 121). Notwithstanding the limitations of the statement, inclusion is seen by many authors and commentators in education as a big opportunity to take discourse beyond integration and special education, and reform a common neighbourhood school.

A TYPOLOGY OF DISCOURSES AND SCHOOL SETTINGS   Perspectives and discourses guide strategies. The perspectives perused by a school in its policy and practices may influence the shape of school settings. There are no empirical evidences to support the typology in Table 8.3, but the literature reviewed by me could be presented in this broad framework. Schools may be following psycho-medical perspectives and using descriptors linked with them in the table,

TABLE 8.3
A TYPOLOGY OF SCHOOL SETTINGS

Discourse	Perspective	Setting	Language/Descriptors Used
Charity	Psycho-medical	Special	Diagnostic, prescriptive, identification, assessment, IQ, not normal, behavioural modifications, labelling, segregated, treatment, professional control, institutional segregation
Rights	Sociological	Integration	Resources, compensatory, remedial, withdrawal, mainstreaming, assimilation, normalisation Individualised Education Programme (IEP), laws, rules, professional superiority, institutional selectivity
Diversity	Institutional	Inclusion	Acceptance, valuing, celebrating, reconstructing curriculum, pedagogy, questioning normality, benefiting all, professional collaboration, institutional reforms
Disability deconstruction, discovering learning, questioning education, redesigning school			Feeling a part and not apart, a sense of belonging, feeling needed and not a child with (special) needs, locational irrelevance, individuality appreciation, mixed-ability study, Multiple Intelligence (MI), a responsive school

but may claim to be integrated or even inclusive largely because of the locational presence of children in the same premises or at times in the same classrooms. But the cultures and ethos of such schools would be non-inclusive, and children in such settings might prefer to be in separate special units rather than in the company of non-disabled and non-labelled peers. A truly inclusive school will not depend upon accurate identification and assessment of special needs, and pedagogy and curriculum will be restructured in a manner that make all feel involved and participating in a rather natural way.

Features of Inclusive Schooling   No precise definition of inclusive education has emerged as yet, but some common themes presented in most of the literature on inclusive education are presented here (for example, Booth 1996; Booth et al. 2000; Brantlinger 1997; Ferguson 1996; Lipsky and Gartner 1999; Thomas et al. 1998; Udvari-Solner and Thousand 1995; Vislie 2003):

1. Inclusion is not a state but a process.
2. Inclusion is not an extension of special or integration, but an entirely new educational enterprise.
3. It does not only refer to children identified as having disabilities or special needs, but *all* children.
4. Inclusive education is designed on the principles of heterogeneity, diversity and mixed-ability class rooms.
5. An inclusive school cannot be a school selecting/sorting children on any criterion.
6. Inclusion benefits and is useful for *all* children.

Some of the pedagogical and curricular features of inclusive education are:

1. Competitive activities encourage an individualistic and ego-centric ethos in students; collaboration, cooperation and mutual support are preferred forms of learning.
2. Learning is not developmentally linear, may not take one sequential step at a time.

3. Some of the core practices would be: outcome-based, multi-cultural, constructivist learning, thematic curriculum, multi-age grouping, team teaching and peer tutoring.

CONCLUSION

Diversity and heterogeneity are the core of inclusive education, and the Indian community by nature is diverse. Therefore, a common school in the neighbourhood may provide a perfect setting for organising inclusive education. Such schools would be addressing concerns of equality and social justice, provided it restructures itself with respect to culture, curriculum and pedagogy. These initiatives call for school reforms and a fresh approach to schooling, and a huge investment in the infrastructure of common schools to begin with. There are many micro initiatives in the country experimenting with a variety of forms of learning, and Tomlinson (2002: 13) says, 'India with a tradition of experimenting with many forms of schooling is well placed to take a lead in developing concept and reality of inclusive education'. The challenge is to plant many forms of learning and schooling into national and state education policy instruments for building common inclusive schools to be attended by *all* in the neighbourhood, irrespective of caste, ability, and social and economic status, and 'compel the rich, privileged and powerful classes to take interest' (Education Commission 1966: 458) in the common school system. This is a 'power struggle', and the form that the (common) school system would take shape, and its inclusivity or exclusivity would finally depend on who 'controls' and 'who decides'?

Notes

1. St. Stephen's College vs. University of Delhi, 1992, AIR (SC) 1630.
2. Professor Anil Sadgopal of Delhi University, in a personal communication.

3. Professor Sally Tomlinson in the Third Memorial Lecture on the Comprehensive Success and Bog-Standard Government in January 2004.
4. The example shared by Professor Alan Rogers in a conference in the Department of Educational Studies of Oxford University.
5. Professor Sally Tomlinson of the University of Oxford, in a personal communication, May 2003.

References

Ahmed, M. 1975. *The Economics of Non-formal Education*. New York: Praeger Publication.
Allan, J. 1999. *Actively Seeking Inclusion: Pupils with Special Needs in Mainstream Schools*. London: Falmer.
Archer, M.S. 1979. *Social Origins of Educational Systems*. London: Sage Publications.
Armstrong, D., F. Armstrong and L. Barton. 2000. 'Introduction: What is this Book About?' In F. Armstrong, D. Armstrong and L. Barton (eds), *Policy, Contexts and Comparative Perspectives*. London: Fulton.
Bailey, J. 1998. 'Medical and Psychological Models in Special Needs Education'. In C. Clark, A. Dyson and A. Millward (eds), *Theorising Special Education*. London: Routledge.
Ballard, K. 1995. 'Inclusion, Paradigms, Power and Participation'. In C. Clark, A. Dyson and A. Millward (eds), *Towards Inclusive Schools?* London: Dewid Fulton.
Barton, L. and S. Tomlinson. 1984. 'The Politics of Integration in England'. In L. Barton and S. Tomlinson (eds), *Special Education and Social Interests*. Kent: Croom Helm.
Beare, H. and R. Salughter. 1993. *Education for the Twenty first Century*. London: Routledge.
Bennison, E.A. 1987. 'Before the Learning Disabled There Were Feeble Minded Children'. In B.M. Franklin (ed.), *Learning Disability: Dissenting Essays*. London: The Falmer Press.
Booth, T. 1987. 'Introduction to the Series: Curricula for All'. In T. Booth, P. Potts and W. Swann (eds), *Preventing Difficulties in Learning*. Milton Keynes: Open University Press.
———. 1996. 'A Perspective on Inclusion from England'. *Cambridge Journal of Education*, 26 (1): 87–98.
———. 1998. 'The Poverty of Special Education: Theories to Rescue?' In C. Clark, A. Dyson and A. Millward (eds), *Theorising Special Education*. London: Routledge.
Booth, T. and M. Ainscow. 1998. 'Making Comparisons Drawing Conclusions'. In T. Booth and M. Ainscow (eds), *From Them to Us: An International Study of Inclusion in Education*. London: Routledge.
Booth, T., M. Ainscow, K. Black-Hawkins, M. Vaughan and L. Shaw. 2000. *Index for Inclusion: Developing, Learning and Participation in Schools*. Bristol: Centre for Studies on Inclusive Education.

Brantlinger, E. 1997. 'Using Ideology: Cases of Non-recognition of the Politics of Research and Practice in Special Education'. *Review of Educational Research*, 67 (4): 425–59.

Central Avisory Board of Education (CABE). 1944. *Post War Education Development in India*. New Delhi: Government of India.

Clark, C., A. Dyson, A. Millward and D. Skidmore. 1997. *New Directions in Special Needs: Innovations in Mainstream Schools*. London: Cassell.

Clark, C., A. Dyson, A. Millward and S. Robson. 1999. 'Theories of Inclusion, Theories of Schools: Deconstructing and Reconstructing the "Inclusive School"'. *British Educational Research Journal*, 25 (2): 157–76.

Clough, P. and J. Corbett (eds). 2000. *Theories of Inclusive Education: A Student's Guide*. London: Paul Chapman.

Daniels, H. and P. Garner (eds). 1999. 'Inclusive Education: Challenges for the New Millenium'. In H. Daniels and P. Garner (eds), *World Year Book of Education, 1999: Inclusive Education*. London: Kogan Page.

Department of Education and Science (DES). 1978. *Special Educational Needs: Report of a Committee of Enquiry into the Education of the Handicapped Children and Young People* (The Warnock Report). London: HMSO.

Dunn, L.M. 1968. 'Special Education for the Mildly Retarded: Is Much of it Justifiable?' *Expected Children*, 35: 5–24.

Education Commission. 1966. *Education and National Development*. New Delhi: Ministry of Education.

Elliott, M. 2002. 'Test Scores Don't Say it All'. *Time Magazine*, 15 April, 159 (14): 52.

Emanuelsson, I. 1998. 'Integration and Segregation: Inclusion and Exclusion'. *International Journal of Educational Research*, 29: 95–105.

Fagg, H. 2002. *Back to Sources: A Study of Gandhi's Basic Education*. New Delhi: National Book Trust.

Farrell, P. 2000. 'The Impact of Research on Developments in Inclusive Education'. *International Journal of Inclusive Education*, 4(2): 153–62.

Ferguson, D.L. 1996. 'Is it Inclusion Yet? Bursting the Bubbles'. In M.S. Berres, D.L. Ferguson, P. Knowblock and C. Woods (eds), *Creating Tomorrow's Schools Today*. New York: Teachers' College Columbia University.

Ford, J. 1969. *Social Class and the Comprehensive School*. Routledge and Kegan Paul.

Fulcher, G. 1999. *Disabling Policies? A Comparative Approach to Education Policy and Disability*. Sheffield: Philip Armstrong.

Galloway, D., D. Armstrong and S. Tomlinson. 1994. *The Assessment of Special Educational Needs: Whose Problem?* London: Longman.

Government of India. 1990. *Towards an Enlightened and Humane Society: Report of the Committee for Review of National Policy on Education, 1986* [i.e., National Policy on Education Review Committee Report (NPERC) or Acharya Ramamurti Committee Report], Department of Education, Ministry of Human Resource Development. New Delhi: Government of India.

———. 1996. *Persons with Disabilities (Equal Opportunities, Protection of Rights and Full Participation) Act 1995*. Ministry of Law and Justice, New Delhi: Government of India.

Government of India. 2004a. Department of Education, http://education.nic.in/htmlweb/ssa/free_compulsory_edu_bill_2004.htm, accessed on 11 July 2004.

———. 2004b. Ministry of Labour, http://labour.nic.in/cwl/welcome.html, accessed on 17 August 2004.

Haq, E. 1989. 'Open Education and Closed Society: A Study of Social and Educational Inequalities in Contemporary India'. In A. Yoger (ed.), *International Perspectives on Education and Society*. London: Jai Press.

Hornby, H., M. Atkinson and J. Howard. 1997. *Controversial Issues in Special Education*. London: David Fulton.

Jangira, N.K. 1997. 'Special Education'. In *Fifth Survey of Educational Research 1988: Trend Report* (Vol.1). New Delhi: NCERT.

Jha, M.M. 2002a. *School Without Walls: Inclusive Education for All*. Oxford: Heinemann.

———. 2002b. 'Foreword'. In H. Fagg, *Back to the Sources: A Study of Gandhi's Basic Education*. New Delhi: National Book Trust.

Kahelnberg, R.D. 2001. *All Together Now: Creating Middle-class Schools through Public School Choice*. Washington, DC: Brookings Institution Press.

Karabel, J. and A.H. Halsey (eds). 1977. *Power and Ideology in Education*. New York: Oxford University Press.

Kumar, K. 1994. 'Mohandas Karamchand Gandhi'. In Z. Morsy (ed.), *Thinkers on Education* (Vol. 2). Paris: UNESCO.

Lipsky, D.K. and A. Gartner. 1999. 'Inclusive Education: A Requirement of a Democratic Society'. In H. Daniels and P. Garner (eds), *World Yearbook of Education 1999: Inclusive Education*. London: Kogan Page.

Lloyd, C. 2000. 'Excellence for All Children: False Promises! The Failure of Current Policy for Education and Implications for Schooling in the 21st Century'. *International Journal of Inclusive Education*, 4(2): 133–51.

Miles, M. 1994. 'Disability Care and Education in 19th Century India: Some Dates, Places and Documentation'. *Action Aid Disability News*, 5(2): 2–22.

———. 1997. 'Disabled Learners in South Asia: Lessons from Past for Educational Experts'. *International Journal of Disability*, 44(2): 97–104.

———. 2002. 'Disability in South Asia: Millennium to Millennium'. *Journal of Religion, Disability and Health*, 6 (2/3): 109–15.

Ministry of Human Resource Development (MHRD). 1990. *Towards an Enlightened and Humane Society: NPE 1986—A Review*. New Delhi: Government of India.

———. 1992. *Report of the CABE Committee on Policy* (Janardhan Reddy Committee Report), Department of Education, Ministry of Human Resource Development. New Delhi: Government of India.

———. 1998. *National Policy on Education (As modified in 1992) with National Policy on Education, 1968*. New Delhi: Government of India.

National Sample Survey Organisation (NSSO). 1994. 'Disability in India: NSS 47th Round'. *Sarvekshana*, July–December.

Norwich, B. 2002. 'Education, Inclusion and Individual Differences: Reconstructing and Resolving Dilemmas'. British Journal of Educational Studies, 50(4): 482–502.

Oliver, M. 1988. 'The Political Context of Educational Decision-making: The Case of Special Needs'. In L. Barton (ed.), *The Politics of Special Needs*. London: Falmer Press.

———. 1990. *The Politics of Disablement*. London: Macmillan.

———. 1995. 'Does Special Education have a Role to Play in the Twenty-first Century?' *REACH, Journal of Special Needs Education in Ireland*, 8(2): 67–76.

Planning Commission. 1998. *Evaluation Study on Impact of Non-Formal Education*. New Delhi: Government of India.

Public Report on Basic Education (PROBE). 1999. *Public Report on Basic Education in India*. New Delhi: Oxford University Press.

Rehabilitation Council of India (RCI). 2000. *Status of Disability in India*. New Delhi: RCI.

Sadgopal, A. 2003. 'Exclusion and Inequality in Education: The State Policy and Globalisation'. *Contemporary India, Journal of the Nehru Memorial Museum and Library*, 2 (3): 1–36.

———. 2004. *Globalization and Education: Defining the Indian Crisis*. New Delhi: Zakir Hussain College.

Sargent, J. 1968. *Society, School and Progress in India*. Oxford: Pergamon.

Scarse, T.J. 1993. *Image, Ideology and Inequality: Cultural Domination, Hegemony and Schooling in India*. New Delhi: Sage Publications.

Simmons, J. 1983. 'Reforming Education and Society: The Enduring Quest'. In J. Simons (ed.), *Better Schools: International Lessons*. New York: Praeger Publications.

Singal, N. and M. Rouse. 2003. '"We Do Inclusion": Practitioner Perspectives in Some "Inclusive Schools" in India'. *Perspectives in Education, (Special Issue: The Inclusion and Exclusion Debate in South Africa and Developing Countries)*, 2 (3): 85–97.

Skidmore, D. 1996. 'Towards an Integrated Theoretical Framework for Research into Special Educational Needs'. *European Journal of Special Needs Education*, 11(1): 33–47.

Skrtic, T.M. 1991. *Behind Special Education: A Critical Analysis of Professional Culture and School Organisation*. Denver: Love Publishing.

Slee, R. 1997. 'Inclusion or Assimilation? Sociological Explorations of the Foundations of Theories of Special Education'. *Educational Foundations*, Winter: 55–71.

Gazette of India. 1996. *The Persons With Disabilities (Equal Opportunities, Protection of Rights and Full Participation) Act, 1995*. New Delhi: Ministry of Law, Justice and Company Affairs.

———. 1999. *National Trust for the Welfare of Persons with Autism, Cerebral Palsy, Mental Retardation and Multiple Disabilities Act, 1999*. New Delhi: Ministry of Law, Justice and Company Affairs.

Thomas, G., D. Walker and J. Webb. 1998. *The Making of the Inclusive School*. London: Routledge.

Thomas, G. and M. Vaughan. 2004. *Inclusive Education: Readings and Collections*. Berkshire: Open University Press.

Tomlinson, S. 1982. *A Sociology of Special Education*. London: Routledge and Kegan Paul.

———. 2001. *Education in a Post-Welfare Society*. Buckingham: Open University Press.

Tomlinson, S. 2002. 'Foreword'. In M. Jha, *School without Walls: Inclusive Education for All.* Oxford: Heinemann.

Udvari-Solner, A. and J. Thousand. 1995. 'Effective Organisational, Instructional and Curricular Practices in Inclusive Schools and Classrooms', in C. Clark, A. Dyson and A. Millward (eds), *Towards Inclusive Schools?* London: David Fulton.

UNESCO. 1994. *The Salamanca Statement and Framework for Action on Special Needs Education.* Paris: UNESCO.

———. 1995. *Review of Present Situations in Special Needs Education.* Paris: UNESCO.

Vislie, L. 2003. 'From Integration to Inclusion: Focusing Global Trends and Changes in the Western European Societies'. *European Journal of Special Needs Education,* 18 (1): 17–35.

Warnock, M. 1980. 'A Flexible Framework'. *Times Educational Supplement,* 26 September.

Watkins, K. 2000. *The Oxfam Education Report.* Oxford: Oxfam International.

Wedell, K. 1995. 'Making Inclusive Education Ordinary'. *British Journal of Special Education,* 22(3): 100–104.

9

EDUCATIONAL DEPRIVATION OF THE MARGINALISED

A VILLAGE STUDY OF THE MUSHAR COMMUNITY IN BIHAR*

Ravi Kumar

EDUCATIONAL INEQUALITY AS A REFLECTION OF STRUCTURAL INEQUALITY

Education has always been an arena of political and ideological contest. It has been used as the most effective tool of consensus building in society. Hence, there has always been a meta-discourse that impeded the formation and sustenance of any radical ideological position trying to look critically at the social processes. Education, apart from being an instrument of creating knowledge, in an informal as well as formal way, came to be treated as an important site of ideological contest, and has been linked to the struggle for liberation. Karl Marx was one such philosopher who saw it as

*I am extremely grateful to Professor Muchkund Dubey for extending all possible help, personal as well as institutional, to me for fieldwork. I must also thank researchers Rakesh and Arjun, who stayed in the villages in most difficult circumstances.

an instrument used by the ruling class to sustain its hegemony in society. He believed:

> The ideas of the ruling class are in every epoch the ruling ideas, i.e. the class which is the ruling material force of society, is at the same time its ruling intellectual force. The class which has the means of material production at its disposal, has control at the same time over the means of mental production, so that thereby, generally speaking, the ideas of those who lack the means of mental production are subject to it. (Marx 1968)

In the 20th century, the Frankfurt School explored and questioned the way ruling ideas of society become more aggressive through their cultural agencies and the techno-bureaucratic mechanisms employed by capitalism (Adorno 2004; Marcuse 1972). Marcuse showed how techno-rational politics induces and seduces us into doing things through 'a comfortable, smooth, reasonable democratic unfreedom'. He argued that people are deprived of criticality in this society, which is effected by a whole functional dynamics of technology, mass media, cultural symbols, education, etc., making people compulsive consumers (Marcuse 1972). Thereafter, postmodernism in a variety of forms challenged the notions of a hegemonic meta-knowledge that seeks to undermine the localised 'not-so-powerful knowledges' (thereby emerged notions of plurality, therefore, *knowledges*). Foucault (1980: 51–52) observed that

> the exercise of power perpetually creates knowledge and, conversely, knowledge constantly induces effects of power.... Diffused, entrenched and dangerous, they operate in other places than in the person of the old professor.... [I]t is not possible for power to be exercised without knowledge, it is impossible for knowledge not to engender power.

Pierre Bourdieu recognised the way power imposes meanings and makes them 'legitimate' through concealing power relations, which constitute the basis of 'pedagogic action' that sustains ruling ideas. He held that:

> In any given social formation the cultural arbitrary which the power relations between the groups or classes making up that social formation put into the

dominant position within the system of cultural arbitraries is the one which most fully, though always indirectly, expresses the objective interests (material and symbolic) of the dominant groups or classes. (Bourdieu and Passeron 1990: 9)

Apart from these scholars, many others like Michel Apple (1990), Samuel Bowles (1976), Krishna Kumar (1989) and Anil Sadgopal (2003, 2004a, 2004b) have argued consistently about the ways in which education is intimately related to the politics in society and, hence, is a field of constant struggle between the dominant discourse and those at the margins. In fact, one aspect that finds space in the discourses on education all along has been the concern with the educational status of people at the margins looked from class, caste, gender and other perspectives.

Education has been seen as a tool invested with power and, therefore, as representing the interests of the ruling class. By virtue of representing ruling ideas, it reproduces existing inequalities through symbols and cultural notions in order to preserve the status quo. Hence, emerge notions, in context of our study, such as 'Mushars do not want to study' or 'They themselves are not interested in their upliftment'. Such 'popular' notions delegitimise their desire to be part of an educational framework and also suppress the fact that they are neglected by the prevailing education system.

In the Indian context, the thoughts of Gandhi on education, in form of his conception of *nayi talim*, provided the essential turn to the education discourse linking the social structural aspects with education. Basing his argument on poverty and the occupational structure of India, he argued, 'It is a crime to make education mere literary and to unfit boys and girls for manual work in after-life.' He argued that every child must be taught dignity of labour (Gandhi 1999). His notion of basic education sought to attain the physical, intellectual and moral development of the child through the medium of a handicraft. It was not conceived as the class-work vulgarised today by 'subjects' such as SUPW (socially useful productive work) for the sake of learning the art, but as a productive engagement. If this is not done, 'it will neglect a very important moral principle, viz., that human labour and material should never be used in a wasteful of unproductive way. The emphasis laid on the principle of spending every minute of one's life usefully is the best education for citizenship and incidentally makes Basic Education self-sufficient' (Gandhi 1999). The concept of basic education

> presents a significant example of the influence of the sociology of knowledge on the school curriculum.... In functional terms, the idea was to relate the school to the processes of production in the local milieu, with the aim of making the school itself a productive institution. In symbolic terms, by proposing the introduction of productive skills and the knowledge associated with them in the curriculum, Gandhi was advocating the allocation of a substantive place in education to systems of knowledge developed by, and associated with, the oppressed groups of Indian society. (Kumar 1989: 70)

The linking of two hitherto presumably disjointed spheres of 'world of knowledge' and 'world of work' was a new conceptualisation.

From the critical concern of knowledge as representing power relations and as a tool of all-round development of the child to the current debates, education has traversed a long path. One of the most significant developments of the post-colonial worldview has been the role attributed to the State for providing education to the child. The older Article 45 of Indian Constitution (before its modification through the 86th Amendment) had been a reflection of the same concern. This aspect became more evident ever since education became an intrinsic part of the development debate. The new discourse (put forth by the so-called 'development sector') completely glossed over the element of criticality as an essential component of education. The only aim that remained has been the target to make everybody literate. The path from 'education' to 'literacy' has been in consonance with the whole development discourse that accompanied it—in terms of 'from state to market'. Gradually, the State is abdicated of its responsibilities, and education is no longer seen critically as part of the social system, which reproduces the existing order of things. However, this is never to deny the innumerable discourses that seek to argue that the crisis in education is a part and parcel of the capitalist system, which is more interested in producing uncritical mechanical beings.

EDUCATION AND THE DEVELOPMENT DISCOURSE

Education became the paramount agenda ever since its recognition as essential for the development of human capital. It came to be seen as an 'enabling' factor that promotes or constrains the freedom that individuals have. Education is important if equal economic opportunities are to be provided to humans. But 'somehow the educational aspects of economic development have continued to be out of the main focus, and this relative neglect has persisted despite the recent radical changes in economic policy' (Dreze and Sen 2002: 38). Dreze argues that 'literacy is an essential tool of self-defense in a society where social interactions include the written media'. It is not only being seen as a tool of facilitating economic opportunities, but is also taken as essential 'to overcome the traditional inequalities of caste, class and gender, just as the removal of these inequalities contributes to the spread of education' (Dreze and Sen 2003: 3).

The documents released by 'international/national development agencies' have constantly been reflecting on the concerns of getting every child into school. Education, interpreted in variety of ways, is being 'monitored' by bodies like UNICEF and the World Bank. Aid is pouring in to expand 'opportunities' and 'freedoms' of individuals, and enhance their capability through adequate provisions of education, health and nutrition. The World Bank (1998) came out with its *World Development Report* 1998/99 titled *Knowledge for Development*, stressing on knowledge as critical for development. However, while dealing with knowledge, it mostly made references to technological know-how and defined knowledge as the art to acquire it. The critical space of enquiry, the ultimate objective of any knowledge, which culminates into innovations and development of knowledge stock, never became the focus. Citing the example of countries that have been 'the vanguard of the world economy', it argued:

Today's most technologically advanced economies are truly knowledge-based. And as they generate new wealth from their innovations, they are creating millions of knowledge related jobs in an array of disciplines that have emerged overnight: knowledge engineers, knowledge managers, knowledge coordinators. (World Bank 1998: 16)

It asked international donor agencies to actively participate in knowledge creation, and governments to narrow knowledge gaps through free market, free trade and ensuring competition (please see chapters 9 and 10 of the report). Education is being seen as a tool to develop the human resource.

In the Indian context, the failure to meet constitutional obligations of educating each and every child led ultimately to formulation of non-formal education. Having tacitly supported the dual education system of private and government schools, the State allowed the section having the capacity to pay for education to get educated, while those not having it remained uneducated and gradually their number accumulated. The government decided to have non-formal schools (a separate category of education) for these out-of-school children, who have been poor, Dalits and girls primarily. Newer 'schemes' have kept adding to this trend. The choice of 'schemes' range from literacy measured in terms of capacity to read bus numbers, do signatures to sitting in dilapidated schools without sufficient infrastructure, and being taught by underpaid and underqualified teachers. The inequality in education essentially reflects the iniquitous social relations, and this is evident in the way more educational facilities are enjoyed by those who have better purchasing power. The problems acquire a serious dimension when this inequality in education, represented by its commodification and, therefore, marginalisation of a vast mass, is endorsed by the State in the name of resource crunch or in the name of achieving targets.

The spate of liberalisation unleashed in the aftermath of structural adjustment programmes (SAP) has been accompanied by radical changes in the educational scenario, with newer initiatives taken up by the State. The understanding of education as an isolated construct has been advocated quite vigorously. The understanding of education as an arena of critical thinking has been negated and replaced by the necessity of literacy. The ideas of the World Bank and other international agencies have percolated down to become

India's state policy. A homogeneous language and uniform set of perspectives are seen omnipresent in all documents—from the World Bank and UN to the Indian state's documents. Public–private partnership is being talked about (Government of India 2001a) and 'alternative' schemes for deprived section of population are being implemented. Programmes and policies such as the Sarva Shiksha Abhiyan among others is a blatant example of institutionalising the educational inequality in India.

The new paradigms have led to conceptualisations developed in haste to achieve the target of literacy. The notion of education has been put on the backburner in this process. Gandhi's rejection of literacy becomes extremely relevant here, and so does the Freirian concern for criticality and dialogicity as the essence of education. The libertarian terminology of Friere, Illich and others has been co-opted *sans* their conceptual underlining. Paulo Friere's ideas were distorted and co-opted by the development programmes and agencies 'for the incorporation of the small peasant into the consumer economy' (Kumar 1989). Terms like 'knowledge society', 'empowerment' and 'disadvantaged' are used without dealing with the meaning that they represent. In fact, meanings of the words have been reformulated in this whole process, as can be seen in Birla–Ambani report on education, which talks of the need for 'revolution' in education system.

SOME EMERGING ISSUES IN THE EDUCATION DEBATE

There are new additions to the issues of non-enrolment and dropout, which continue to be Herculean tasks. Objective categories of enrolments and measurement of literacy had inbuilt contradictions, which have emerged as issues of quality education. Long-pending aims of universalising elementary education culminated into target-oriented programmes. The issue of 'targets' become important and relevant because UNESCO defines it as a sign of commitment of states. It also enables external partners to support the programmes of 'education'. The World Bank talks extensively in context of 'aid-worthiness' of countries and 'target requirements' as important to get funding and technical support. Target achievements become necessary criteria for grants or loans (Goldstein 2004). The learning target also means centralisation of control 'even within the rhetoric of diversity and local decision-making' (ibid.: 4998).

Now it has been realised that 'enrolment is obviously not a big issue anymore... attendance, transition, completion and learning outcomes are emerging as bigger issues' (Ramachandran et al. 2003: 4994–5002). The issue of education, it is being debated, is more than merely literary campaigns. Scholars have argued that 'equality in educational opportunities and conditions of success' have been the constitutional rights of every child, which has been denied by the Indian state. Now, educational inequality is, instead, being institutionalised through parallel systems of education (Kumar et al. 2002; Sadgopal 2004a, 2004b). The pressure generated by the 'judiciary' and 'civil society' led the government to enact the 86th Amendment making education a fundamental right, though it is being seen as an eyewash (Sadgopal 2001), while many see it as a step forward towards expanding educational services to the whole country. Whether the new constitutional promulgation will effect any changes in the educational deprivation of the marginalised section is a very significant question that needs to be debated. However, it does not constitute the subject matter of this paper.

MORE EMPHASIS ON DEVELOPMENT: CONCERN FOR THE COMMUNITY'S PARTICIPATION

The condition of the marginalised sections, Dalits and the poor (because their economic condition coincides) has not improved much in more than 50 years of Indian independence. Now, the 'new' developmental agenda of 'decentralisation' and 'partici-pation' is being cited as the panacea of all underdevelopment symp-toms. The discourse on development witnessed a major shift since the 1980s in India, when the *processes* of economic liberalisation began. This discourse was complemented by new direction provided by scholars like Amartya Sen, who argued in favour of measuring development on the basis of human development indicators (Dreze and Sen 1995). As part of this new direction, the issues of hunger, poverty, lack of 'basic education', basic health facilities, marginalisation on the basis of caste and gender, etc. acquired greater significance. International pressure as well as movements from within created conditions that have been compelling the State to frame newer constitutional provisions taking such issues into account. Efforts towards translating many ideals laid down in the Directive Principles of State Policy into constitutional amendments and Acts have been made. One such example is Article 40 of the Indian Constitution, which was translated into the 73rd Amendment in 1992.

These new developments have taken place in the context of an increasing emphasis on decentralisation of governance throughout the world, under pressure from a variety of 'new social movements' as well as international donor agencies. India, of course, is not alone in this process. Decentralisation has emerged as a dominant trend in world politics. In 1998 the World Bank, for example, estimated that all but 12 of the 75 developing and transitional countries with populations greater than 5 million had embarked on a process of political devolution (Johnson 2003). The emphasis on decentralisation and its purpose is evident in the documents of World Bank when it claims that 'successful decentralization improves the efficiency and responsiveness of the public sector while accommodating potentially explosive political forces' (World Bank 2000a: 107). It is seen as an instrument to tackle the pressures of localisation and bring oppositional forces into a formal framework through institutionalising their actions and ideas.

Decentralisation to smaller units increases the scope for interaction with the citizenry served. It makes state institutions more responsive to poor people, but only if it allows poor people to hold public servants accountable, and ensures their participation in the development process (World Bank 2000b). The issues of participatory budgeting, dissemination of information, greater transparency and accountability featured prominently in the World Bank doctrines. It also started citing market as a major force which through its competitive mechanism creates instruments of accountability (World Bank 2003). These ideas percolated down to the Indian state and the *National Human Development Report, 2001* (Government of India 2002a), which says that 'governance for human development relates to the management of all such processes that, in any society, define the environment which permits and enables individuals to raise their capacity levels, on the one hand, and provide opportunities to realize their potential and enlarge the available choices, on the other'. It emphasises the need to 'conceptually reposition' the role of the state. The Vision 2020 document of the Indian government also sees decentralisation as an important aspect of development in future through devolution of political and financial power to local bodies as well as enhanced participation of the local masses in the distribution of resources and building and managing local projects (ibid.: 2002b).

Hence, on 24 April 1993, the 73rd Amendment Act (1992) came into force (Ministry of Rural Development Web site; http://www.rural.nic.in/panch.htm). 'Since this time, the process of decentralization has been highly variable, ranging from ambitious attempts at *Gram Swaraj* (or village self-rule) in Madhya Pradesh to political *re-centralization* in Karnataka' (Johnson 2003). This thrust on decentralisation bases itself on a wider critique of centralised state planning, on grounds of inefficiency, corruption and persistent marginalisation, in terms of resource generation and distribution, over years of state-controlled development (ibid.: Bardhan 2002). Even the State began accepting the drawbacks of centralisation and bureaucracy and lack of transparency (Government of India 2001b).

It has been argued that decentralisation would improve the condition of masses as their participation increases in the issues concerning them directly. The constitutional amendments have been lauded in different quarters in this regard for enhancing the participation of marginalised sections in local decision-making processes, and also for their impact on administrative transparency and problems such as corruption (Raman 2000). India has been recognised as doing exceptionally well in terms of democratic institutions and

> the *main* limitations of Indian democracy do not ... relate so much to democratic institutions as to democratic practice. The performance of democratic institutions is contingent on a wide range of social conditions, from educational levels and political traditions to the nature of social inequalities and popular organizations. (Dreze and Sen 2002: 350)

The recent changes through constitutional amendments are being taken as its continuation.

However, decentralisation need not necessarily mean participation. Fears have been expressed (based on empirical evidences by different World Bank reports as well as by Dreze and Sen [2002]) that when the aspect of participation is ignored and only decentralisation is emphasised, democratic institutions become a tool for the local elite. It can merely imply shifting of power from the national to local elite (Mathew and Nayak 1996). If governance means emergence of various actors that participate in the governing process apart from the state, then it also needs to be ensured that people at the margins of society get space in the changing political landscape. Unless this happens it will be only an *apparently* (and not real) reformed landscape of power equations where the new and dominant social elite enjoy privileges. The traditionally marginalised castes and women remain mute witnesses to the whole process. However, it is also being accepted that the change is gradually taking place. 'Over time, the forces of repression seem to be losing some ground, with good prospects of further advance in the direction of both greater social equity and more vibrant local democracy in the near future' (Dreze and Sen 2002). The aim at this juncture, however, remains to ensure how the sections located at the margins of society get an opportunity to participate in the development process. This becomes more pertinent because of the dialectical relationship between participation of human beings in democratic processes and the indicators of development such as education. Both enhance the scope of one another towards attaining a higher end.

India's education policy, as indicated by its justifications for the opening of innumerable parallel educational streams for the under-privileged, also celebrates the idea of decentralisation and participation. After the 86th Amendment, decentralised education is being highlighted as the hallmark of the new policies in education. The Sarva Shiksha Abhiyan (SSA) focuses on 'community ownership', participatory 'community based planning process' at grassroots level, 'community based monitoring with full transparency' etc. (Government of India, undated). Local participation and the decen-tralised aspect of education is aimed at involving people in the education process and also mitigating the fallacies that hampered the attainment of educating every citizen of India as laid down in Article 45 of Indian Constitution. This new framework emerges out of the 86th Amendment and the pending Free and Compulsory Education Bill. But the question that still remains is whether it will be able to incorporate the most marginalised sections in its scope of empowerment. It has been argued that it is difficult to empower people without realising and addressing the structural constraints that do not allow 'fuller realisation of human potentiality in the case of the deprived sections'. These constraints operate at the level of 'socio-economic structure, ideology and political process, which the omnibus concept of "empowerment" does not capture' (Mohanty 2001: 22–30). Such critical perspectives indicate the complexities of the social system and the critical need to study the reasons why a section of population is constantly marginalised in the local dynamics of political and social processes.

The marginalisation of a vast population because of their eco-nomic deprivation as well as social discrimination has to be what any doctrine of empowerment and participation needs to base itself. It is on the basis of this marginalisation that their cultural exclusion or reasons for non-participation can be understood. This also im-plies that there is a dialectical relationship between cultural exclu-sion, socio-economic status and participation in the local society. The basis for exclusion is constructed in a local context, which em-erges out of the complex interplay of the local contest of power. There is a cultural paradigm, dominant and overwhelming in char-acter, which infuses certain images and motivates certain discourses to establish and sustain the hegemony of certain sections and marginalise others. In our context of the Mushar community, the same holds true as of any other community. It becomes relevant in this context to recall what Bourdieu writes about the ways and means through which culture is reproduced through education system, which he gives a wider space through notion of 'pedagogic action':

> Reproduction sought to propose a model of the social mediations and processes which tend, behind the backs of the agents engaged in the school system—teachers, students and their parents—and often *against their will*, to ensure the transmission of cultural capital across generations and to stamp pre-existing differences in inherited cultural capital with a meritocratic seal of academic consecration by virtue of the special symbolic potency of the *title* (credential). Functioning in the manner of a huge classificatory machine which inscribes changes within the purview of the structure, the school helps to make and to impose the legitimate exclusions and inclusions which form the basis of the social order. (Bourdieu 1990: ix–x)

At this juncture one needs to question whether the exclusionist provisions of education being instituted by the state *fail* (meaning unconsciously) to take into consideration the basis of people's education or seeks to *sustain* and *reproduce* (that is, consciously, because of inherent character of the state, which represents the dominant elite of society) the existing deprivation. If the Indian state, despite having accepted the deprivation of the masses, ventures into such discriminatory policy measures, then it becomes obvious about the interests which it represents.

DALITS: CAUGHT IN THE WHIRLPOOL OF CASTE AND CLASS

Within this larger context of marginalisation, the condition of Dalits needs to be located. From the geographical exclusion of Dalits to their economic impoverishment, there are numerous factors that play a determining role in their educational deprivation. SC dwellings, geographically and therefore conceptually declared outcaste, continue to be deprived and denied of basic amenities and services. The denial of basic minimum services, necessary for human beings to exist, negatively impacts their capabilities, capacity, confidence and efforts to join the mainstream.

Therefore, if on the one hand Dalits are confronted with immediate consequences of social discrimination, then on the other hand their economic condition has also not been showing signs of improvement.

> There has been a decrease in the number of SC cultivators from 28.17 per cent in 1981 to 25.44 per cent in 1991 and an increase in the percentage of agricultural labourers from 48.22 per cent in 1981 to 49.06 per cent in 1991. It is also likely that some of the SCs who have lost their lands may have also joined the ranks of labourers. Evidently, their hold on agrarian economy has also been declining as the number of cultivators has declined from 38 per cent in 1961 to 25.44 per cent in 1991. (Government of India 2001c)

Their participation in the other sectors of economy, which is being highlighted as the symbol of growth, is also negligible 'as SCs can neither compete nor sustain in the liberalised market economy, wherein the national/multi-national companies with their cost effective products are causing a serious threat to the tradition-based economy of SCs'. They are, consequently, 'being further marginalised in the new economic regime'. (ibid.)

The fundamental right to education

> has come at a time when the poorest sections of society face exclusion from the production process itself. Increasing unemployment, casualisation and large-scale retrenchment of labour and suicide by indebted farmers—at times by consuming the same poison that is supposed to save their crops and bring prosperity—form the context in which this constitutional amendment has been made. (Kumar et al. 2002)

The provisions of the Bill and amendment will also have wider and significant ramifications.

> Despite the noticeable silence in the Amendment with regard to a commitment to quality, the freezing of the contested terrain of education as a legal entity

is likely to reinforce a particular turn towards teaching as an evidence-based activity. Teaching functionaries in government schools, wary of the legal action that they may become liable to, may shun efforts towards creative pedagogy. In debates on education, empirical testing for outcomes is likely to triumph over the more qualitative process-based approaches. (Kumar et al. 2002)

To further understand the educational marginalisation of Dalits, despite the policies making great promises of decentralisation and community participation, it is necessary that we look at the dynamics of the interface between Dalit communities and education at the micro level.

The Indian educational scenario has been characterised by extreme inequality, and this has been established beyond doubt by the quantitative data generated by the State as well as many other independent researches. The NCERT's Sixth Educational Survey made it amply clear that there were 135,208 Dalit habitations which did not have a primary school within 1 km (NCERT 1997). Their overall education in terms of literacy also presents a dismal picture. The NFHS-2 (IIPS and ORC Macro 2000) as well as NSSO data clearly reflects the situation of Dalit education in rural Bihar.

One can derive an interesting aspect of Dalit's socio-economic status and link it with their educational status. The social and economic deprivation of Dalits goes hand in hand. It is because of this reason that the references to poverty become important, especially if one talks of the rural areas of the Indian society. The Scheduled Castes have the lowest monthly per capita consumption expenditure (MPCE) in Bihar as shown by the NSSO survey (Table 9.1).

The Dalits also fare poorly in landownership. Most of them are landless or barely manage to own a small patch of land (Table 9.2), and, therefore, their survival largely depends on the daily wage activities.

If a correlation between their economic status and educational status is to be derived using the MPCE and landownership pattern, we find that Dalits are deprived of education at all levels. SCs fall largely in the lowest MPCE category as well as possess little or no land. The categories of lowest MPCE as well as that of lower land possessed are the ones that have more illiterates, and even if they are literate the educational level is largely below primary level. The inequality becomes starker once we look at the higher education (Tables 9.3 and 9.4).

TABLE 9.1
POPULATION DISTRIBUTION BY MPCE CLASS AND AVERAGE MPCE
FOR DIFFERENT SOCIAL GROUPS IN RURAL BIHAR (%)

MPCE Class (Rs.)	Social Group				
	ST	SC	OBCs	Others	All
0–225	14.0	14.4	6.1	3.9	7.9
225–55	13.4	11.9	8.0	4.2	8.4
255–300	17.4	19.7	16.6	8.3	15.6
300–40	18.0	16.7	14.8	12.2	14.9
340–80	12.5	12.0	14.4	11.5	13.2
380–420	6.3	7.7	10.2	12.8	10.0
420–70	6.2	7.4	9.7	13.7	9.8
470–525	4.1	4.4	7.4	8.4	6.7
525–615	3.5	3.8	5.9	11.2	6.4
615–775	3.6	1.7	4.4	7.3	4.4
775–950	0.4	0.2	1.5	3.5	1.6
>950	0.5	0.1	0.8	3.0	1.1
All classes	99.9	100	99.8	100	100
Average MPCE	337.16	329.32	384.66	457.59	384.45

Source: NSSO (2001b).

TABLE 9.2
DISTRIBUTION OF HOUSEHOLDS BY SIZE OF LAND POSSESSED
IN RURAL BIHAR (%)

Social Group	Land Owned (hectare)					
	0.0	0.01–0.40	0.41–1.00	1.01–2.00	2.01–4.00	> 4.01
ST	2.0	35.5	32.0	23.5	5.5	0.5
SC	23.8	67.1	6.4	2.1	0.6	0
OBC	8.8	58	19.5	9.5	3.5	0.7
Others	6.0	49.2	23.0	12.6	6.1	3.1

Source: NSSO (2001a).

Table 9.3

Distribution of Population Aged 7 and Above by Level of Education According to MPCE Class in Rural Bihar (%)

MPCE Class (Rs.)	Not Literate	Literate	Level of Education Among Literates					
			Below Primary	Primary	Middle	Secondary	Higher Secondary	Graduate and Above
0–225	73.9	26.1	56.32	16.86	18.77	5.36	1.92	1.15
225–55	71.5	28.5	58.60	17.19	13.68	7.37	1.40	1.40
255–300	68.2	31.8	50.63	19.18	17.92	9.12	1.89	1.57
300–340	61.5	38.5	46.23	19.48	20.00	9.87	2.34	2.34
340–80	60.7	39.3	43.00	19.59	19.85	10.94	3.82	2.80
380–420	55.6	44.4	40.54	19.37	21.17	13.51	4.05	1.35
420–70	49.8	50.2	38.84	19.52	20.92	13.35	4.38	3.19
470–525	50.5	49.5	35.56	16.57	23.03	15.35	5.05	4.24
525–615	42.5	57.5	30.61	16.35	24.17	16.00	6.78	6.09
615–775	42.3	57.7	31.20	16.46	21.66	15.25	8.84	6.59
775–950	29.8	70.2	27.35	11.40	20.94	25.07	8.55	6.70
>950	23.7	76.3	17.56	9.96	22.41	15.86	12.32	21.89
All	58.2	41.8	41.39	17.94	20.33	12.44	4.31	3.59

Source: NSSO (2001c).

Table 9.4

Distribution of Population Aged 7 and Above by Level of Education According to Land Possessed in Rural Bihar (%)

Size of Land Possessed (ha)	Not Literate	Literate	Level of Education Among Literates					
			Below Primary	Primary	Middle	Secondary	Higher Secondary	Graduate and Above
<0.01	76.8	23.2	48.71	16.81	20.26	9.48	2.16	2.59
0.01–0.40	64.5	35.5	47.32	18.31	18.03	10.14	3.38	2.82
0.41–1.00	49	51	37.25	19.41	23.73	12.55	4.12	2.94
1.01–2.00	44.7	55.3	35.62	17.72	21.88	15.37	4.88	4.52
2.01–4.00	34.4	65.6	29.73	16.46	21.65	18.29	8.08	5.64
>4.01	32.1	67.9	28.57	13.55	21.06	18.70	9.43	8.84
All Classes	58.2	41.8	41.39	17.94	20.33	12.44	4.31	3.59

Source: NSSO (2001c).

Leave aside the issue of holistic education, even literacy rate among SCs has been dismal in Bihar. As per the Primary Census Abstracts of 2001 (Government of India 2000d), the literacy rate among Scheduled Caste men was 40.2 per cent, among women 15.6 per cent, and overall literacy among SCs was 28.5 per cent, which is only a slight improvement over 1991 figures. The situation of inequity in education has been blatant. The reasons, as we have seen earlier, have been the poor economic condition of Dalits supplemented by social discrimination. The local schooling system has been consistently reproducing this inequality, and as a result we find the overall educational status of Dalits in shambles (Table 9.5).

TABLE 9.5
DISTRIBUTION OF POPULATION AGED 7 AND ABOVE BY LEVEL OF EDUCATION ACCORDING TO SOCIAL GROUP IN RURAL BIHAR (%)

Social Group	Not Literate	Literate	Level of Education Among Literates					
			Below Primary	Primary	Middle	Secondary	Higher Secondary	Graduate and Above
Scheduled Tribe	65.6	34.4	36.05	23.55	25.58	8.72	3.20	2.91
Scheduled Caste	74.3	25.7	53.31	16.34	16.34	10.12	2.33	1.56
Other Backward Class	57.6	42.4	42.69	18.87	20.75	11.56	3.54	2.83
Others	40.8	59.2	34.63	16.22	20.61	15.71	6.76	5.91
Not recorded	61.6	38.4	31.51	19.27	25.00	13.02	0.00	11.46
All	58.2	41.8	41.39	17.94	20.33	12.44	4.31	3.59

Source: NSSO (2001c).

There are innumerable studies that point to discrimination that Dalits have to face in schools, which is complemented by the situation outside as well. If one applies the notion of 'pedagogic action' of Bourdieu, which would include 'education in the broadest sense, encompassing more than the process of formal education' (Bottomore 1990: XIV–XV), then one needs to take into consideration the socio-economic and cultural environment that impedes Dalits from attending school. It has been observed that 'school participation on the part of children from disadvantaged castes is a major challenge to the conservative upper-caste notion that knowledge is not important or appropriate for members of the lower orders' (Dreze and Sen 2003: 4). Underprivileged students also drop out more than the other students before class V. 'This phenomenon is far more pronounced among the children from the most disadvantaged sections of our society, most of whom rely on the government primary school system' (Ramachandran 2003: 4).

There is a cultural setting, a social construct that dominates the life of villagers. This construct categorises Dalits as lacking merit and not having 'respect' or 'dignity'. As a consequence, children from disadvantaged sections are never asked the typical question of 'what do you want to be'? (Rampal 2000). Similarly, on many occasions in the course of current fieldwork as well as previous ones, if a question such as 'Who are the respected people of your village' (*Tum apne gaon ke kuch sammanit vyaktiyon ke naam geenwa sakte ho?*) was asked of children, they could hardly name anyone from the Dalit community. There is an omnipresent cultural framework constructed by the dominant power of the village, enforced by different mediums in everyday life. It is through these mediums, inside as well as outside the school, that the hegemonic culture and ethos is reproduced.

It is this construct that institutionalises discrimination in society through its various instruments. Hence, the unequal structural realities of village life play a very important role in producing and reproducing educational inequality in the village. This gets reflected in every aspect of schooling, from curriculum to the pedagogy (Apple 1990). And that is why the learning process becomes disinteresting for the child. The subjects taught and the way they are taught are alien to the child, held synonymous with monotony and un-freedom by them. 'A venture in education, to be meaningful, must integrate the words, sounds and images of the learner. This is more relevant in the case of the oppressed whose life does not "naturally" find its expression and portrayal in the vocabulary and thoughts of the privileged in society' (Talib 1998: 208).

Mushars and Their Educational Marginalisation

The situation becomes more acute when one narrows down to certain communities within the larger category of Scheduled Castes. One such community is that of Mushars in Bihar. Their educational status represents a negation of the recent stress on decentralisation in service delivery, reflected in all policy documents concerning education such as DPEP, SSA, Tenth Five-Year Plan, among many others. The analysis of data shows that their literacy has not even crossed the 5 per cent mark (see Table 9.6). The literacy percentage of other scheduled castes is also low but even slight growth shown by them over decades is visible among the Mushars.

Table 9.6
LITERACY RATES FOR DIFFERENT CATEGORIES NATIONALLY AND IN BIHAR (%)

Categories	Total	Male	Female
National (total)*	64.8	75.3	53.7
Bihar (total)*	47.0	59.7	33.1
National (SCs)*	45.2	55.1	34.6
Bihar (SCs)*	28.5	40.2	15.6
Mushars (Bihar)**	4.63	7.67	1.25

Sources: *Primary Census Abstract (2001); **Calculated on the basis of Census (1991), Special Tables on Scheduled Castes, Part VIII (1), Volume-1. This data is for population of 7 years and above.

Of late many intervention programmes have been initiated by donor agencies and consequent researches have also been done. Such researches have thrown light on the certain vital ethnographic dimensions of Mushars' life and have in fact at certain junctures also argued that 'if Mushars have to be pulled out from the clutches of this plight, the only means to accomplish this task is education' (Sundarani 2002: 71). The arguments have fallen in the trap of giving education an unsurpassed autonomy in terms of being an agency of transformation. Education is, indubitably, a major source of development of self as well as collective, but there are a variety of factors that impinge on the underdevelopment of the self as well as the community. Mushars' underdevelopment and educational deprivation in specific can be understood fully only if we consider their location within the local social structural framework. Education, being the focus here, must be looked at the way the social relations in their totality interact and impact this community. Hence, the local culture and social and economic conditions of the Mushars become vital in understanding their educational deprivation.

REFLECTION ON EDUCATION INEQUALITY: EVIDENCES FROM THE FIELD

Based on this given situation, an effort was made to randomly select a village with Mushar population to find out the dynamics of such educational deprivation. One month of fieldwork was undertaken to collect basic information about the community and generate qualitative data through group discussions and intensive interaction with the village community. However, in the course of fieldwork it was decided to look at two adjoining villages, in Jehanabad district— Kasain and Godiha. Situated on the road connecting Jehanabad with Arwal district, these villages are about 6 km from the district headquarters. In the two villages, questionnaires to collect basic information were randomly administered among different castes (Table 9.7). An effort was made to engage in dialogue more with members of Mushar community.

The total questionnaires administered in Kasain village were 55, whereas in Godiha village the number was 39. Out of this, two communities had substantial representation—27 Mushar households in Kasain and eight in Godiha, 10 and four households of Dusadhs in Kasain and Godiha respectively, and 25 Chamar households in Godiha. Apart from the questionnaires, which also helped in making inroads into the village community as well as in establishing a rapport with the local villagers, group discussions and informal interviews were the other major source of information and local perspective that we derived. An effort was also made to look at the comparative situation of the different Dalit communities.

TABLE 9.7
DISTRIBUTION OF CASTES (%)

Castes	Kasain	Godiha	Total
Mushar	49.1	20.5	37.6
Dusadh	18.2	10.3	15.1
Brahmin	1.8	0.0	1.1
Bhumihar	9.1	0.0	5.4
Mahto	12.7	0.0	7.5
Yadav	7.3	0.0	4.3
Kahar	1.8	0.0	1.1
Chamar	0.0	64.1	25.8
Pasi	0.0	5.1	2.2
Total	100.0	100.0	100.0

Source: Field data.

The two villages represented a mixture of different castes such as Mushar, Dusadh, Brahmin, Bhumihar, Mahto, Yadav, Kahar, Chamar and Pasi. The presence of the upper caste, mainly Bhumihars, can be felt in Kasain despite their smaller number. Though they are small in number, the *mukhiya* of the Larsa panchayat, within which these two villages fall, is a Bhumihar and the *up-mukhiya* is a Mahto (OBC) by caste. The two ward members from Kasain are also Mahto. OBCs and the so-called *savarna* castes dominate as evident from their numerically high presence in the bodies such as panchayat *samitis* and local *puja samitis*. The symbols of power are vested with the non-Dalit castes, except for the relatively higher representation of Chamar caste in the Village Education Committee of Godiha village (five of a total of 14 members, with the president being a Chamar). When one says symbols of power, it refers to the way decision making is carried out during Dussehra *puja*, panchayat meetings or village education committee meetings, especially in Kasain village. It is also seen in terms of notions about certain communities, which are constructed and popularised leading to maintenance of status quo.

Mushars in the Local Context

As the study was primarily focused on the Mushar community, trying to look at their educational marginalisation, it becomes important to dwell upon the status of this community. Mushars belong to the lowest rung of the caste hierarchy and have been considered 'untouchable' by the traditional notions of caste belief. They are distributed in different parts of Bihar like Bhagalpur, Munger, Purnea, Gaya, Jehanabad, Arwal, Patna, Darbhanga and other districts. Risley considered them as 'offshoot of the Bhuiya tribe of Chota Nagpur' (Singh 1993: 2403). Some interpret their names as *Masu+hera* = flesh-seeker/hunter, while some others consider them as *Musa+har* = rat-eaters. They are divided into clans (*gotras*) such as Balakumuni/Balakmum, Daitinia, Sohlaut, Pail, Rikh-mun, Rishimuni, Tisbaria, Bansghat, Danharia, Sarpurkha and Kasmeta. Majhi, Mandar and Mushar are their surnames. They do not have inhibitions in accepting water or food from Hindu communities except Chamar (ibid.).

They are predominantly agricultural labourers, with the ability to measure and assess the quality of soil. Gradually there has been a sharp decline in employment opportunities for them. Their traditional job market has been squeezed. Consequently, they get work for only three to four months a year and that too primarily the women. This scarcity creates financial crisis for which they approach moneylenders and get trapped in the vicious cycle of debt. It has been argued that their economic plight affects their educational status as well (Sharma 1999).

As a very specific and common feature of the geographical location of different caste groups, the Dalits have generally been placed on the fringes of village, and the farthest location, as per the rules of purity/pollution, is allocated to the Mushars, Doms, etc. Their participation in village affairs is negligible and they are treated as non-identities in the local socio-political processes of governance and administration.

The only contact that the villages generally have with them is in context of the purchase of their labour power. Because of their historical alienation, they have failed to be part of various schemes, with certain exceptions, and development planning. Most of the Mushars are landless (Tables 9.8 and 9.9) and work as agricultural labour, with even their children working at a very early age of 12–14 years. Around 8 to 10 per cent of children of this community have started going to school. Marriage takes place at a very early age, for boys 12 to 14 years, and by the age of 20, the married couple sets up a separate household. The hardships of life and of earning a livelihood forces them to remain outside the house allowing little time for them to interact with the children (Lokshala and CDI 2003).

TABLE 9.8
OCCUPATIONAL PATTERNS IN KASAIN

Caste	Landless	Landed (not working for others)	Sharecroppers	Traditional
Mushar	67	0	3	0
Dusadh	13	0	0	0
Bhumihar	0	8	0	0
Mahto	5	3	8	0
Yadav	0	9	3	0
Kahar	0	2	0	0
Brahmin	0	0	0	1
Total	85	22	14	1

Source: Based on field study data.

TABLE 9.9
OCCUPATIONAL PATTERNS IN GODIHA

Caste	Landless	Landed (not working for others)	Sharecroppers
Mushar	13	0	0
Chamar	66	0	8
Dusadh	1	0	0
Pasi	0	1	1
Total	80	1	9

Source: Based on field study data.

In fact, the actual test of any decentralised planning rests in its capability to incorporate such groups into the system. Even if the claims to 'impartial' disbursement of development schemes are made by the state, their economic and social condition stands in sharp contrast to it. If the educational status of the country, and Dalits and women in specific, has become a subject of major concern, it becomes imperative to explore the reasons behind near-static literacy rate of this community.

The Educational Status of Villages

The composition of the two villages shows that the maximum illiteracy is among the Mushars in the age group of 5 to 14 (Tables 9.10 and 9.11). The number is higher also because of the higher number of Mushar respondents. However, noticeable in Table 9.10 is absence of illiterates among the Mahto, Bhumihars, Brahmin and Kahar. On the other hand, the number of Mushars in the category of primary to class XII decreases because they are not able to continue schooling even if they get enrolled in schools.

TABLE 9.10
EDUCATIONAL STATUS OF KASAIN (PERSONS)

Caste	Illiterate (5–14 years)	Illiterate (15+ years)	Below Primary	Primary	Literate Middle	Class X	Class XII	Above Class XII
Mushar	20	59	46	7	3	2	1	0
Dusadh	3	19	16	4	1	1	0	0
Brahmin	0	0	1	0	1	1	1	1
Bhumihar	0	2	8	5	2	8	5	5
Mahto	0	6	17	4	11	6	3	0
Yadav	3	6	6	4	2	4	3	0
Kahar	0	1	2	1	0	2	1	0
Total	26	93	96	25	20	24	14	6

Source: Based on field study data.

In the case of Godiha village, where all the respondents belonged to the Dalit community, one finds the overall number decreases as one moves further from below primary schooling category. In this the number of Mushars, as in the case of Kasain, also shows a decline.

Table 9.11
Educational Status of Godiha (Persons)

Caste	Illiterate (5–14 years)	Illiterate (15+ years)	Literate Below Primary	Primary	Middle	Class X	Class XII	Graduate and Above
Mushar	5	15	2	1	1	1	0	0
Chamar	15	69	55	13	12	3	0	0
Dusadh	0	3	9	1	4	1	0	0
Pasi	1	3	4	1	2	0	1	0
Total	21	90	70	16	19	5	1	0

Source: Based on field study data.

The illiteracy or lower educational level among Dalits and Mushars in general does not reflect absence of desire to study among them. There are many more reasons than mere non-interest of parents, as many argue. There are notions such as *Mushars are disinterested or not interested in upward mobility* made popular in the local society. However, one needs to go into the dynamics of why such notions emerge only about certain particular communities and that too, made popular only by certain communities.

Kasain village has a middle school, which has five rooms. One room serves as the office and four rooms are used for teaching. There are a total of five teachers, including a woman and one *shiksha mitra*. There are two toilets and three hand pumps (out of which one is not functional). There is no games teacher. In the school compound one could see villagers' animals tied to posts.

The students get enrolled here for classes I to VIII. Total enrollment was 321 and there were only five teachers. One teacher had to give two classes simultaneously. Leave aside the dismal teacher-student ratio here (64.2:1), the basic infrastructure of rooms are also lacking.

Table 9.12 shows that there were less Dalit students enrolled in the school than others. This number reduced by classes V to VIII, which had the lowest figure of five students. This shows how Dalits drop out before reaching class V, even if enrolled at earlier stages.

There was one primary school in Godiha village, with two rooms. There was one hand pump and two toilets, which had been constructed in 2004, but did not start functioning because some portions collapsed due to bad material. There were no sports items for the children. There were two teachers, out of which one was a *shiksha mitra*. What is interesting in Table 9.13 is that the overall situation of education is disappointing. There are only seven children in class V. The condition of Mushars has been the worst, and in 2002, there was only one Mushar child enrolled who never attended the school whereas, in the years 2003 and 2004, out of two Mushar children enrolled only one attended school.

TABLE 9.12
ENROLMENT IN KASAIN MIDDLE SCHOOL, 2004

Class	SC	Others	Total
I	23	59	82
II	17	42	59
III	7	32	39
IV	10	25	35
V	5	40	45
VI	5	20	25
VII	5	31	36
Total	72	249	321

Source: Based on figures provided by the local school.

TABLE 9.13
ENROLMENT IN GODIHA PRIMARY SCHOOL, 2004

Class	SC			Others			Total		
	Boys	Girls	Total	Boys	Girls	Total	Boys	Girls	Total
I	12	17	29	24	20	44	36	37	73
II	16	9	25	8	13	21	24	22	46
III	4	8	12	6	10	16	10	18	28
IV	9	3	12	7	3	10	16	6	22
V	1	2	3	3	1	4	4	3	7
Total	42	39	81	48	47	95	90	86	176

Source: Data collected from the school register.

A close look at Table 9.14 reveals a complete picture of the total number of children in the surveyed households and the number of children enrolled. It was seen that even though the .children were enrolled, many of them did not go school. However, one finds that the enrollment is near 53.8 per cent among Mushars, compared to 57.1 per cent among Dusadhs, 90.9 per cent among Bhumihars, 95.5 per cent among Mahtos and 76.9 per cent among Yadavs. Hence, even if one goes by the enrolment rates the educational status of Mushars have been worst.

TABLE 9.14
SCHOOLGOING CHILDREN IN THE AGE GROUP 0 TO 18 YEARS IN KASAIN

Caste	0–4 Years			5–18 Years			School-going Children			Non-school Going Children			Total Children
	Boys	Girls	Total	Boys	Girls	Total	Boys	Girls	Total	Boys	Girls	Total	
Mushar	12	14	26	36	29	65	22	13	35	14	16	30	91
Dusadh	3	2	5	9	5	14	8	0	8	1	5	6	19
Brahmin	0	2	2	0	1	1	0	1	1	0	0	0	3
Bhumihar	4	3	7	7	4	11	6	4	10	1	0	1	18
Mahto	5	4	9	12	10	22	11	10	21	1	0	1	31
Yadav	0	6	6	11	2	13	8	2	10	3	0	3	19
Kahar	2	0	2	0	2	2	0	2	2	0	0	0	4
Total	26	31	57	75	53	128	55	32	87	20	21	41	185

Source: Based on field study data.

On the other hand, the picture that emerges from Godiha (see Table 9.15) is that the enrolment among Mushars is a mere 9.09 per cent, compared to 61.3 per cent among Chamars, 100 per cent among Dusadhs and 66.6 per cent among Pasis.

TABLE 9.15
SCHOOLGOING CHILDREN IN THE AGE GROUP 0 TO 18 YEARS IN GODIHA

Caste	0–4 Years			5–18 Years			School-going Children			Non-school Going Children			Total Children
	Boys	Girls	Total	Boys	Girls	Total	Boys	Girls	Total	Boys	Girls	Total	
Mushar	2	3	5	6	5	11	1	0	1	5	5	10	16
Chamar	18	7	25	37	38	75	25	21	46	12	17	29	100
Dusadh	3	2	5	2	4	6	2	4	6	0	0	0	11
Pasi	1	1	2	4	2	6	4	0	4	0	2	2	8
Total	24	13	37	49	49	98	32	25	57	17	24	41	135

Source: Based on field study data.

Desire for Education among Mushars

The study also tried to look at: (*a*) whether people perceived education as having 'utility'; (*b*) what they expect from education; and (*c*) whether the universalising discourse of 'English' as a necessary language and subject to be studied has made its inroads.

It will be erroneous to consider that parents are least interested in sending their children to school. The school and education as a whole has come to be recognised as an essential means to be upwardly mobile. When we tried to quantify the very fundamental perspective about the reasons they think education is necessary, most of them either saw it as a means of better employment opportunities or as a tool that introduces them to new things. One respondent from the Mushar community in Kasain village remarked:

> If children go to school they will learn to be neat and clean and live a better life. They will learn new things. We want our children to study. Can any parent not want its child to study? It is only after studying that he will earn a livelihood and live comfortably. It will also bring fame to us.

Another respondent from the same community said:

> My son will study, move ahead with studies and gain knowledge. It will be only through studying that his development will take place and then only he will get a job.... I will not have to go to other people with my letters.

Most of the respondents believed that education is important to learn new things, which would equip the child better to live in this world, and also for employment (Tables 9.16 and 9.17). With such opinionated views about education, it is difficult to hold parents responsible, especially without taking into consideration the other reasons for the absence of education among them.

They even responded to questions about the quality of teaching in the village school. Most of them looked at the school as offering good education. However, some were even sceptical about the way teachers behave with Mushar students. Some villagers remarked that the teachers did not pay sufficient attention to children and

Table 9.16
Importance of Sending Children to School (Kasain)

Caste	To be Good Human Beings	To Learn New Things	For Employment
Mushar	1	23	16
Dusadh	0	9	8
Brahmin	1	0	0
Bhumihar	3	1	2
Mahto	0	3	6
Yadav	2	1	3
Kahar	0	0	1
Total	7	37	36

Source: Based on field study data.
Note: Many people expressed more than one opinion about the importance of going to school.

Table 9.17
Importance of Sending Children to School (Godiha)

Caste	To be Good Human Beings	To Learn New Things	For Employment
Mushar	1	6	3
Chamar	0	15	24
Dusadh	0	4	2
Pasi	0	0	1
Total	1	25	30

Source: Based on field study data.

generally came to school to sign their attendance sheet and not to perform their duty. Some informed that in many cases teachers refused to enrol their children as well. There were other issues that hampered the enrolment of children in school. In fact in Kasain the current headmaster introduced a school uniform, which was accepted by most of the villagers, but some of the respondents said that they could not afford it and therefore had to withdraw their children from the school. The headmaster said that wearing a uniform was not compulsory and that he had told the poorer sections that if they could not afford one immediately they could get one made for their children during festivals instead of buying other kinds of clothes.

The respondents were asked about whether learning English was necessary in today's world. They looked at English as a tool that would enable one to interact with the outside world more easily, to read signboards, read the name of medicines, and would also bring better employment opportunities (Tables 9.18 and 9.19).

TABLE 9.18
VILLAGERS' PERCEPTION OF THE NECESSITY OF TEACHING ENGLISH (IN KASAIN)

| Caste | Is English Necessary | | Don't Know |
	Yes	No	
Mushar	17	0	14
Dusadh	8	0	5
Brahmin	1	0	0
Bhumihar	5	0	0
Mahto	7	0	0
Yadav	4	0	0
Kahar	1	0	0
Total	43	0	19

Source: Based on field study data.
Note: One person gave multiple responses to our questions.

TABLE 9.19
VILLAGERS' PERCEPTION OF THE NECESSITY OF TEACHING ENGLISH (IN GODIHA)

| Caste | Is English Necessary | | Don't Know |
	Yes	No	
Mushar	3	0	8
Chamar	22	0	10
Dusadh	3	0	2
Pasi	1	0	0
Total	29	0	20

Source: Based on field study data.

Economic Deprivation of Mushars and Their Educational Status

The local economy is primarily agriculture based. Hence, the major source of livelihood is agricultural activities—the landed engaged in extracting maximum possible surplus, and the landless left to wage-based income, which is not available to them throughout the year (see Tables 9.8 and 9.9).

Mushars hardly possess any land apart from the small plots on which they live (see Tables 9.20 and 9.21). They are generally landless labourers or engage in other kinds of casual labour to earn their livelihood making their life more precarious.

TABLE 9.20
LANDOWNERSHIP PATTERNS IN KASAIN

Caste	Land Owned (Bigha¹ / Person)				
	0–1	1.01–2	2.01–5	5.01–10	10+
Mushar	0	0	0	0	0
Dusadh	0	0	0	0	0
Brahmin	0	0	0	0	0
Bhumihar	0	1	1	2	1
Mahto	4	1	2	0	0
Yadav	1	1	1	1	0
Kahar	0	0	1	0	0
Total	5	3	5	3	1

Source: Based on field study data.
Note: ¹ 1 Bigha = 0.25 hectare (approx.)

TABLE 9.21
LANDOWNERSHIP PATTERNS IN GODIHA

Caste	Land Owned (Bigha* / Person)				
	0–1	1.01–2	2.01–5	5.01–10	10+
Mushar	0	0	0	0	0
Chamar	7	0	0	0	0
Dusadh	4	0	0	0	0
Pasi	0	0	1	0	0
Total	11	0	1	0	0

Source: Based on field study data.
Note: * 1 Bigha = 0.25 hectare (approx.)

They do not even migrate to other towns in search of jobs. Migration from Kasain village was relatively negligible compared to Godiha, where the Chamars migrated to work in factories outside the state (see Tables 9.22 and 9.23). In fact, this could be one of the reasons of their better educational status in terms of enrolment compared to Mushars. Migration not only means a better affordability to educate children because of relatively better and regular

TABLE 9.22
MIGRATION PATTERNS IN KASAIN

Caste	Factory Worker	Driver	Others	Total
Mushar	0	2	0	2
Dusadh	1	1	0	2
Brahmin	0	0	1	1
Bhumihar	0	0	0	0
Mahto	3	0	0	3
Yadav	1	0	0	1
Kahar	0	0	0	0
Total	5	3	1	9

Source: Based on field study data.

TABLE 9.23
MIGRATION PATTERNS IN GODIHA

Caste	Factory Worker	Driver	Others	Total
Mushar	0	0	0	0
Chamar	10	2	1	13
Dusadh	1	0	0	1
Pasi	0	0	1	1
Total	11	2	2	15

Source: Based on field study data.

income, but also means an exposure to a new worldview, which encourages education as a means of upward social mobility.

A correlation between economic condition and educational status has been found, as evident from Mushars' unaffordability of education due to economic deprivation. It has been established that education, despite claims of 'free' government education, costs a substantial amount, especially when even minimum wages are not implemented. Studies and analysis of data have revealed that households have to bear a minimum cost for educating a child even if primary education is argued to be free. The cost of dress material, exercise books, bags, pen, pencil, etc. are some of the many things that a child needs. Within the current educational set-up, the only truth is that the cost of education in government schools is lower than the local body schools or government-aided schools (Nair 2004; Tilak 1996, 2001).

The expenditure on education becomes a major hurdle for Mushars when it comes to sending their children to school because of their low income (Table 9.24). This wage received in kind, once translated into money, is less than the minimum wage announced by the state—3.5 kg of rice gets translated into a maximum of Rs. 21–22 (if rice sells at Rs. 6 per kg), which is much below the Rs. 48.71 per day of official minimum wage (AIPWA 2003). Above all, they do not get work throughout the year, but only during the agricultural season.

TABLE 9.24
WAGES PAID IN THE TWO VILLAGES

Sector of Employment	Type of Work	Mode of Payment	Wage Received
Agricultural labour	Ploughing	Land, rice, flour	9 kathhas[1] of land,[2] 2.5 kg of rice/flour or 3.5 kg of rice/flour
	Harvesting	Bundle of harvested crops	One bundle out of every 12
	Sowing	Grain	2.5 kg of rice
	Normal Wage	Rice, flour	3.5 kg of rice

Source: Study data based on surveyed households.
Notes: [1] 1 kathha = 0.013 hectare (approx.)
[2] This is in case of 'attached labour'.

It is economic hardship that makes the husband and wife leave the house early in the morning and come back in the evening. They hardly have enough time to make a focused attempt at educating their children. Though not many children were found to be involved in full-time occupations, there were some looking after younger siblings or engaged in grazing cattle. Some of the Mushar respondents put forth their views on why their children do not go to schools even if enrolled. They said that because the non-Mushar women largely stayed at home, they looked after the children even when the men went out to work, whereas it was impossible in their case because both men and women went out to work.

In fact, one respondent put forth the point of 'facilities' available more to the badkan ke laikan (children of other castes with higher ritual position). His notion of facility encompassed the issues of poverty and affluence, when he said that upper-caste (which is a relative term because it would include OBCs as well as *savarna* castes) children did not have to graze cattle or look after younger children. Even a morning breakfast before going to school is something other castes get but not Mushars.

The Everyday Life of Mushars and Their Participation in Local Culture

The everyday life of Mushars shows that they have not been part of village affairs as other castes. Culturally, it would be flawed to presume a homogeneous framework with all communities integrated as one, especially when local societies are structurally so divided. However, after the onset of the democratisation processes and percolation of slogans of development and equity, one has seen the integration of OBCs and other Scheduled Caste communities taking place in bodies such as village education committees (VEC) and *panchayati raj* institutions (PRIs). But, one finds no such enhanced participation of Mushars in local village affairs.

We tried to look at their participation in village festivals. In fact, Mushars, in other villages of the district, have been found to be participating more religiously in only one festival—Jitiya. In other festivals such as Dussehra or Diwali, their participation has been negligible. In fact, one of the respondents said that this community does not have any festival to celebrate.

The Mushars participate in Dussehra festivals in Kasain, but in a limited fashion. When asked, all of them said that they participated in the *puja* as all other villagers. However, a closer look told us that their participation is in the form of musclemen, used when funds are to be collected, when security is to be maintained during cultural programmes, or when immersion of the idol takes place. Their role is negligible in management of funds, rituals, etc. Hence, the participation, which respondents happily acknowledged as if there was no discrimination, was predefined and functioned within a set dominant cultural and social framework. The discrimination persisted but in a changed manner.

In the panchayat meetings, some close to the camp of the *mukhiya* said that the people were informed of the general body meeting through beating the drum, but nobody turns up and ultimately the powerful people take decisions and get the quorum register signed. A Mushar respondent said that they were seldom invited for the meeting and even if they went, they did not speak much because the *mukhiya* assured them that all the proposed activities or the agenda was for the benefit of the village and therefore should be supported. They were never explained in detail the mechanism of how PRIs work. Similarly, the Mushars hardly knew about the existence of VECs. The information about meetings, which were not held frequently, was limited primarily to members of VECs. The VEC met only when there was pressure from the district or when certain kind of purchases were to be done or financial matters were to be discussed. The VECs were not popularly elected. At least the Mushar community was never taken into confidence when the VEC was constituted. Many respondents seemed casual about it, which reflected on the need to popularise the notions and concepts of why decentralisation and community participation is needed. If such an exercise is not undertaken, it is also in the interest of the local elite, because once done it will threaten their entrenched position. However, in the case of Kasain village, the numerical strength of Mushars did provide them some space in the committees and meetings. Many respondents said that they did not have time for such meetings because earning livelihood was more important for them.

The non-participation of Mushars also emerges from the cultural construct that portrays them as 'different', 'other'. They are treated as a community incapable of doing 'intelligent' things. During group discussions, the Mushars said that one important reason for their children not being able to go to or remain in schools was absence of a Mushar teacher. They felt that had there been a teacher from their community he would have been sensitive to the needs of their children. Other caste teachers looked down upon them and even thrashed their children for no reason, which forced many children to stay out of school. On one occasion when this point was raised by Mushars while sitting with other castes, it was commented sarcastically by the Bhumihars that 'should somebody from the Mushar community be made a teacher?'

The discriminatory attitude towards Mushars was also clear among the teachers. The headmaster of the Godiha school repeatedly made the point that the Mushars would never come to school because 'they do not have any tension about life [*sic*], neither about what to wear or about future'. He believed that the Mushars 'don't think about studying. Their children start earning at an early age.... They neither understand their duties nor their rights'. We asked the teachers to write an essay on why Mushars do not come to school, and a majority of them believed that they were not interested in studying and that they were unaware about the advantages of education. The headmaster of the Kasain school went to the extent of saying that they did not know the meaning of education. He believed that their poverty, bad company and lack of respect for good work deprived them of education. Interestingly, some respondents believed that it was because of teachers that their children did not study. They had strong opinions about education in the local school, and education in general as seen before.

CONCLUSION

The educational crisis in India has two interlinked dimensions: on the one hand the State does not seem very committed to *educating* people, in terms of a critical full-time education process, which is also liberating; and on the other hand the notions of *empowerment* and *participation* do not get realised because the urge in people to become part of the process is not generated due to the strict bureaucratic and hierarchical framework of the process. Knowledge, which is inherently related to power structures in society, is enmeshed in a constant battle being fought between the meta-narratives conceptualised and enforced from the top by the ruling elite and the striving bodies of local and marginalised knowledge, which are pushed to the periphery. It is largely due to theses processes that apprehension is expressed about the SSA becoming a movement. Mobilisations are generally based on conscientisation, which cannot be achieved through a tailored programme, run by paid staff with predefined goals and formula (see Saxena 2004). Education in India is confronted with many dilemmas and contradictions, especially in its content and form of implementation. An effort has been made to understand these dilemmas and contradictions through fieldwork in one of the most backward communities of the country, namely, the Mushars in Bihar.

We have seen that Mushars generally do not go to school, and even if they do, as in the case of the two villages studied here, their number is less than other communities or they do not even complete primary schooling. This is in consonance with the overall scenario of Dalits in the state, as shown through NSS data. Even within the Dalit conglomerate, Mushar enrolment is less than others.

It has been seen in this paper that one fundamental reason for their educational marginalisation is their poverty and the un-affordability of education. It is fundamental to have a certain income, which can facilitate the learning process among their children. The same poverty never allows them sufficient time to devote to their children. The other reason has been lack of facilities in the local school, especially the basic requirements of rooms or teachers. The Mushars have not been able to become part of the development discourse, even if it mutilates the notion of 'education' and highlights 'literacy', because of their alienation from the local setting. Their participation in traditional festivals as well as in modern decentralised democratic mechanisms is minimal. It is a completely subjective investigation that is required to look at how a cultural construct has been created that categorises them as responsible for their educational backwardness. They are seen as people disinterested in education, who are always drunk, and least bothered about the future of their children. Notions of this 'otherness' are so entrenched that even teachers believe that their children will not study. Though an illusion is created that provides a sense of participation to them during festivals, that participation itself is limited and predefined, which does not let the significant variables of power (such as participation in decision making or management) percolate to them.

Such a cultural construct, in fact, plays a significant role in what Bourdieu would call cultural reproduction. The developments that take place outside the school, the overarching 'pedagogic action', play a significant role in the participation or withdrawal of Mushar children in the educational process. The educational process needs to be sensitive to such elements, which lead to marginalisation of the whole community. But the question that still remains is, why does this happen? Is it because the dominant elite in society seeks to maintain the status quo of structural inequalities, which in turn gets reflected in educational realities? One needs to locate the whole educational paradigm that exists in terms of an enterprise created by certain interests and with certain perspectives and purposes. Unless that is understood it will be difficult to ascertain why for so long issues of teaching pedagogy, local cultural variance, structural inequalities and so on have not been addressed in a manner to incorporate communities at the margins of society.

References

Adorno, Theodor, W. 2004. *The Culture Industry*. London: Routledge.
All India Progressive Women's Association (AIPWA). 2003. 'Women Agricultural Labourers' Struggles: Key Issues', http://www.cpiml.org/liberation/year_2003/february/aadhi%20zameen%202.htm, accessed in November 2004.
Apple, Michel, W. 1990. *Ideology and Curriculum*. New York: Routledge.
Bardhan, Pranab. (2002). 'Decentralization of Governance and Development', *Journal of Economic Perspectives* (Fall 2002), also http://www.globetrotter.berkeley.edu/mcarthur/inequality/papers/BardhanGovt.pdf, accessed in February 2005.
Bottomore, Tom. 1990. 'Foreword'. In Pierre Bourdieu and Jean-Claude Passeron (eds). *Reproduction in Education, Society and Culture*. London: Sage Publications.
Bourdieu, Pierre. 1990. 'Preface'. In Pierre Bourdieu and Jean-Claude Passeron. *Reproduction in Education, Society and Culture*. London: Sage Publications.
Bowles, Samuel. 1976. 'Unequal Education and the Reproduction of the Social Division of Labor'. In Roger Dale, Geoff Esland and Madeleine MacDonald (eds). *Schooling and Capitalism: A Sociological Reader*. London: Routledge and Kegan Paul.
Dreze, Jean and Amartya Sen. 1995. *India: Economic Development and Social Opportunity*. New Delhi: Oxford University Press.

Dreze, Jean and Amartya Sen. 2002. *India: Development and Participation*. New Delhi: Oxford University Press.

———. 2003. 'Basic Education as a Political Issue'. In B.G. Jandhyala (ed.), *Education, Society and Development: National and International Perspectives*. New Delhi: APH Publishing Corporation and NIEPA.

Foucault, Michel. 1980. *Power/Knowledge: Selected Interviews and Other Writings 1972–1977*. London: Harvester Wheatsheaf.

Gandhi, M.K. 1999. *India of My Dreams*. Ahmedabad: Navjivan Publishing House.

Government of India. Undated. *Sarva Shiksha Abhiyan: A Programme for Universal Elementary Education—Framework for Implementation*. New Delhi: Department of Elementary Education and Literacy, Ministry of Human Resource Development, Government of India.

———. 2000. *A Policy Framework for Reforms in Education* (Mukesh Ambani and Kumar Mangalam Birla), Prime Minister's Council on Trade and Industry. New Delhi: Government of India.

———. 2001a. *Tenth Five Year Plan 2002–2007*, Chapter 2.2, pp. 23–40. New Delhi: Planning Commission.

———. 2001b. *Approach Paper to the Tenth Five Year Plan (2002–2007)*. New Delhi: Planning Commission.

———. 2001c. *Tenth Five Year Plan 2002–2007* (Chapter 4.1). New Delhi: Planning Commission.

———. 2001d. *Primary Census Abstracts 2001*, Registrar General and Census Commissioner, India. New Delhi: Government of India.

———. 2002a. *National Human Development Report, 2001*. New Delhi: Planning Commission and Oxford University Press.

———. 2002b. *Report of the Committee on Vision 2020*. New Delhi: Planning Commission, Government of India.

Goldstein, Harvey. 2004. 'Education for All: The Globalization of Learning Targets', *Comparative Education*, 40(1): 7–14.

IIPS and ORC Macro (2000).

Johnson, Craig. 2003. *Decentralization in India: Poverty, Politics and Panchayati Raj* (Working Paper No. 199). London: Overseas Development Institute.

Kumar, Krishna. 1989. *Social Character of Learning*. New Delhi: Sage Publications.

Kumar Krishna, Manisha Priyam and Sadhna Saxena. 2002. 'A New Right for the Poor'. *Frontline*, 19(11). Avilable at http://www.frontlineonnet.com, accessed in May 2004.

Lokshala and Centre for Development of India (CDI). 2003. *Shiksha Ke Samaajik Charitra Ki Kahani*. Patna: CDI.

Majumdar, Diptosh. 2003. 'Buddha's Bengal Gets Red on Primary Education Report Card'. *Indian Express*, 2 October.

Marx, Karl. 1968. *The German Ideology*. Moscow: Progress Publishers.

Marcuse, Herbert. 1972. *One Dimensional Man*. London: Abacus.

Mathew, George and Ramesh Nayak. 1996. 'Panchayats at Work: What it Means for the Oppressed?', *Economic and Political Weekly*, 30(27): 1765–71.

Mohanty, Manoranjan. 2001. 'On the Concept of Empowerment'. In Debal K. Singh Roy (ed.), *Social Development and the Empowerment of Marginalized Groups: Perspectives and Strategies*. New Delhi: Sage Publications.

Nair, N. Gopalkrishnan. 2004. *Household Cost of School Education* (Discussion Paper No. 64). Thiruvananthapuram: Centre for Development Studies.

National Council of Educational Research and Training (NCERT). 1997. *Sixth All India Education Survey* (National Tables, Vol. 1). New Delhi: NCERT.

National Sample Survey Organization (NSSO). 55th Round. 2001a. *Employment & Unemployment Situation among Social Groups in India* (NSS 55th Round, Report No. 469 (55/10/7), July 1999–June 2000, Ministry of Statistics and Programme, Implementation. New Delhi: Government of India.

————. 2001b. *Difference in Levels of Consumption Among Socio Economic Groups 1999–2000*, NSS 55th Round, Report No. 472, Ministry of Statistics and Programme Implementation. New Delhi: Government of India.

————. 2001c. *Literacy and Levels of Education in India 1999–2000*, NSS 55th Round, Report No. 473 (55/10/11), Ministry of Statistics and Programme Implementation. New Delhi: Government of India.

Raman, Vasanthi. 2000. 'Globalization, Sustainable Development and Local Self-government Challenges of the 21st Century: The Indian Experience'. Konrad Adenauer Stiftung Foundation, http://www1.kas.de/publikationen/2000/entwicklung/raman.pdf, accessed in December 2004.

Ramachandran, Vimla. 2003. 'Overview: Backward and Forward Linkages that Strengthen Primary Education'. In Vimla Ramachandran (ed.), *Getting Children Back to School: Case Studies in Primary Education*. New Delhi: Sage Publications.

Ramachandran, Vimla, Kameshwari Jandhyala and Aarti Sailyee. 2003. 'Through the Life Cycle of Children: Factors the Facilitate/Impede Successful Primary School Completion', *Economic and Political Weekly*, 38(47): 4994–5002.

Rampal, Anita. 2000. 'Education for Human Development in South Asia', *Economic and Political Weekly*, 35(30): 2623–31.

Sadgopal, Anil. 2001. 'Political Economy of the Ninety Third Amendment Bill', *Mainstream*. Annual Issue, pp. 43–50.

————. 2003. 'Education for Too Few', *Frontline*, 20 (24), http://www.frontlineonnet.com/fl2024/stories/20031205002809700.htm, accessed in January 2005.

————. 2004a. *Globalization and Education: Defining the Indian Crisis* (XVI Zakir Hussain Memorial). New Delhi: Zakir Hussain College, University of Delhi.

————. 2004b. *Globalization: Demystifying its Knowledge Agenda for India's Education Policy* (Durgabai Deshmukh Memorial Lecture). New Delhi: Council for Social Development.

Saxena, Sadhna. 2004. 'Revisiting Ajmer Total Campaign'. In Malavika Karlekar (ed.), *Paradigms of Learning: The Total Literacy Campaign in India*. New Delhi: Sage Publications.

Sharma, Mukul. 1999. 'Everyday Life of Mushars in North Bihar', *Economic and Political Weekly*, 34(49): 3465–70.

Singh, K.S. 1993. *The Scheduled Castes* (in *The People of India (National Series), Volume II*). New Delhi: Oxford University Press.

Sundarani, Dwarko. 2002. 'Education is the Foundation of Culture'. In Hemant Joshi and Sanjay Kumar (eds), *Asserting Voices: Changing Culture, Identity and Livelihood of the Mushars in the Gangetic Plains*. New Delhi: Deshkal Publications.

Talib, Mohammad. 1998. 'Educating the Oppressed: Observations in a Working Class Settlement in Delhi'. In Sureshchandra Shukla and Rekha Kaul (eds), *Education, Development and Underdevelopment*. New Delhi: Sage Publications.

Tilak, J.B.G. 1996. 'How Free is "Free" Primary Education in India?', *Economic and Political Weekly*, 31(4–5): 275–82.

———. 2001. 'Household Expenditure on Education: A Few Stylised Facts'. In S. Mahendra Dev, Piyush Antony, V. Gayathri and R.P. Mamgain (eds), *Social and Economic Security in India*. New Delhi: Institute for Human Development.

World Bank. 1998. *Knowledge for Development: World Development Report 1998/99*. New York: Oxford University Press.

———. 2000a. *World Development Report 1999/2000: Entering the 21st Century*. Washington, DC: Oxford University Press.

———. 2000b. *World Development Report 2000/2001: Attacking Poverty*. Washington, DC: Oxford University Press.

———. 2003. *World Development Report 2004: Making Services Work for Poor People*. Washington, DC: Oxford University Press.

About the Editor and Contributors

Editor

Ravi Kumar is currently working as Associate Fellow, Council for Social Development, New Delhi. He has done extensive fieldwork on education and Dalits, and writes for national dailies and magazines. He has recently edited *The Politics of Imperialism and Counterstrategies* (Aakar Books, 2004). He can be contacted at ravik05@gmail.com.

Contributors

Karuna Chanana was Professor at the faculty of Zakir Hussain Centre for Educational Studies, Jawaharlal Nehru University, New Delhi. She has been a member of the Regional Scientific Committee for Asia and the Pacific of the UNESCO Forum on Higher Education, Research and Knowledge. She has authored many research papers and her publications include *Socialisation, Education and Women: Explorations in Gender Identity* (Orient Longman, 1998) and *Transformative Links between Higher and Basic Education: Mapping the Field* (Sage, 2004).

Vasudha Dhagamwar received a B.A. in philosophy, politics and economics at Oxford, an M.A. in English and a LL.B. at the University of Bombay, and a Ph.D. in law at the University of London. She is Founding Member and Executive Director of an NGO, Multiple Action Research Group (MARG), and she has been a Visiting Fellow at the Human Rights Program, Harvard Law School. Her publications include *Law, Power and Justice: The Protection of Personal Rights in the Indian Penal Code* (Sage, 1992), *Industrial Development and Displacement: The People of Korba* (Sage, 2003), *Role and Image of Law in India: The Tribal Experience* (Sage, 2006), and various articles.

Madan Mohan Jha is a member of the Indian Administrative Service (IAS). He has done his Ph.D. on inclusive education from University of Cambridge, and is currently the Secretary, Education, Government of Bihar. He writes regularly for many national newspapers, and his earlier works include *School Without Walls: Inclusive Education for All* (Heinemann, 2002).

Geetha B. Nambissan is Professor at Zakir Hussain Centre for Educational Studies, Jawaharlal Nehru University, New Delhi. She has authored many research papers in distinguished journals and edited *Year for Child Labour and the Right to Education in South Asia: Needs Versus Rights* (Sage, 2003).

Anil Sadgopal organised a rural education and development programme through Kishore Bharati in Hoshangabad district, Madhya Pradesh, and initiated the Hoshangabad Science Teaching Programme in 1972 with the Friends Rural Centre, Rasulia. He also conceived and led the Lokshala Programme for demonstrating an alternative vision of universalisation of elementary education through social intervention in the government school system. He has served as member of various commissions on education and is presently member of Central Advisory Board on Education. He has served as Professor of Education in University of Delhi and as Senior Fellow, Nehru Memorial Museum and Library. Author of numerous articles in English and Hindi dailies, research papers and two books in Hindi: *Sangharsh aur Nirman* (Rajkamal 1993) and *Shiksha Mein Badlav ka Sawal* (Granth Shilpi 2000), he is engaged in writing a book on tools for analysis of education policy and the impact of globalisation on Indian education, with focus on elementary education.

Sadhna Saxena is a Reader, Department of Education, Delhi University. She was a senior member of Kishore Bharati, a well-known voluntary organisation that worked in the field of innovative science education, non-formal education, adult literacy and rural development in Madhya Pradesh for more than 18 years. She has also been engaged in education research for more than a decade, and has written extensively on the issues confronting education today.

Amarjeet Sinha is a member of Indian Administrative Service (IAS), and has done extensive work on literacy, education, health care and empowerment through community organisations. He was actively associated in the process of making elementary education a fundamental right and in designing the sector-wide rights-based national programme for universal elementary education, the Sarva Shiksha Abhiyan, and has published extensively on a variety of themes in social development. He was involved in the Public Report on Basic Education in India (PROBE). His publications include *Primary Schooling in India* (Vikas, 1998) and *India: Democracy and Well-Being?* (Rupa, 2005).

INDEX